1-04

Teen

Table of Contents

by
Osamu Tezuka

translation
Frederik L. Schodt

lettering and retouch
Digital Chameleon

Dark Horse Comics®

publisher
MIKE RICHARDSON

editor
CHRIS WARNER

consulting editor
TOREN SMITH for STUDIO PROTEUS

collection designers
DAVID NESTELLE and LANI SCHREIBSTEIN

English-language version produced by **DARK HORSE COMICS** and **STUDIO PROTEUS**

ASTRO BOY® VOLUME 5

The artwork of this volume has been produced as a mirror-image of the original Japanese edition to conform to English-language standards.

Published by
Dark Horse Comics, Inc.
10956 SE Main Street
Milwaukie, OR 97222

WWW.DARKHORSE.COM

To find a comics shop in your area, call the Comic Shop Locator Service toll-free at 1-888-266-4226.

First edition: July 2002
ISBN: 1-56971-680-3

10 9 8 7 6 5 4 3 2 1
Printed in Canada

A NOTE TO READERS

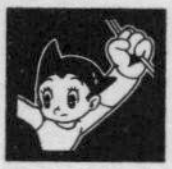

Many non-Japanese, including people from Africa and Southeast Asia, appear in Osamu Tezuka's works. Sometimes these people are depicted very differently from the way they actually are today, in a manner that exaggerates a time long past or shows them to be from extremely undeveloped lands. Some feel that such images contribute to racial discrimination, especially against people of African descent. This was never Osamu Tezuka's intent, but we believe that as long as there are people who feel insulted or demeaned by these depictions, we must not ignore their feelings.

We are against discrimination, in all its forms, and intend to continue to work for its elimination. Nonetheless, we do not believe it would be proper to revise these works. Tezuka is no longer with us, and we cannot erase what he has done, and to alter his work would only violate his rights as a creator. More importantly, stopping publication or changing the content of his work would do little to solve the problems of discrimination that exist in the world.

We are presenting Osamu Tezuka's work as it was originally created, without changes. We do this because we believe it is also important to promote the underlying themes in his work, such as love for mankind and the sanctity of life. We hope that when you, the reader, encounter this work, you will keep in mind the differences in attitudes, then and now, toward discrimination, and that this will contribute to an even greater awareness of such problems.

— Tezuka Productions and Dark Horse Comics

CRUCIFIX ISLAND

First serialized between January and April
1957 in *Shonen* magazine.

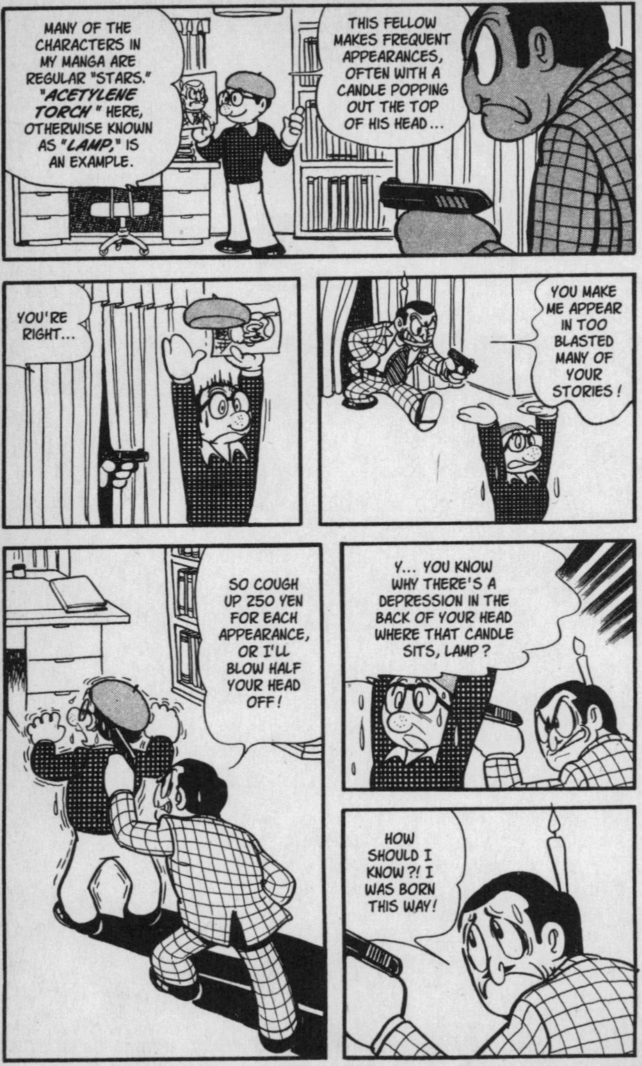
MANY OF THE CHARACTERS IN MY MANGA ARE REGULAR "STARS." "ACETYLENE TORCH" HERE, OTHERWISE KNOWN AS "LAMP," IS AN EXAMPLE.
THIS FELLOW MAKES FREQUENT APPEARANCES, OFTEN WITH A CANDLE POPPING OUT THE TOP OF HIS HEAD...
YOU'RE RIGHT...
YOU MAKE ME APPEAR IN TOO BLASTED MANY OF YOUR STORIES!
SO COUGH UP 250 YEN FOR EACH APPEARANCE, OR I'LL BLOW HALF YOUR HEAD OFF!
Y... YOU KNOW WHY THERE'S A DEPRESSION IN THE BACK OF YOUR HEAD WHERE THAT CANDLE SITS, LAMP?
HOW SHOULD I KNOW?! I WAS BORN THIS WAY!

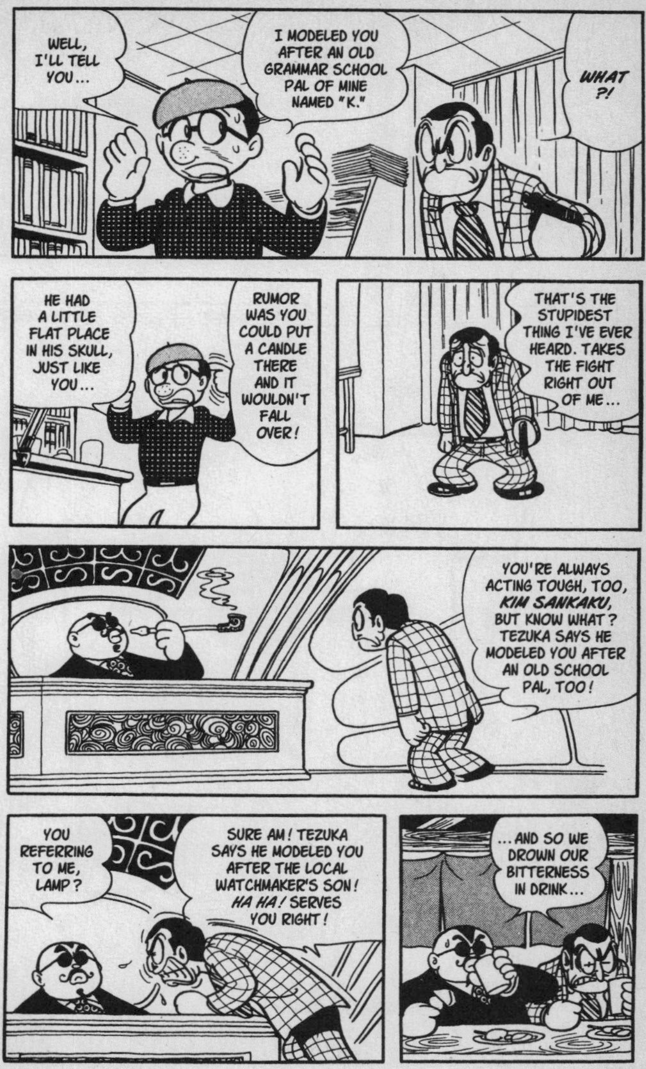
WELL, I'LL TELL YOU...
I MODELED YOU AFTER AN OLD GRAMMAR SCHOOL PAL OF MINE NAMED "K."
WHAT ?!
HE HAD A LITTLE FLAT PLACE IN HIS SKULL, JUST LIKE YOU...
RUMOR WAS YOU COULD PUT A CANDLE THERE AND IT WOULDN'T FALL OVER!
THAT'S THE STUPIDEST THING I'VE EVER HEARD. TAKES THE FIGHT RIGHT OUT OF ME...
YOU'RE ALWAYS ACTING TOUGH, TOO, KIM SANKAKU, BUT KNOW WHAT? TEZUKA SAYS HE MODELED YOU AFTER AN OLD SCHOOL PAL, TOO!
YOU REFERRING TO ME, LAMP?
SURE AM! TEZUKA SAYS HE MODELED YOU AFTER THE LOCAL WATCHMAKER'S SON! HA HA! SERVES YOU RIGHT!
...AND SO WE DROWN OUR BITTERNESS IN DRINK...

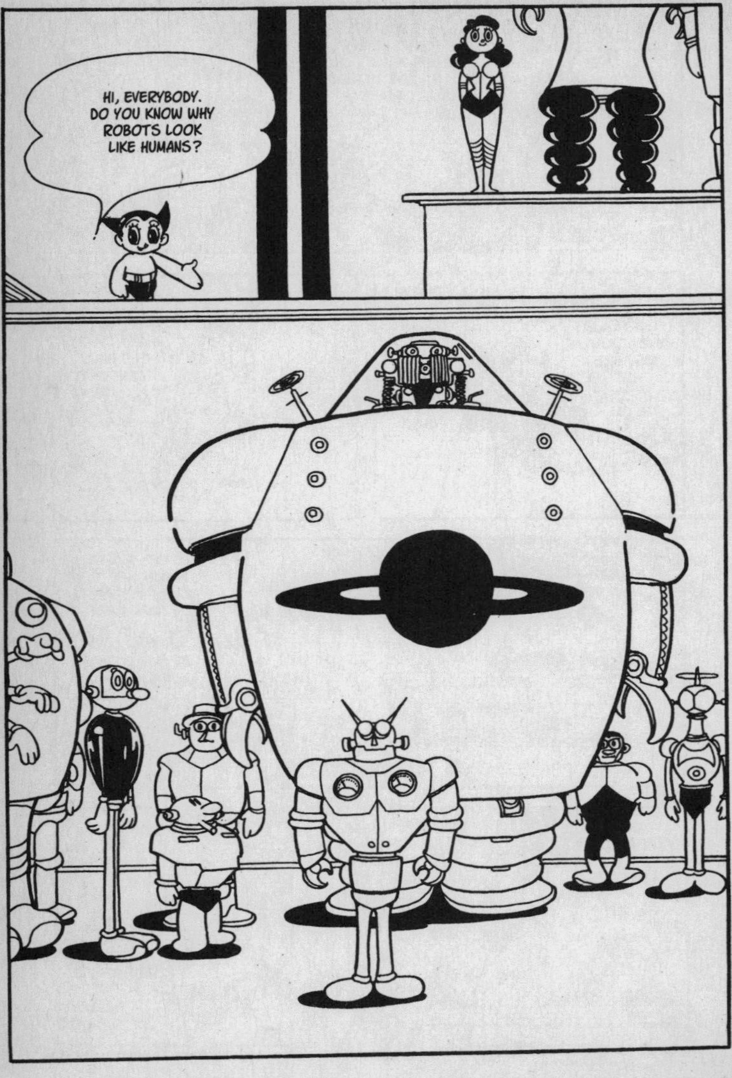
HI, EVERYBODY. DO YOU KNOW WHY ROBOTS LOOK LIKE HUMANS?

WELL, I'LL TELL YOU. THEY LOOK LIKE HUMANS 'CUZ IT'S EASIER FOR THEM TO DO HUMAN WORK THAT WAY...

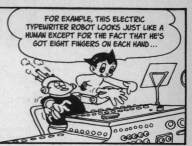

FOR EXAMPLE, THIS ELECTRIC TYPEWRITER ROBOT LOOKS JUST LIKE A HUMAN EXCEPT FOR THE FACT THAT HE'S GOT EIGHT FINGERS ON EACH HAND...

THIS FAMOUS ROBOT ACTRESS, SOYOKO MINAMIKAZE, HAS JUST WON AN AWARD. SHE'S JUST LIKE A HUMAN, DOWN TO THE WAY SHE BREATHES...

"BUT SOMETIMES IT'S BETTER NOT TO HAVE ROBOTS LOOK LIKE HUMANS..."

"MR. YARIKURI, THE HEAD OF THE *MARS DEVELOPMENT COMMISSION*, WAS DRIVEN BY A REAL NEED..."

"...SO HE CREATED A ROBOT THAT COULD TRANSFORM INTO A TRACTOR AT THE FLICK OF A SWITCH!"

AFTER THAT, TRANSFORMING ROBOTS BECAME ALL THE RAGE!

"THERE WERE BELLCAP ROBOTS WHO COULD CHANGE INTO JET AIRCRAFT..."

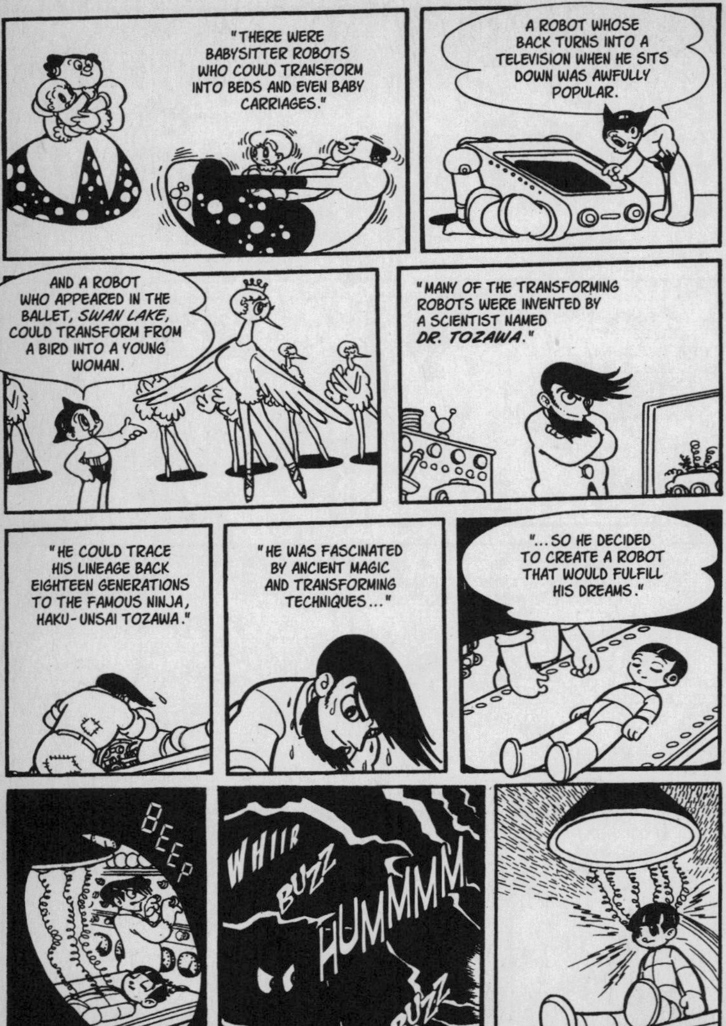
"THERE WERE BABYSITTER ROBOTS WHO COULD TRANSFORM INTO BEDS AND EVEN BABY CARRIAGES."
A ROBOT WHOSE BACK TURNS INTO A TELEVISION WHEN HE SITS DOWN WAS AWFULLY POPULAR.
AND A ROBOT WHO APPEARED IN THE BALLET, *SWAN LAKE*, COULD TRANSFORM FROM A BIRD INTO A YOUNG WOMAN.
"MANY OF THE TRANSFORMING ROBOTS WERE INVENTED BY A SCIENTIST NAMED ***DR. TOZAWA***."
"HE COULD TRACE HIS LINEAGE BACK EIGHTEEN GENERATIONS TO THE FAMOUS NINJA, HAKU-UNSAI TOZAWA."
"HE WAS FASCINATED BY ANCIENT MAGIC AND TRANSFORMING TECHNIQUES..."
"...SO HE DECIDED TO CREATE A ROBOT THAT WOULD FULFILL HIS DREAMS."
BEEP
WHIIR
BUZZ
HUMMMM
BUZZ

"BUT BEFORE TOZAWA COULD COMPLETE HIS ROBOT..."

"HE WAS ARRESTED FOR STEALING MONEY FROM THE MINISTRY OF SCIENCE."

"AND HE WAS THROWN INTO PRISON AS A CLASS-A CRIMINAL..."

"TOZAWA'S ROBOT WAS THUS LEFT UNFINISHED."

"AND SO OUR STORY BEGINS..."

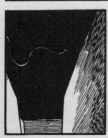

CLANK

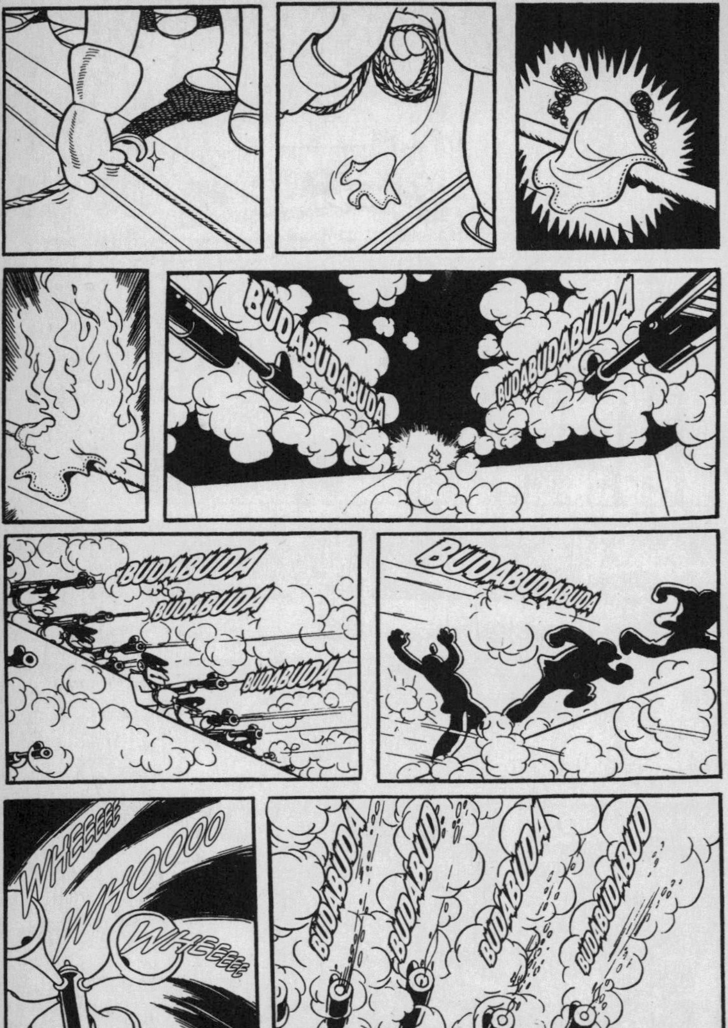
BUDABUDABUDA
BUDABUDABUDA
BUDABUDA
BUDABUDA
BUDABUDA
BUDABUDABUDA
WHEEEEE
WHOOOOO
WHEEEEE
BUDABUDA
BUDABUD
BUDABUDA
BUDABUDABUD

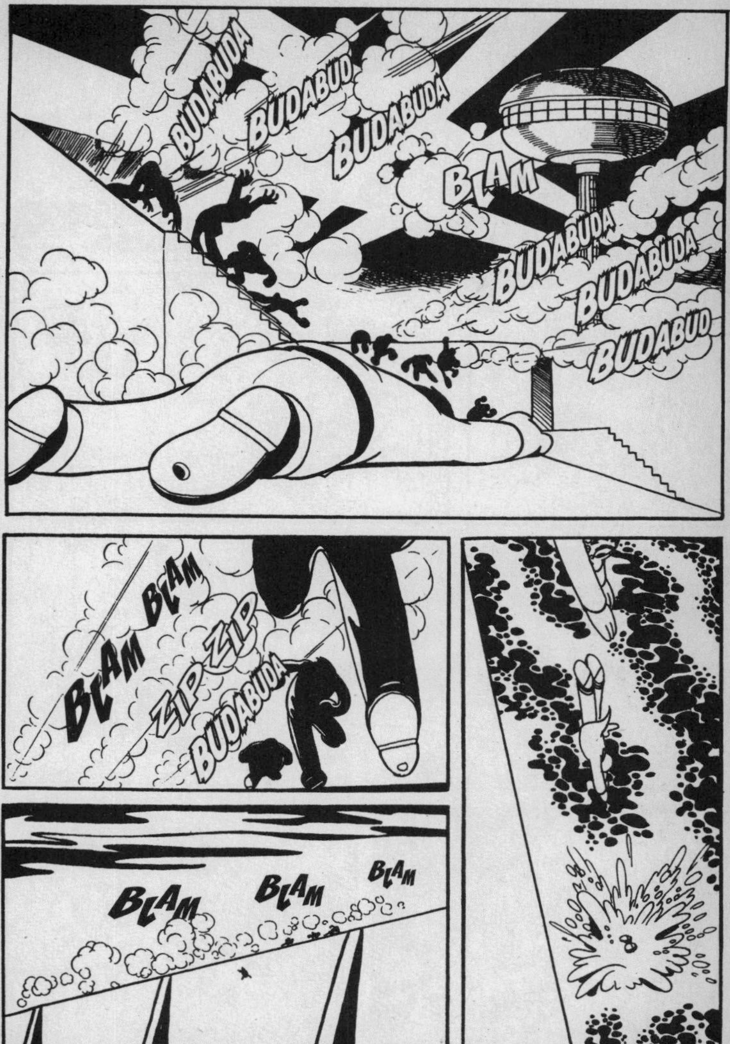
BUDABUDA
BUDABUD
BUDABUDA
BLAM
BUDABUDA
BUDABUDA
BUDABUD
BLAM
BLAM
ZIP ZIP
BUDABUDA
BLAM
BLAM
BLAM

OKAY, GUYS... REGROUP OVER HERE!

YOU MEAN WE'RE THE ONLY ONES WHO GOT OUT ALIVE?

EVERYONE ELSE WAS SHOT, BOSS, AND WE WILL BE TOO UNLESS WE GET OUT OF HERE...

HEY... I SEE THREE FISH SWIMMING...

SHOULD WE OPEN FIRE ON 'EM?

NAW... LET 'EM GO...

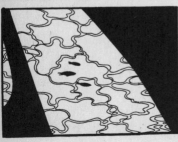

HEH HEH. GOOD THING WE MADE THESE FAKE FISH SKINS OUT OF OLD RUBBER...

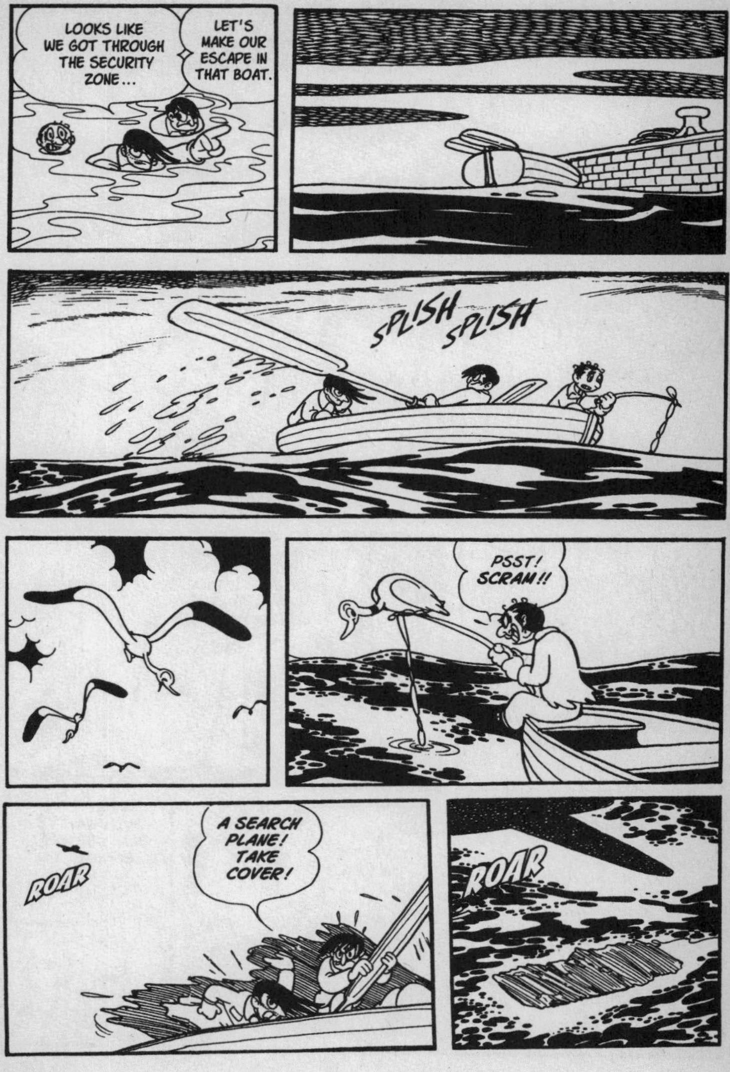
LOOKS LIKE WE GOT THROUGH THE SECURITY ZONE...
LET'S MAKE OUR ESCAPE IN THAT BOAT.
SPLISH SPLISH
PSST! SCRAM!!
ROAR
A SEARCH PLANE! TAKE COVER!
ROAR

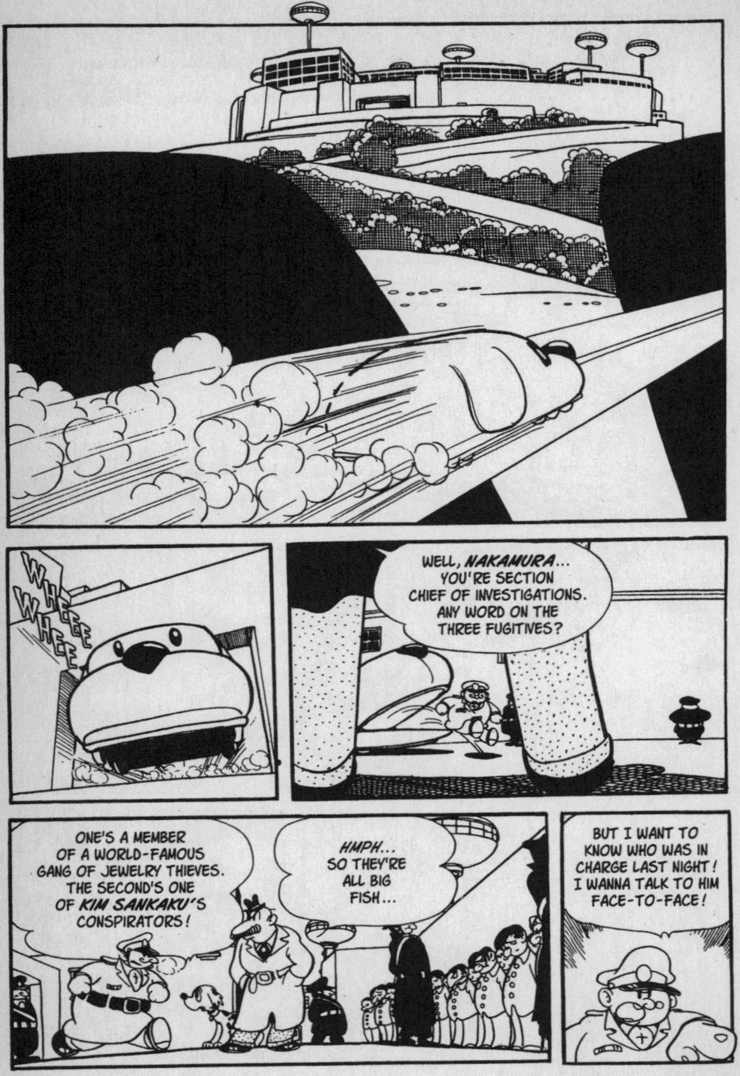
WHEEEE
WHEE
WELL, NAKAMURA... YOU'RE SECTION CHIEF OF INVESTIGATIONS. ANY WORD ON THE THREE FUGITIVES?
ONE'S A MEMBER OF A WORLD-FAMOUS GANG OF JEWELRY THIEVES. THE SECOND'S ONE OF KIM SANKAKU'S CONSPIRATORS!
HMPH... SO THEY'RE ALL BIG FISH...
BUT I WANT TO KNOW WHO WAS IN CHARGE LAST NIGHT! I WANNA TALK TO HIM FACE-TO-FACE!

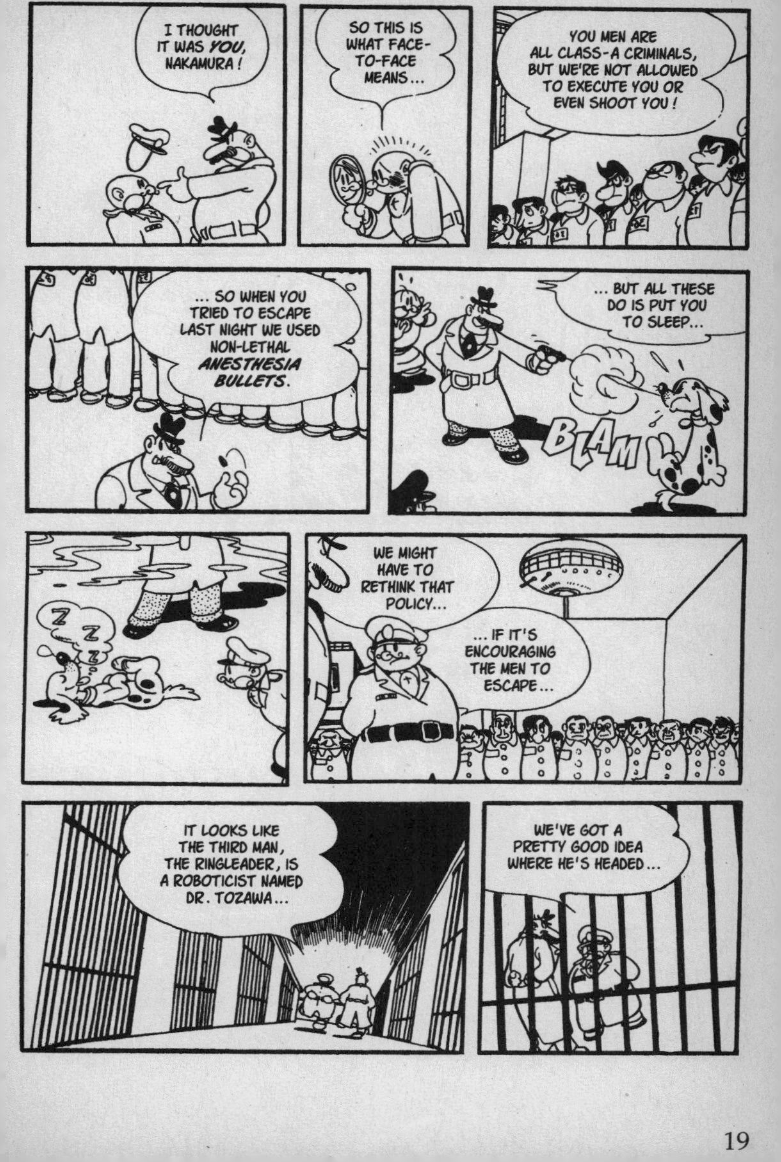
I THOUGHT IT WAS *YOU*, NAKAMURA!
SO THIS IS WHAT FACE-TO-FACE MEANS...
YOU MEN ARE ALL CLASS-A CRIMINALS, BUT WE'RE NOT ALLOWED TO EXECUTE YOU OR EVEN SHOOT YOU!
... SO WHEN YOU TRIED TO ESCAPE LAST NIGHT WE USED NON-LETHAL ***ANESTHESIA BULLETS***.
... BUT ALL THESE DO IS PUT YOU TO SLEEP...
BLAM
Z Z Z
WE MIGHT HAVE TO RETHINK THAT POLICY...
... IF IT'S ENCOURAGING THE MEN TO ESCAPE...
IT LOOKS LIKE THE THIRD MAN, THE RINGLEADER, IS A ROBOTICIST NAMED DR. TOZAWA...
WE'VE GOT A PRETTY GOOD IDEA WHERE HE'S HEADED...

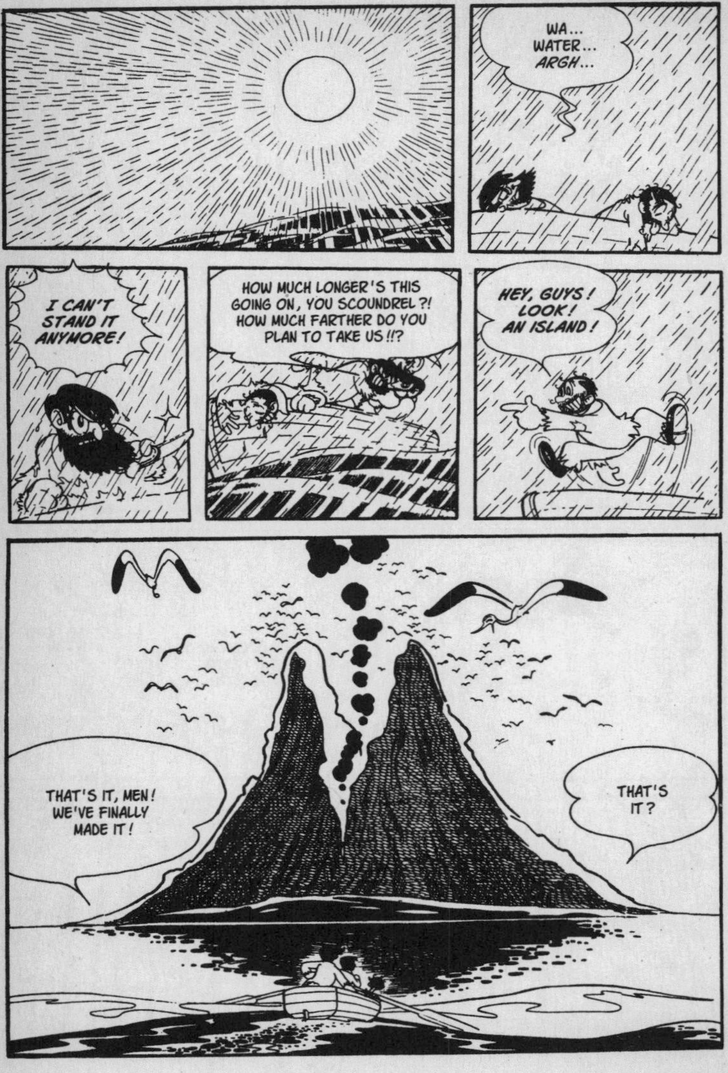

WA... WATER... ARGH...
I CAN'T STAND IT ANYMORE!
HOW MUCH LONGER'S THIS GOING ON, YOU SCOUNDREL?! HOW MUCH FARTHER DO YOU PLAN TO TAKE US!!?
HEY, GUYS! LOOK! AN ISLAND!
THAT'S IT, MEN! WE'VE FINALLY MADE IT!
THAT'S IT?

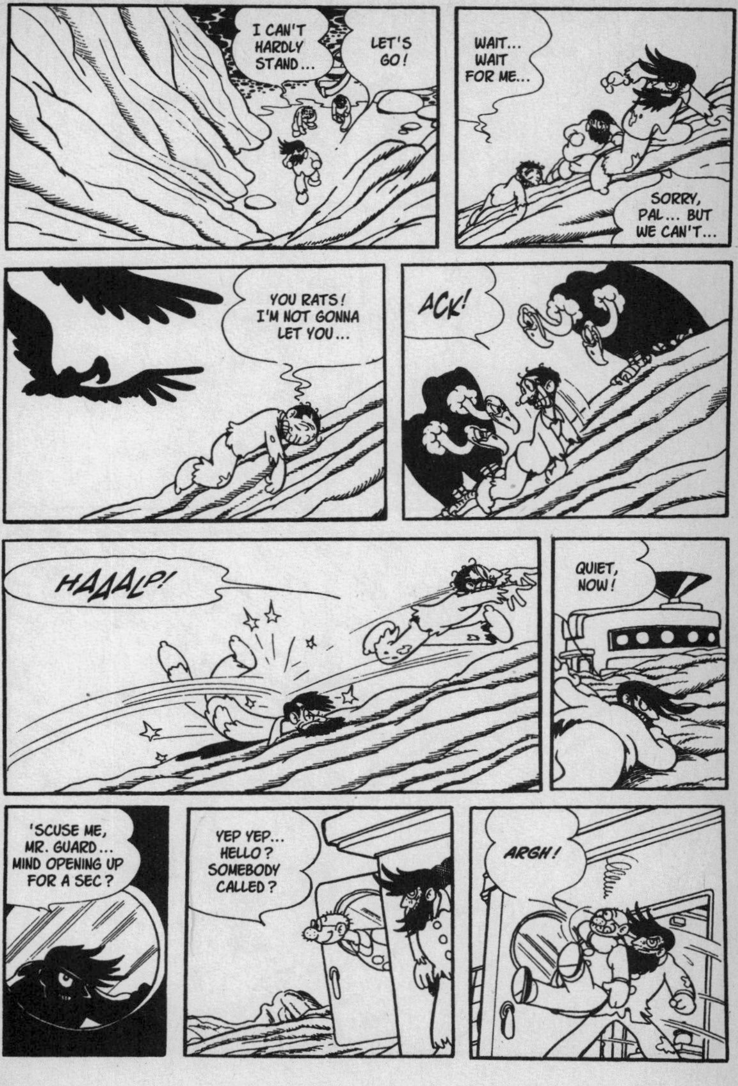
I CAN'T HARDLY STAND...
LET'S GO!
WAIT... WAIT FOR ME...
SORRY, PAL... BUT WE CAN'T...
YOU RATS! I'M NOT GONNA LET YOU...
ACK!
HAAALP!
QUIET, NOW!
'SCUSE ME, MR. GUARD... MIND OPENING UP FOR A SEC?
YEP YEP... HELLO? SOMEBODY CALLED?
ARGH!

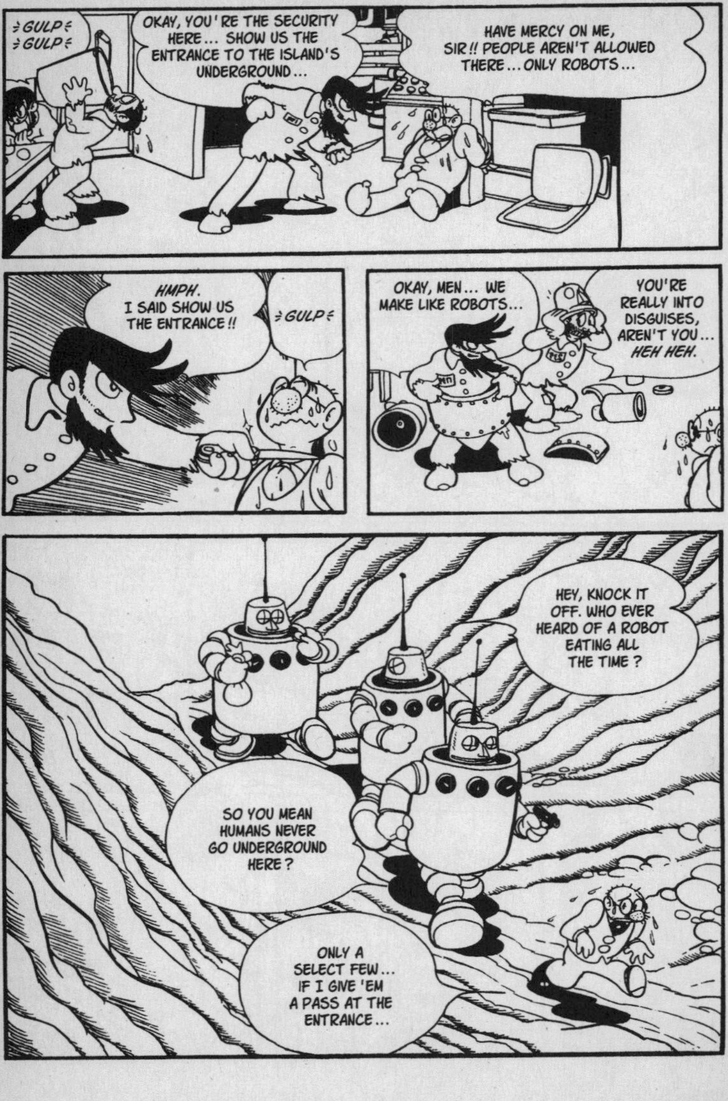

≑GULP≑ ≑GULP≑
OKAY, YOU'RE THE SECURITY HERE... SHOW US THE ENTRANCE TO THE ISLAND'S UNDERGROUND...
HAVE MERCY ON ME, SIR!! PEOPLE AREN'T ALLOWED THERE... ONLY ROBOTS...
HMPH. I SAID SHOW US THE ENTRANCE!!
≑GULP≑
OKAY, MEN... WE MAKE LIKE ROBOTS...
YOU'RE REALLY INTO DISGUISES, AREN'T YOU... HEH HEH.
HEY, KNOCK IT OFF. WHO EVER HEARD OF A ROBOT EATING ALL THE TIME?
SO YOU MEAN HUMANS NEVER GO UNDERGROUND HERE?
ONLY A SELECT FEW... IF I GIVE 'EM A PASS AT THE ENTRANCE...

SO WHO HAVE YOU GIVEN PASSES TO?

WELL, LIKE *MR. MUSTACHIO*... HE'S TEACHING AT THE ROBOT SCHOOL...

THAT SETTLES IT. WE'VE GOT THE RIGHT ISLAND!

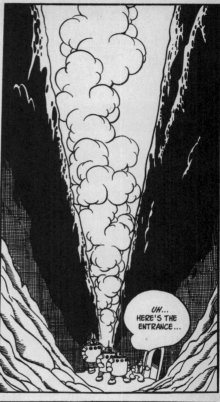

UH... HERE'S THE ENTRANCE...

NOW BEAT IT, POPS!

WE DON'T NEED YOU ANYMORE!!

HAALP!

23

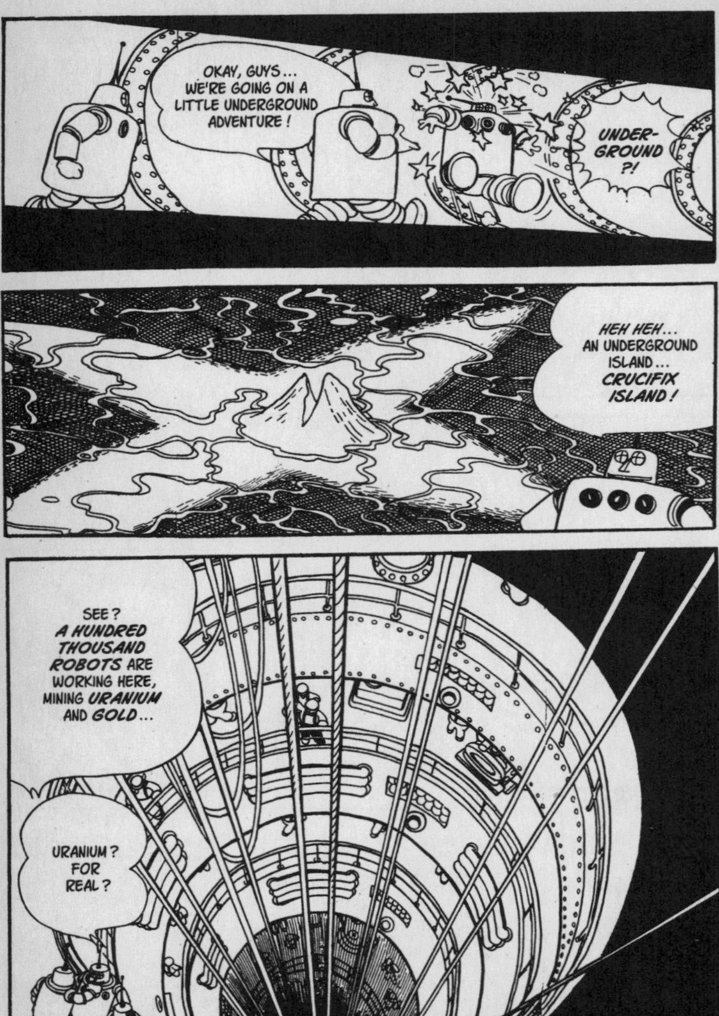
OKAY, GUYS... WE'RE GOING ON A LITTLE UNDERGROUND ADVENTURE!
UNDER-GROUND ?!
HEH HEH... AN UNDERGROUND ISLAND... CRUCIFIX ISLAND!
SEE? A HUNDRED THOUSAND ROBOTS ARE WORKING HERE, MINING URANIUM AND GOLD...
URANIUM? FOR REAL?

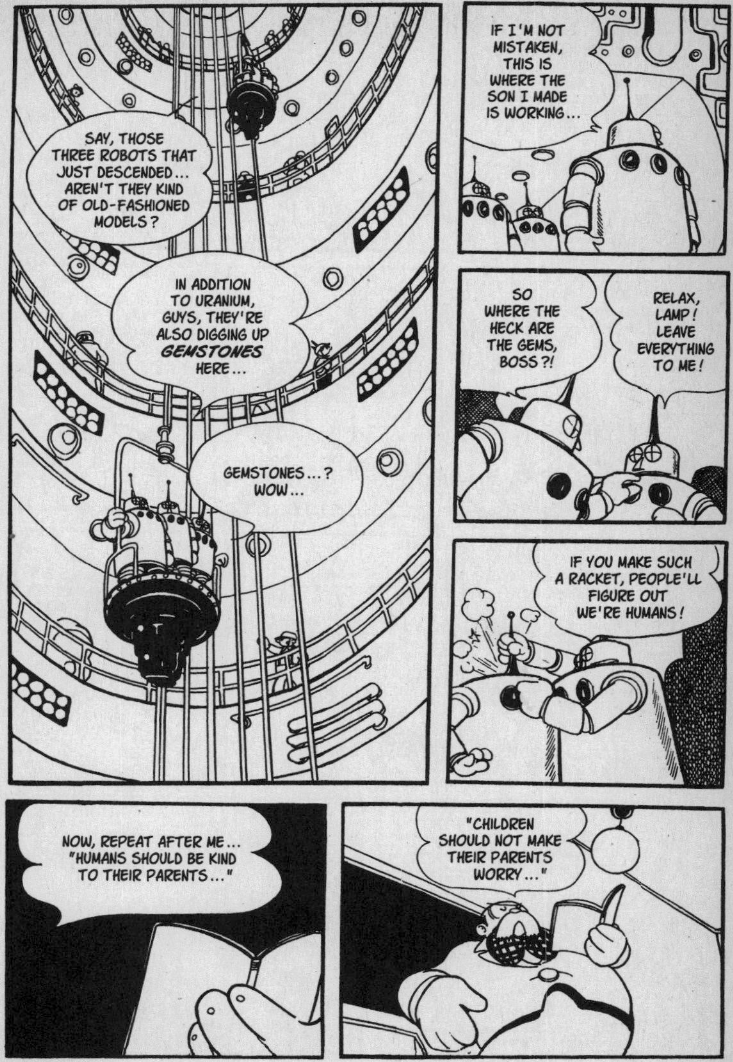
SAY, THOSE THREE ROBOTS THAT JUST DESCENDED... AREN'T THEY KIND OF OLD-FASHIONED MODELS?
IN ADDITION TO URANIUM, GUYS, THEY'RE ALSO DIGGING UP *GEMSTONES* HERE...
GEMSTONES...? WOW...
IF I'M NOT MISTAKEN, THIS IS WHERE THE SON I MADE IS WORKING...
SO WHERE THE HECK ARE THE GEMS, BOSS?!
RELAX, LAMP! LEAVE EVERYTHING TO ME!
IF YOU MAKE SUCH A RACKET, PEOPLE'LL FIGURE OUT WE'RE HUMANS!
NOW, REPEAT AFTER ME... "HUMANS SHOULD BE KIND TO THEIR PARENTS..."
"CHILDREN SHOULD NOT MAKE THEIR PARENTS WORRY..."

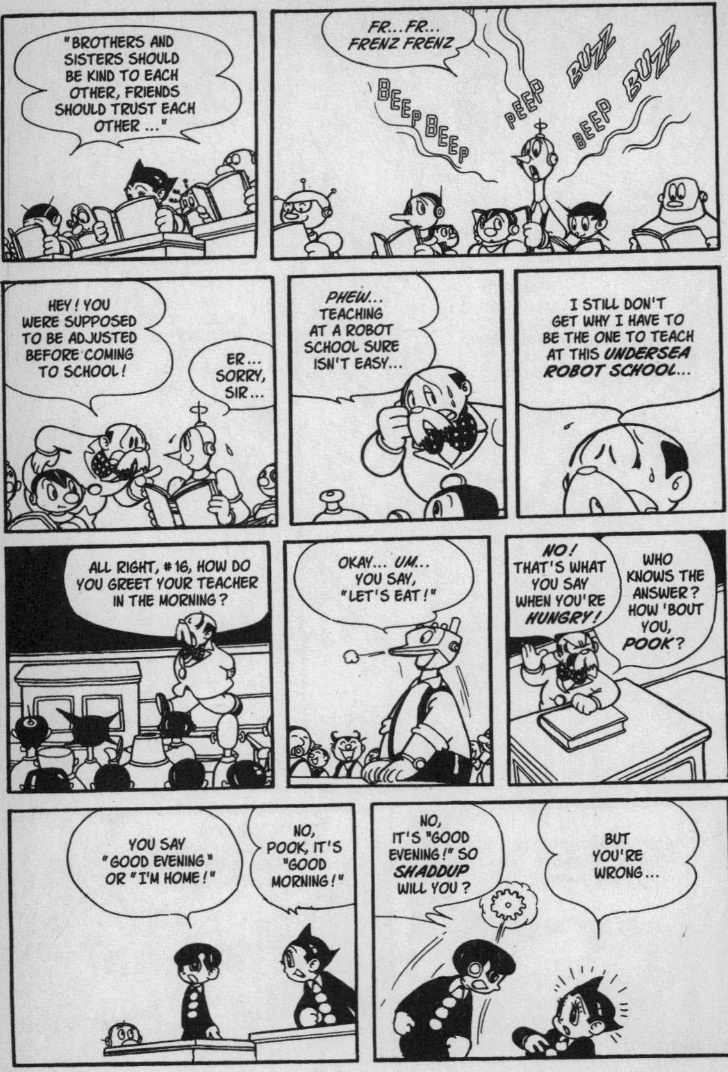
"BROTHERS AND SISTERS SHOULD BE KIND TO EACH OTHER, FRIENDS SHOULD TRUST EACH OTHER ..."
FR... FR... FRENZ FRENZ
BEEP BEEP
PEEP BUZZ
BEEP BUZZ
HEY! YOU WERE SUPPOSED TO BE ADJUSTED BEFORE COMING TO SCHOOL!
ER... SORRY, SIR...
PHEW... TEACHING AT A ROBOT SCHOOL SURE ISN'T EASY...
I STILL DON'T GET WHY I HAVE TO BE THE ONE TO TEACH AT THIS UNDERSEA ROBOT SCHOOL...
ALL RIGHT, #16, HOW DO YOU GREET YOUR TEACHER IN THE MORNING?
OKAY... UM... YOU SAY, "LET'S EAT!"
NO! THAT'S WHAT YOU SAY WHEN YOU'RE HUNGRY!
WHO KNOWS THE ANSWER? HOW 'BOUT YOU, POOK?
YOU SAY "GOOD EVENING" OR "I'M HOME!"
NO, POOK, IT'S "GOOD MORNING!"
NO, IT'S "GOOD EVENING!" SO SHADDUP WILL YOU?
BUT YOU'RE WRONG...

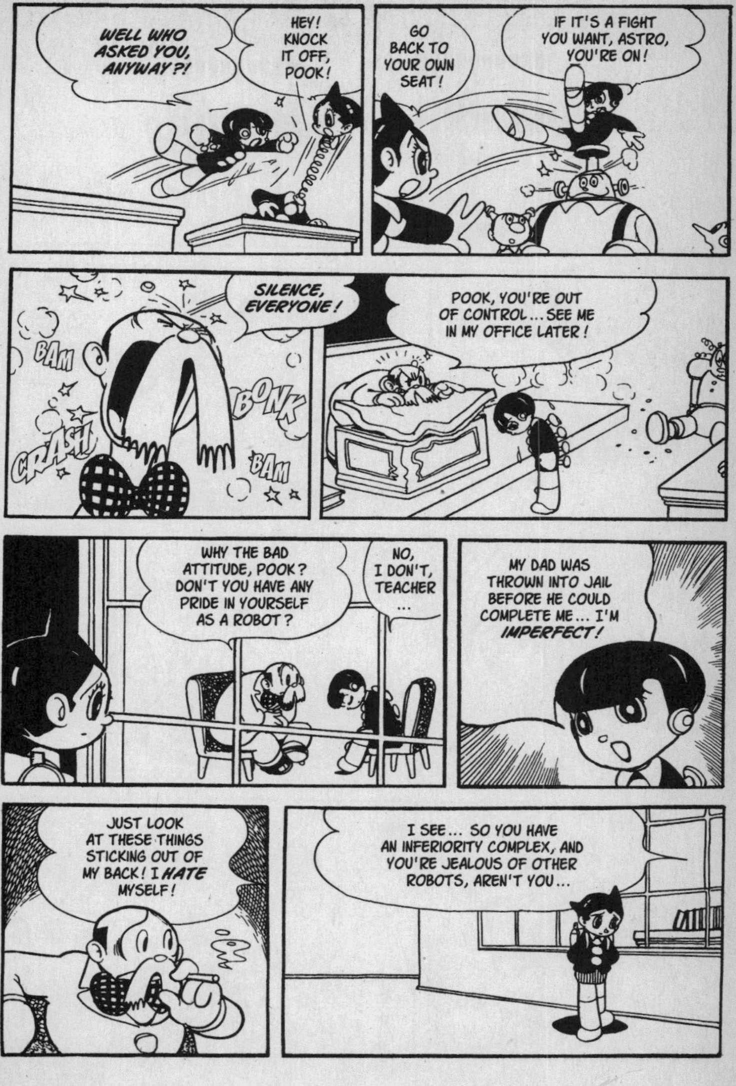
WELL WHO ASKED YOU, ANYWAY?!
HEY! KNOCK IT OFF, POOK!
GO BACK TO YOUR OWN SEAT!
IF IT'S A FIGHT YOU WANT, ASTRO, YOU'RE ON!
BAM
CRASH
SILENCE, EVERYONE!
BONK
BAM
POOK, YOU'RE OUT OF CONTROL... SEE ME IN MY OFFICE LATER!
WHY THE BAD ATTITUDE, POOK? DON'T YOU HAVE ANY PRIDE IN YOURSELF AS A ROBOT?
NO, I DON'T, TEACHER ...
MY DAD WAS THROWN INTO JAIL BEFORE HE COULD COMPLETE ME... I'M IMPERFECT!
JUST LOOK AT THESE THINGS STICKING OUT OF MY BACK! I HATE MYSELF!
I SEE... SO YOU HAVE AN INFERIORITY COMPLEX, AND YOU'RE JEALOUS OF OTHER ROBOTS, AREN'T YOU...

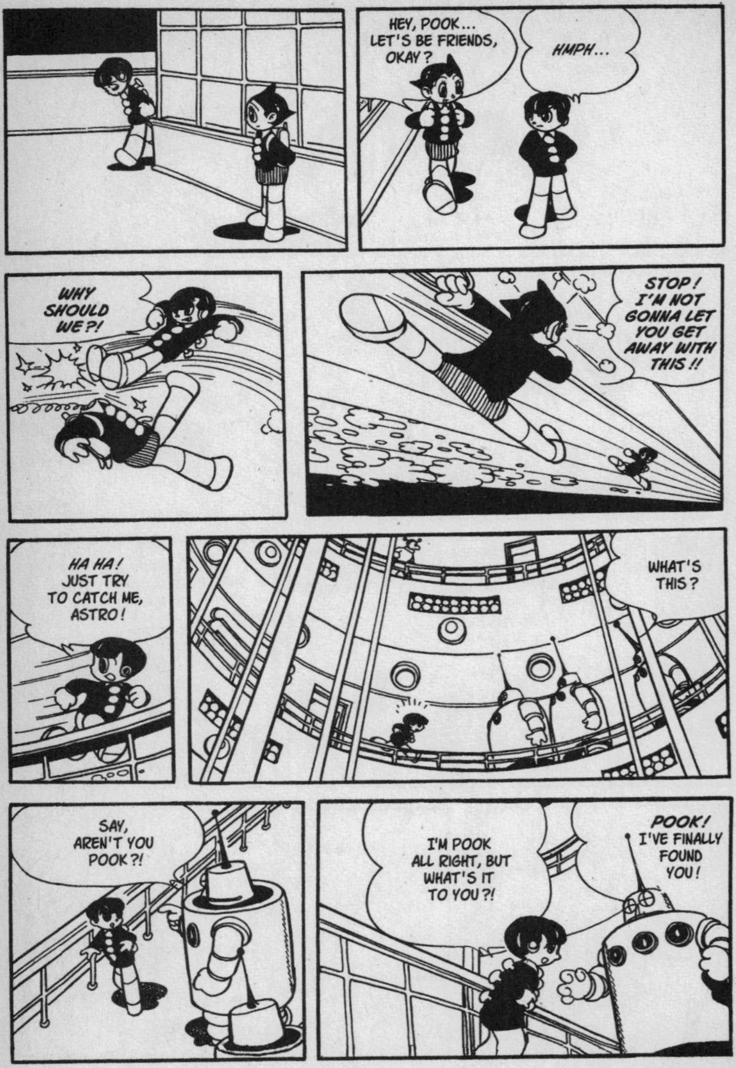
HEY, POOK... LET'S BE FRIENDS, OKAY?
HMPH...
WHY SHOULD WE?!
STOP! I'M NOT GONNA LET YOU GET AWAY WITH THIS!!
HA HA! JUST TRY TO CATCH ME, ASTRO!
WHAT'S THIS?
SAY, AREN'T YOU POOK?!
I'M POOK ALL RIGHT, BUT WHAT'S IT TO YOU?!
POOK! I'VE FINALLY FOUND YOU!

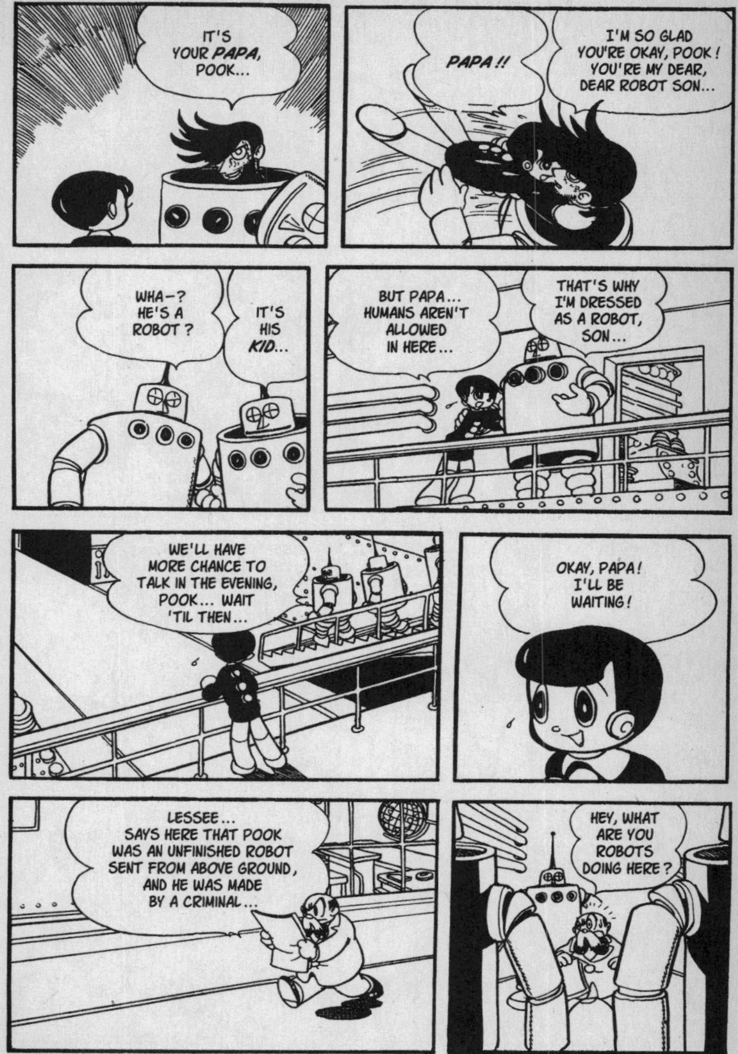
IT'S YOUR PAPA, POOK...
PAPA!!
I'M SO GLAD YOU'RE OKAY, POOK! YOU'RE MY DEAR, DEAR ROBOT SON...
WHA-? HE'S A ROBOT?
IT'S HIS KID...
BUT PAPA... HUMANS AREN'T ALLOWED IN HERE...
THAT'S WHY I'M DRESSED AS A ROBOT, SON...
WE'LL HAVE MORE CHANCE TO TALK IN THE EVENING, POOK... WAIT 'TIL THEN...
OKAY, PAPA! I'LL BE WAITING!
LESSEE... SAYS HERE THAT POOK WAS AN UNFINISHED ROBOT SENT FROM ABOVE GROUND, AND HE WAS MADE BY A CRIMINAL...
HEY, WHAT ARE YOU ROBOTS DOING HERE?

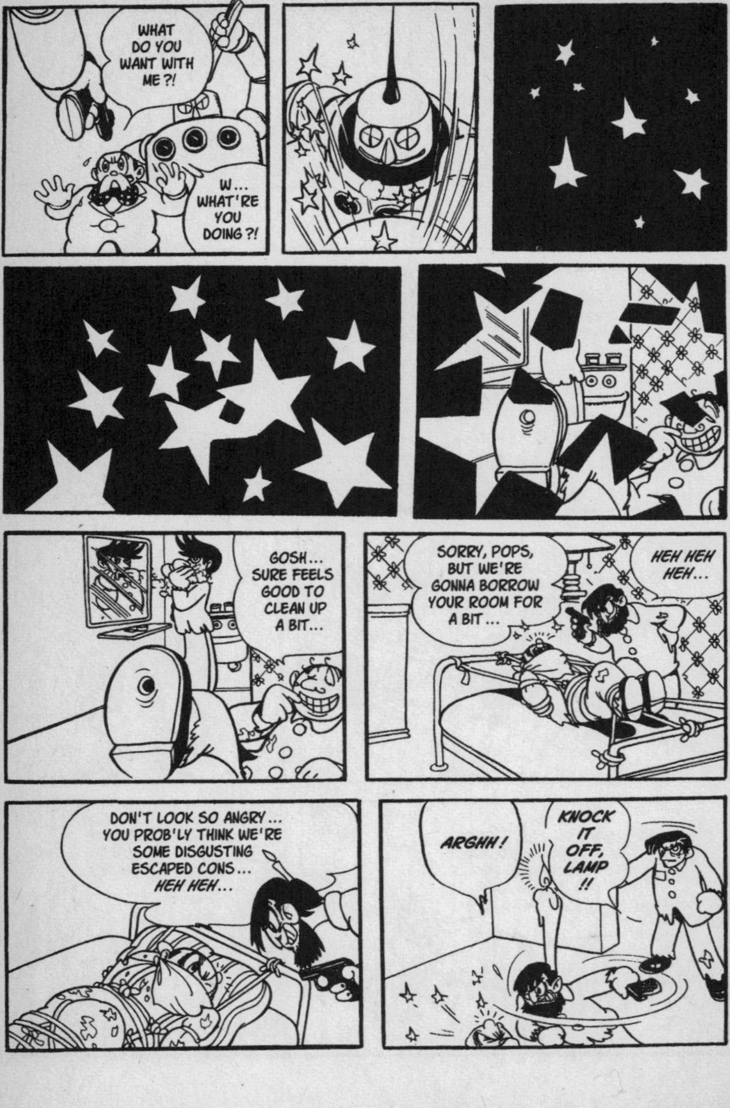
WHAT DO YOU WANT WITH ME ?!
W... WHAT'RE YOU DOING ?!
GOSH... SURE FEELS GOOD TO CLEAN UP A BIT...
SORRY, POPS, BUT WE'RE GONNA BORROW YOUR ROOM FOR A BIT...
HEH HEH HEH...
DON'T LOOK SO ANGRY... YOU PROB'LY THINK WE'RE SOME DISGUSTING ESCAPED CONS... HEH HEH...
ARGHH!
KNOCK IT OFF, LAMP !!

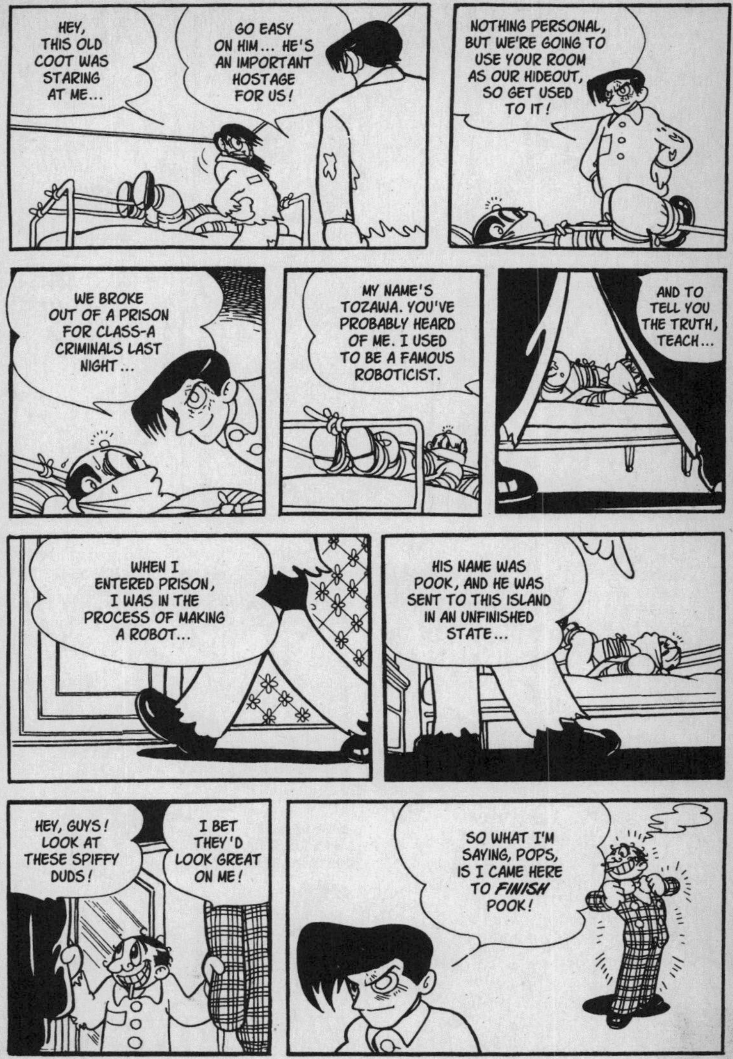
HEY, THIS OLD COOT WAS STARING AT ME...
GO EASY ON HIM... HE'S AN IMPORTANT HOSTAGE FOR US!
NOTHING PERSONAL, BUT WE'RE GOING TO USE YOUR ROOM AS OUR HIDEOUT, SO GET USED TO IT!
WE BROKE OUT OF A PRISON FOR CLASS-A CRIMINALS LAST NIGHT...
MY NAME'S TOZAWA. YOU'VE PROBABLY HEARD OF ME. I USED TO BE A FAMOUS ROBOTICIST.
AND TO TELL YOU THE TRUTH, TEACH...
WHEN I ENTERED PRISON, I WAS IN THE PROCESS OF MAKING A ROBOT...
HIS NAME WAS POOK, AND HE WAS SENT TO THIS ISLAND IN AN UNFINISHED STATE...
HEY, GUYS! LOOK AT THESE SPIFFY DUDS!
I BET THEY'D LOOK GREAT ON ME!
SO WHAT I'M SAYING, POPS, IS I CAME HERE TO *FINISH* POOK!

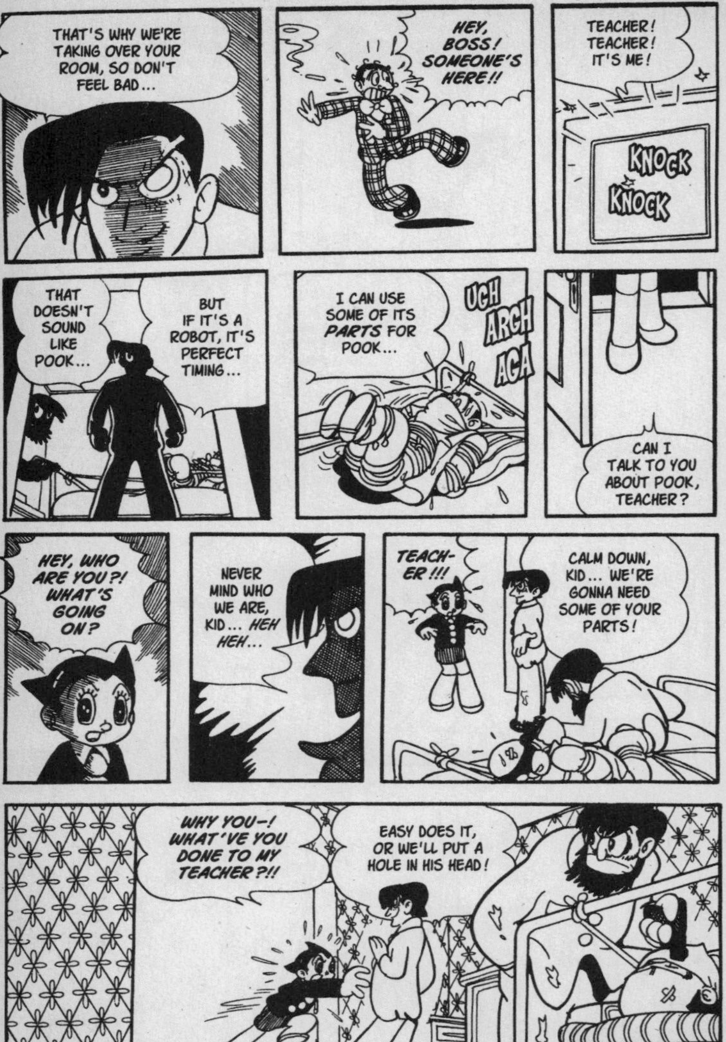
THAT'S WHY WE'RE TAKING OVER YOUR ROOM, SO DON'T FEEL BAD...
HEY, BOSS! SOMEONE'S HERE!!
TEACHER! TEACHER! IT'S ME!
KNOCK
KNOCK
THAT DOESN'T SOUND LIKE POOK...
BUT IF IT'S A ROBOT, IT'S PERFECT TIMING...
I CAN USE SOME OF ITS PARTS FOR POOK...
UGH
ARGH
AGA
CAN I TALK TO YOU ABOUT POOK, TEACHER?
HEY, WHO ARE YOU?! WHAT'S GOING ON?
NEVER MIND WHO WE ARE, KID... HEH HEH...
TEACH-ER!!!
CALM DOWN, KID... WE'RE GONNA NEED SOME OF YOUR PARTS!
WHY YOU–! WHAT'VE YOU DONE TO MY TEACHER?!!
EASY DOES IT, OR WE'LL PUT A HOLE IN HIS HEAD!

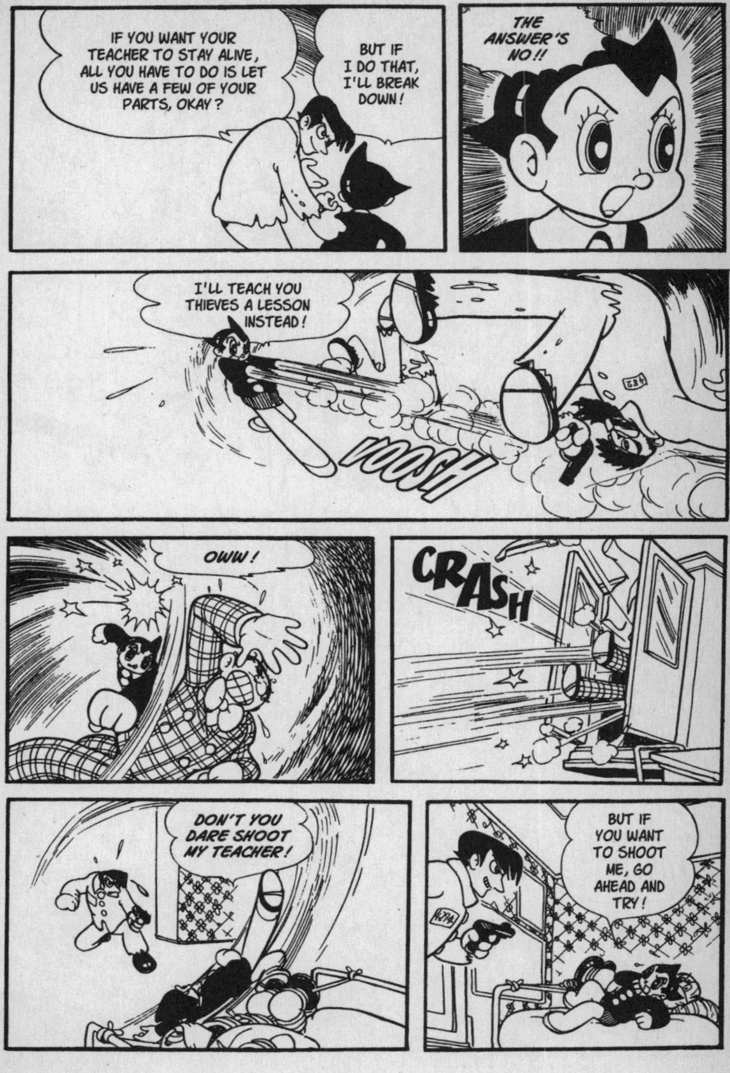
IF YOU WANT YOUR TEACHER TO STAY ALIVE, ALL YOU HAVE TO DO IS LET US HAVE A FEW OF YOUR PARTS, OKAY?
BUT IF I DO THAT, I'LL BREAK DOWN!
THE ANSWER'S NO!!
I'LL TEACH YOU THIEVES A LESSON INSTEAD!
VOOSH
OWW!
CRASH
DON'T YOU DARE SHOOT MY TEACHER!
BUT IF YOU WANT TO SHOOT ME, GO AHEAD AND TRY!

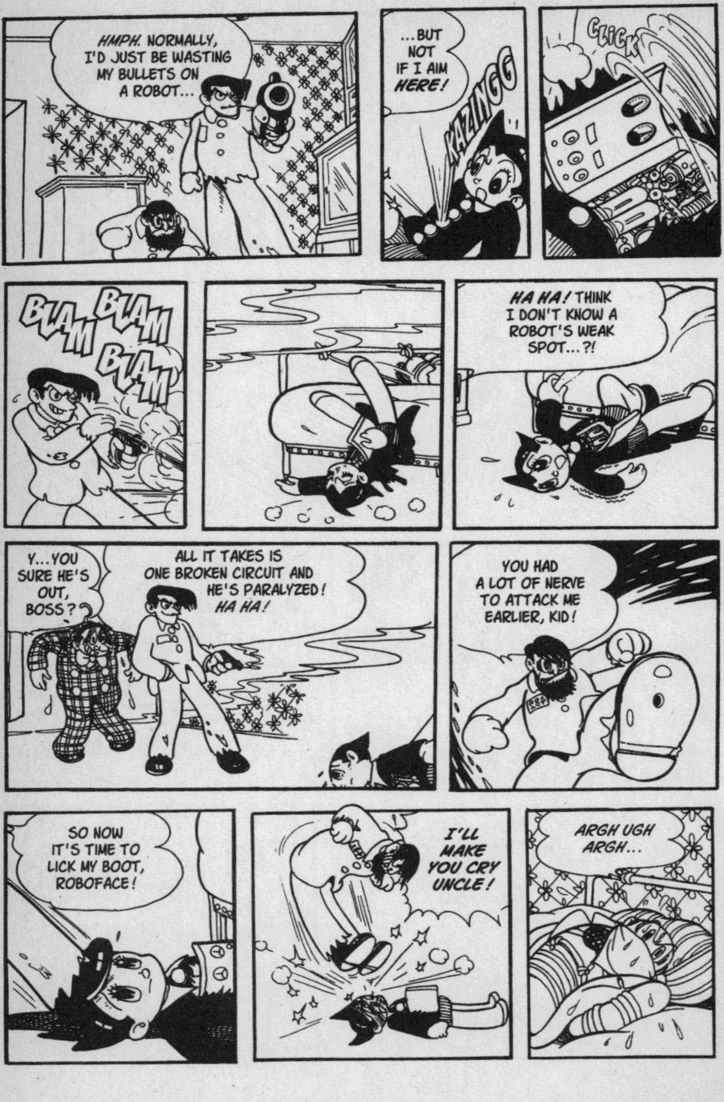
HMPH. NORMALLY, I'D JUST BE WASTING MY BULLETS ON A ROBOT...
...BUT NOT IF I AIM HERE!
KAZINGG
CLICK
BLAM BLAM BLAM
HA HA! THINK I DON'T KNOW A ROBOT'S WEAK SPOT...?!
Y...YOU SURE HE'S OUT, BOSS?
ALL IT TAKES IS ONE BROKEN CIRCUIT AND HE'S PARALYZED! HA HA!
YOU HAD A LOT OF NERVE TO ATTACK ME EARLIER, KID!
SO NOW IT'S TIME TO LICK MY BOOT, ROBOFACE!
I'LL MAKE YOU CRY UNCLE!
ARGH UGH ARGH...

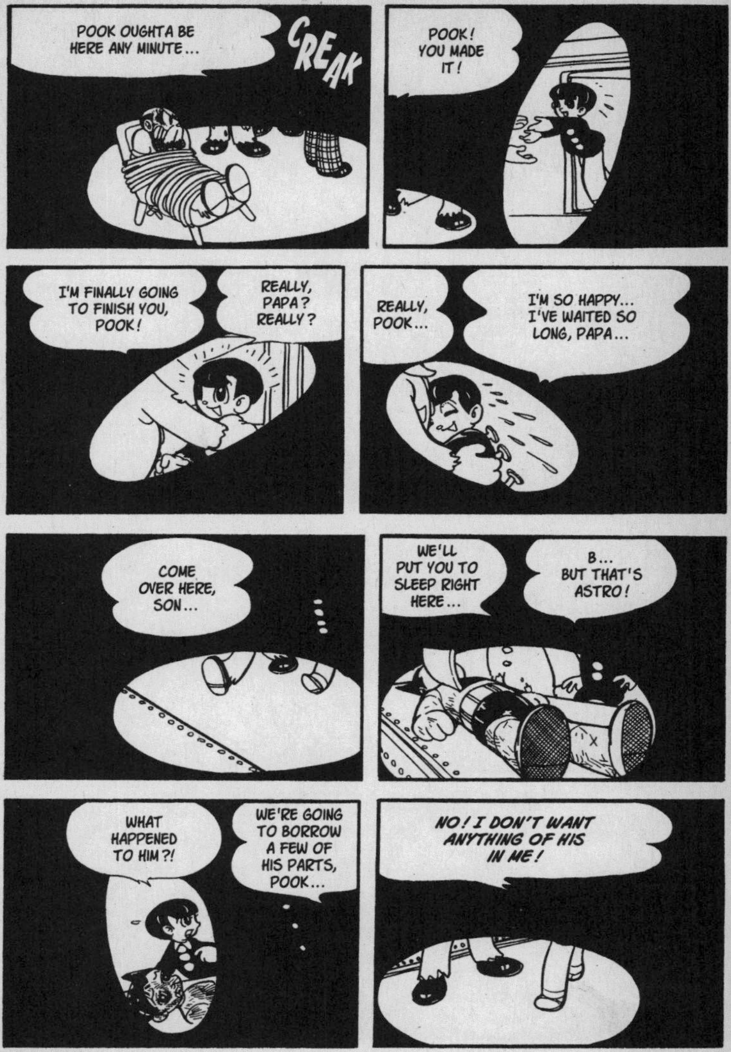
POOK OUGHTA BE HERE ANY MINUTE...
CREAK
POOK! YOU MADE IT!
I'M FINALLY GOING TO FINISH YOU, POOK!
REALLY, PAPA? REALLY?
REALLY, POOK...
I'M SO HAPPY... I'VE WAITED SO LONG, PAPA...
COME OVER HERE, SON...
WE'LL PUT YOU TO SLEEP RIGHT HERE...
B... BUT THAT'S ASTRO!
WHAT HAPPENED TO HIM?!
WE'RE GOING TO BORROW A FEW OF HIS PARTS, POOK...
NO! I DON'T WANT ANYTHING OF HIS IN ME!

BUT IF YOU USE THEM FOR AWHILE THEY'LL BE YOURS, POOK.

OKAY... IF THAT'S THE CASE, HURRY UP AND DO IT...

HEY... YOU CAN'T DO THAT TO A...A...ASTRO! WHO DO YOU THINK YOU'RE DEALING WITH HERE?

THIS IS NONE OF YOUR BEESWAX, TEACH!!

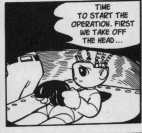

TIME TO START THE OPERATION. FIRST WE TAKE OFF THE HEAD...

STOP! THIEF!

OVER MY DEAD BODY...

OVER YOUR LIVE BODY!

ZAP ZAP ZAP

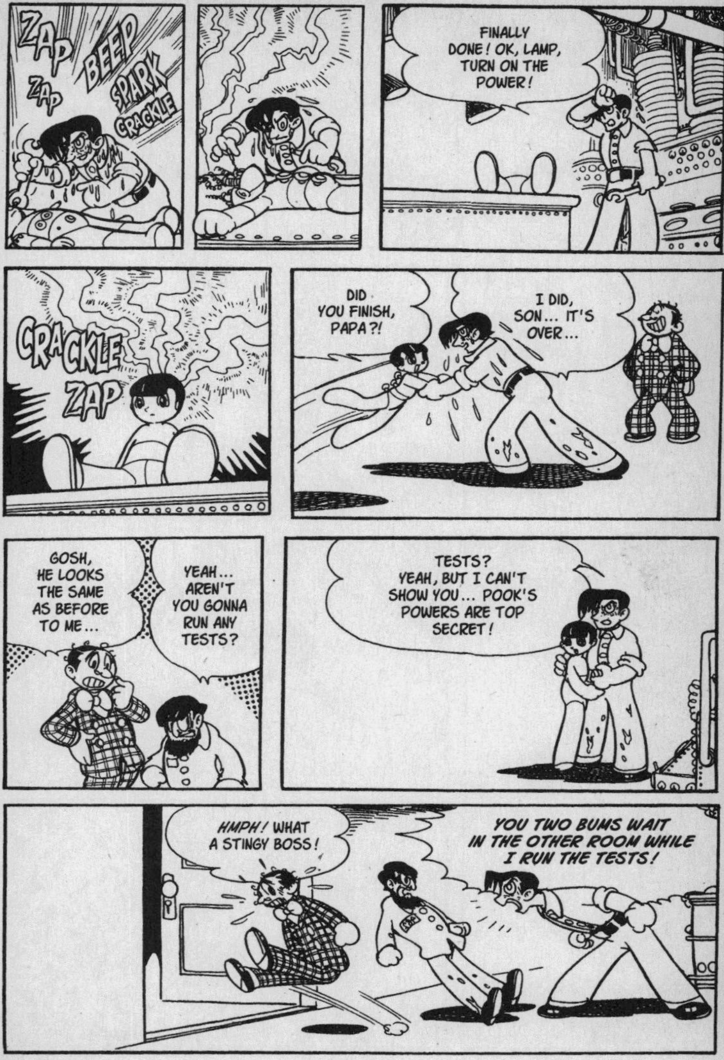
ZAP
ZAP
BEEP
SPARK
CRACKLE
FINALLY DONE! OK, LAMP, TURN ON THE POWER!
CRACKLE
ZAP
DID YOU FINISH, PAPA?!
I DID, SON... IT'S OVER...
GOSH, HE LOOKS THE SAME AS BEFORE TO ME...
YEAH... AREN'T YOU GONNA RUN ANY TESTS?
TESTS? YEAH, BUT I CAN'T SHOW YOU... POOK'S POWERS ARE TOP SECRET!
HMPH! WHAT A STINGY BOSS!
YOU TWO BUMS WAIT IN THE OTHER ROOM WHILE I RUN THE TESTS!

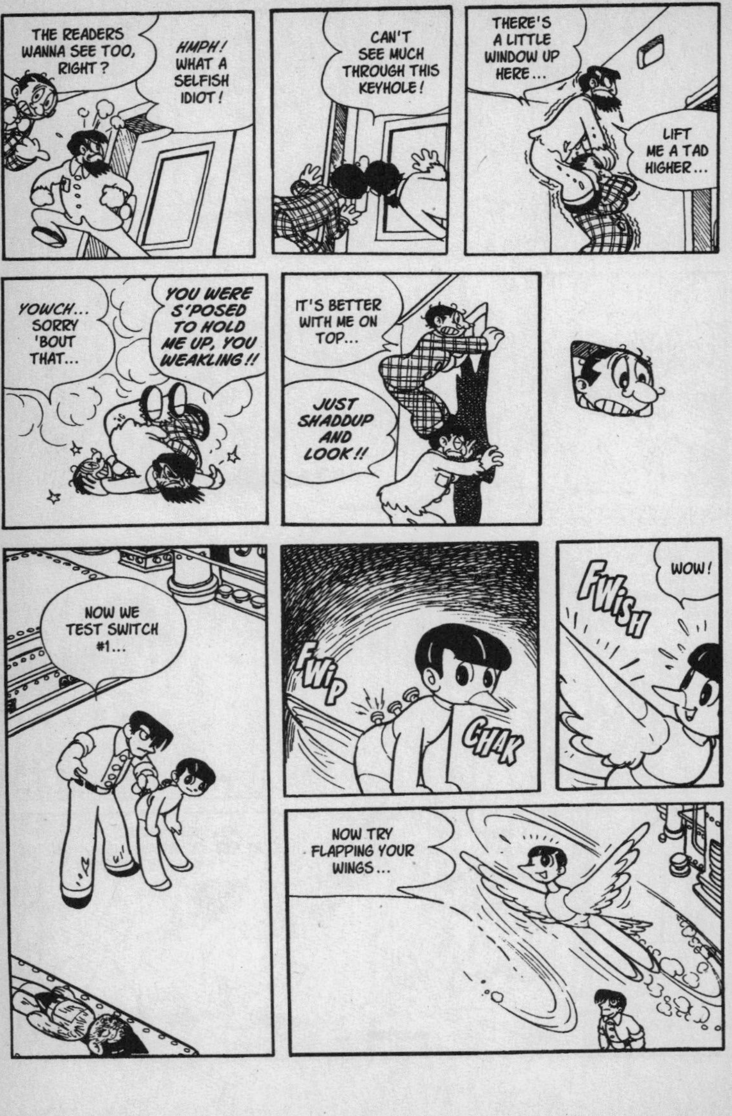
THE READERS WANNA SEE TOO, RIGHT?
HMPH! WHAT A SELFISH IDIOT!
CAN'T SEE MUCH THROUGH THIS KEYHOLE!
THERE'S A LITTLE WINDOW UP HERE...
LIFT ME A TAD HIGHER...
YOWCH... SORRY 'BOUT THAT...
YOU WERE S'POSED TO HOLD ME UP, YOU WEAKLING!!
IT'S BETTER WITH ME ON TOP...
JUST SHADDUP AND LOOK!!
NOW WE TEST SWITCH #1...
FWIP
CHAK
FWISH
WOW!
NOW TRY FLAPPING YOUR WINGS...

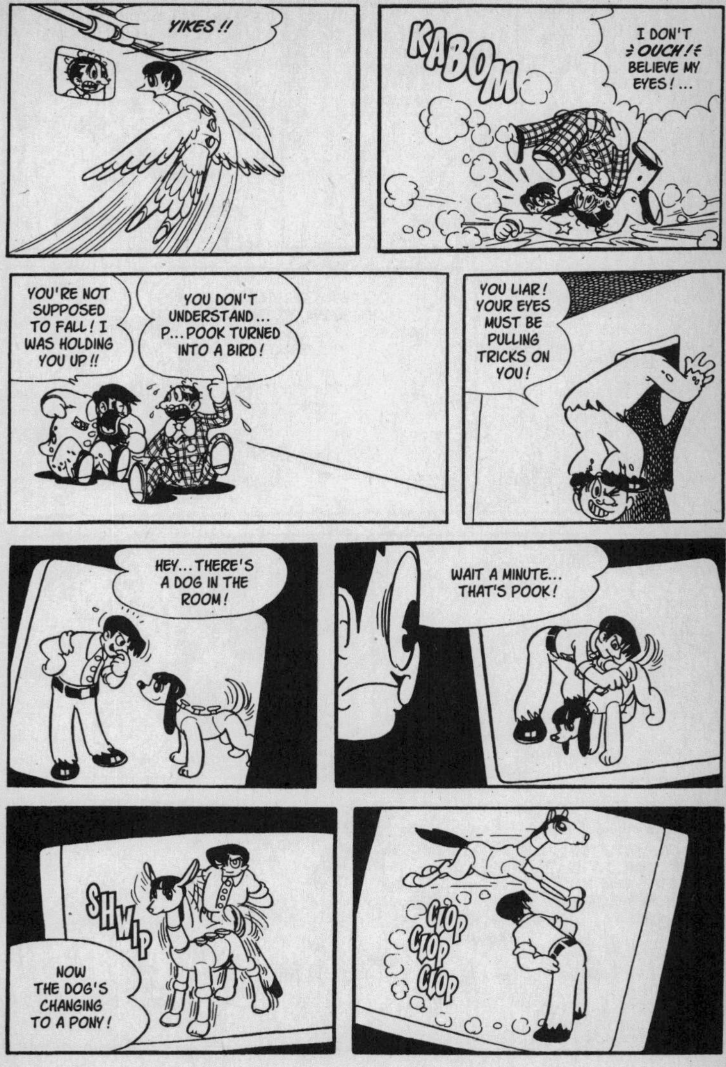
YIKES !!
KABOM
I DON'T
OUCH!
BELIEVE MY EYES! ...
YOU'RE NOT SUPPOSED TO FALL! I WAS HOLDING YOU UP!!
YOU DON'T UNDERSTAND... P...POOK TURNED INTO A BIRD!
YOU LIAR! YOUR EYES MUST BE PULLING TRICKS ON YOU!
HEY... THERE'S A DOG IN THE ROOM!
WAIT A MINUTE... THAT'S POOK!
SHWIP
NOW THE DOG'S CHANGING TO A PONY!
CLOP
CLOP
CLOP

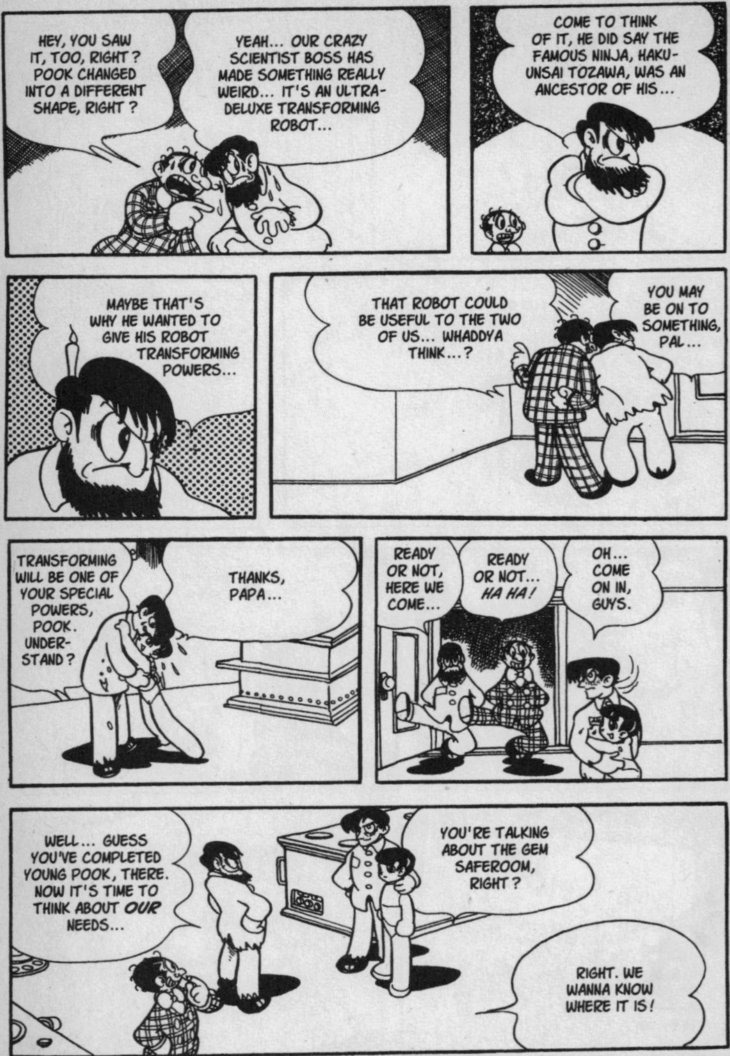
HEY, YOU SAW IT, TOO, RIGHT? POOK CHANGED INTO A DIFFERENT SHAPE, RIGHT?
YEAH... OUR CRAZY SCIENTIST BOSS HAS MADE SOMETHING REALLY WEIRD... IT'S AN ULTRA-DELUXE TRANSFORMING ROBOT...
COME TO THINK OF IT, HE DID SAY THE FAMOUS NINJA, HAKU-UNSAI TOZAWA, WAS AN ANCESTOR OF HIS...
MAYBE THAT'S WHY HE WANTED TO GIVE HIS ROBOT TRANSFORMING POWERS...
THAT ROBOT COULD BE USEFUL TO THE TWO OF US... WHADDYA THINK...?
YOU MAY BE ON TO SOMETHING, PAL...
TRANSFORMING WILL BE ONE OF YOUR SPECIAL POWERS, POOK. UNDER-STAND?
THANKS, PAPA...
READY OR NOT, HERE WE COME...
READY OR NOT... *HA HA!*
OH... COME ON IN, GUYS.
WELL... GUESS YOU'VE COMPLETED YOUNG POOK, THERE. NOW IT'S TIME TO THINK ABOUT *OUR* NEEDS...
YOU'RE TALKING ABOUT THE GEM SAFEROOM, RIGHT?
RIGHT. WE WANNA KNOW WHERE IT IS!

BEFORE EXPLAINING THE GEM SAFEROOM, SOME BACKGROUND INFORMATION ON CRUCIFIX ISLAND MAY BE HELPFUL. YEARS AGO, WHEN AN UNDERSEA SURVEY WAS BEING DONE OF THE AREA...

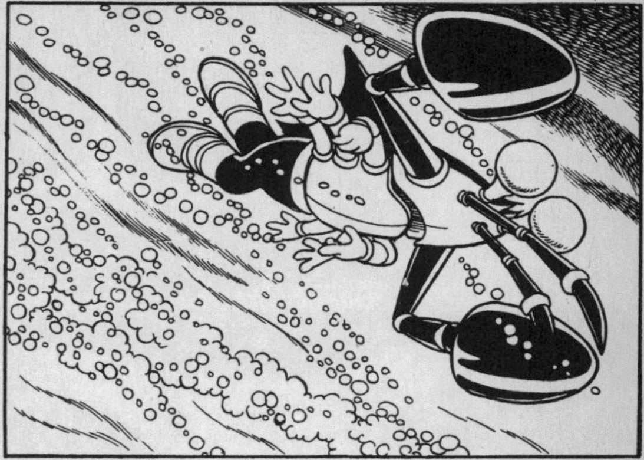

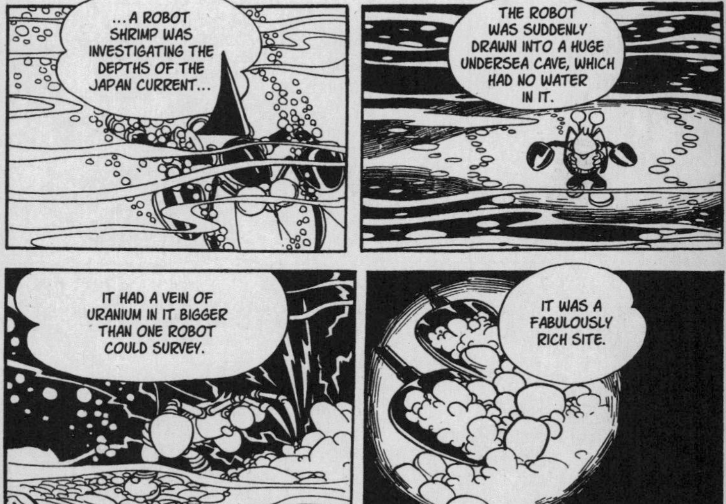

...A ROBOT SHRIMP WAS INVESTIGATING THE DEPTHS OF THE JAPAN CURRENT...
THE ROBOT WAS SUDDENLY DRAWN INTO A HUGE UNDERSEA CAVE, WHICH HAD NO WATER IN IT.
IT HAD A VEIN OF URANIUM IN IT BIGGER THAN ONE ROBOT COULD SURVEY.
IT WAS A FABULOUSLY RICH SITE.

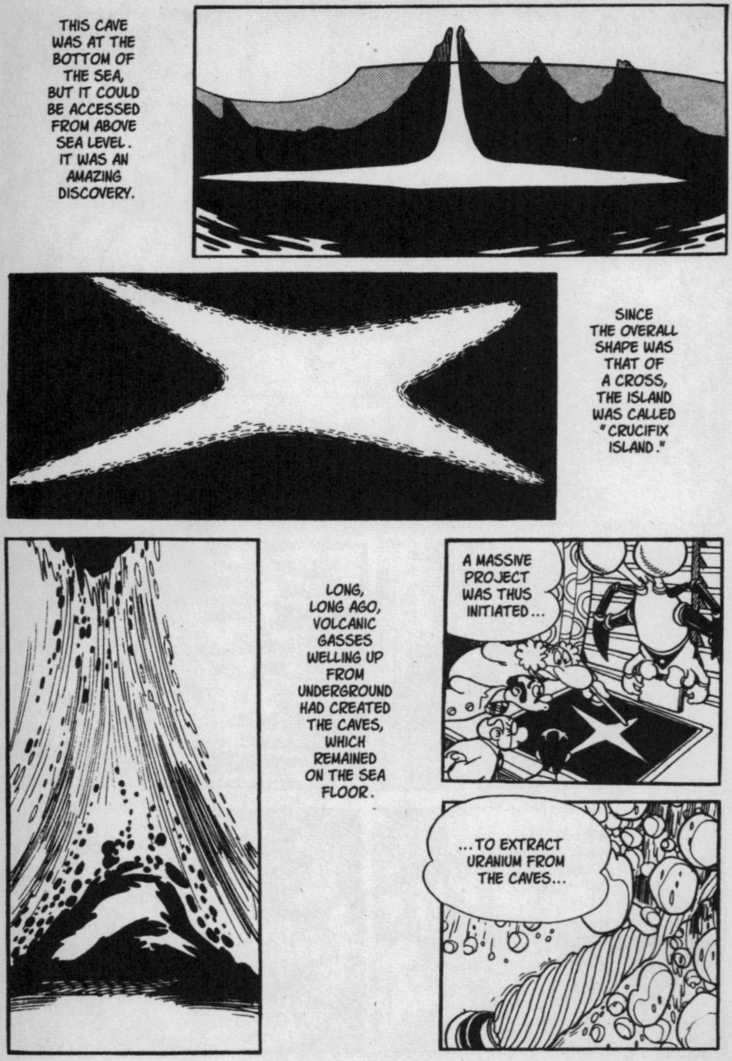
THIS CAVE WAS AT THE BOTTOM OF THE SEA, BUT IT COULD BE ACCESSED FROM ABOVE SEA LEVEL. IT WAS AN AMAZING DISCOVERY.
SINCE THE OVERALL SHAPE WAS THAT OF A CROSS, THE ISLAND WAS CALLED "CRUCIFIX ISLAND."
LONG, LONG AGO, VOLCANIC GASSES WELLING UP FROM UNDERGROUND HAD CREATED THE CAVES, WHICH REMAINED ON THE SEA FLOOR.
A MASSIVE PROJECT WAS THUS INITIATED...
...TO EXTRACT URANIUM FROM THE CAVES...

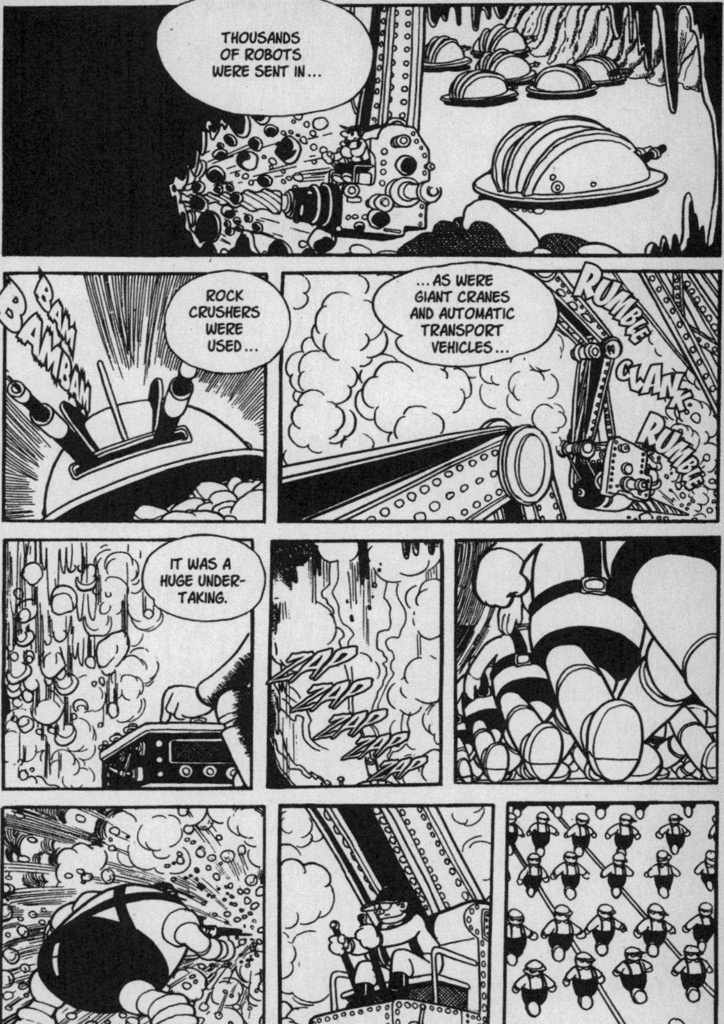
THOUSANDS OF ROBOTS WERE SENT IN...
BAM BAM BAMBAM
ROCK CRUSHERS WERE USED...
...AS WERE GIANT CRANES AND AUTOMATIC TRANSPORT VEHICLES...
RUMBLE
CLANK
RUMBLE
IT WAS A HUGE UNDER-TAKING.
ZAP ZAP ZAP ZAP ZAP

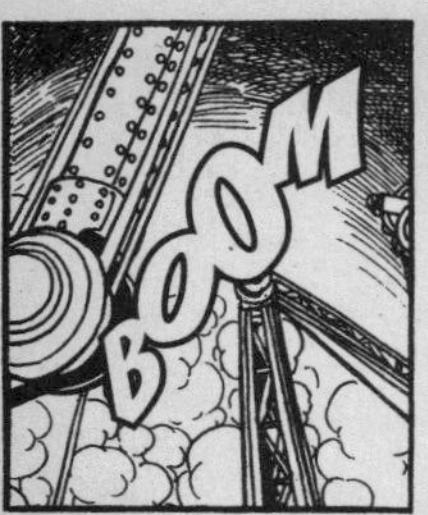
BOOM
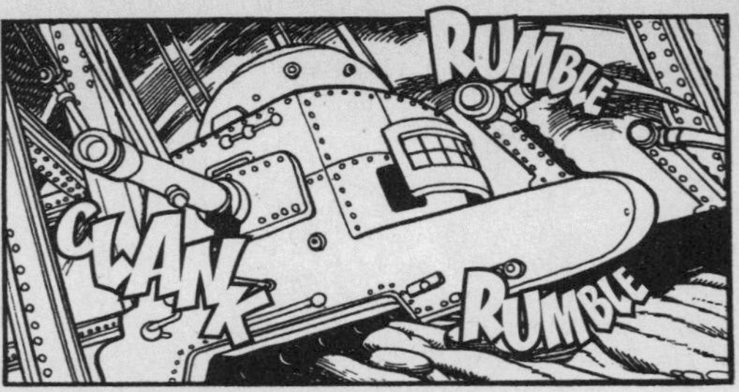
RUMBLE
CLANK
RUMBLE
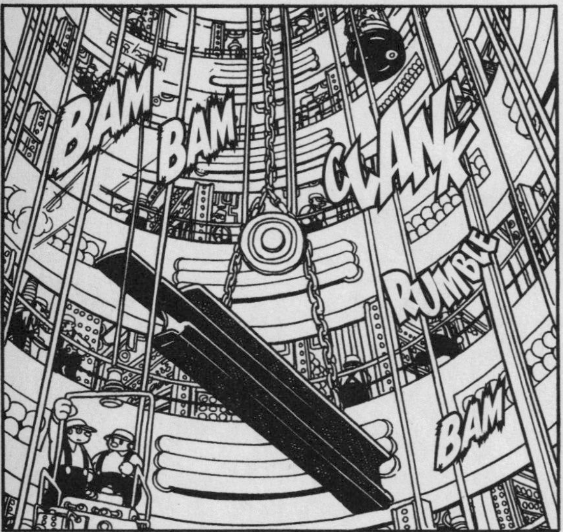
BAM
BAM
CLANK
RUMBLE
BAM

MORE PRECIOUS GEMSTONES AND ORE WERE EXTRACTED FROM THE BOTTOM OF CRUCIFIX ISLAND THAN ANYONE COULD COUNT. IT WAS AS THOUGH JAPAN HAD DISCOVERED A GIANT TREASURE TROVE. THE URANIUM WAS SOON SENT TO JAPAN'S MAIN ISLANDS, BUT THE GOLD AND GEMS WERE STORED IN A SPECIAL SAFE-ROOM DEEP ON THE ISLAND.

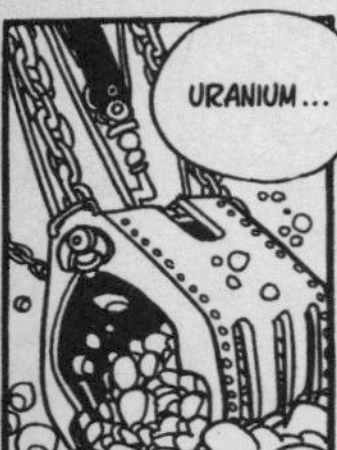
URANIUM...
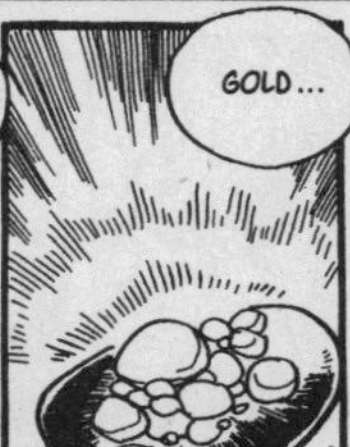
GOLD...
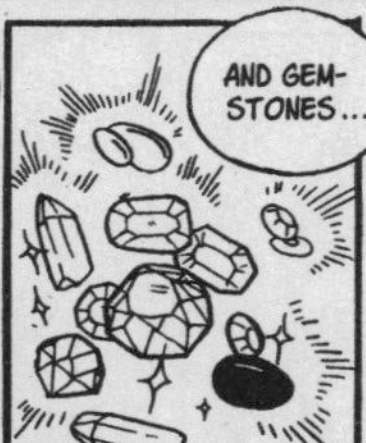
AND GEM-
STONES...

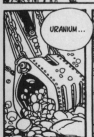

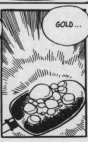

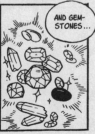

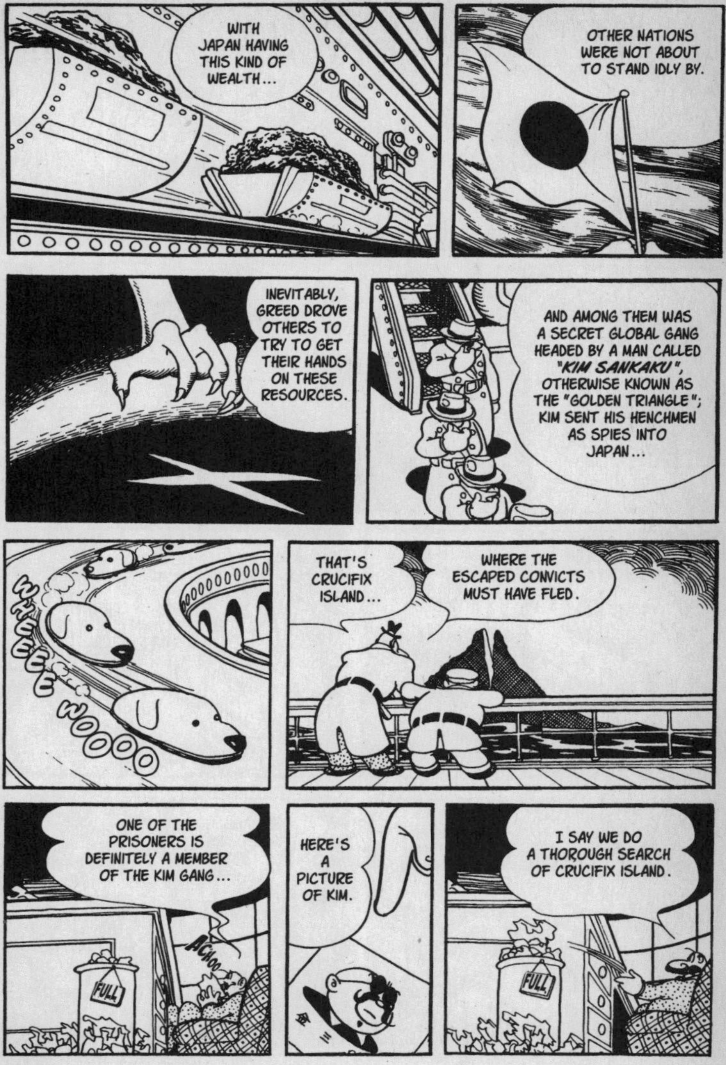
WITH JAPAN HAVING THIS KIND OF WEALTH...
OTHER NATIONS WERE NOT ABOUT TO STAND IDLY BY.
INEVITABLY, GREED DROVE OTHERS TO TRY TO GET THEIR HANDS ON THESE RESOURCES.
AND AMONG THEM WAS A SECRET GLOBAL GANG HEADED BY A MAN CALLED "KIM SANKAKU", OTHERWISE KNOWN AS THE "GOLDEN TRIANGLE"; KIM SENT HIS HENCHMEN AS SPIES INTO JAPAN...
WHEEEE
WOOOO
THAT'S CRUCIFIX ISLAND...
WHERE THE ESCAPED CONVICTS MUST HAVE FLED.
ONE OF THE PRISONERS IS DEFINITELY A MEMBER OF THE KIM GANG...
ACHOO
FULL
HERE'S A PICTURE OF KIM.
I SAY WE DO A THOROUGH SEARCH OF CRUCIFIX ISLAND.
FULL

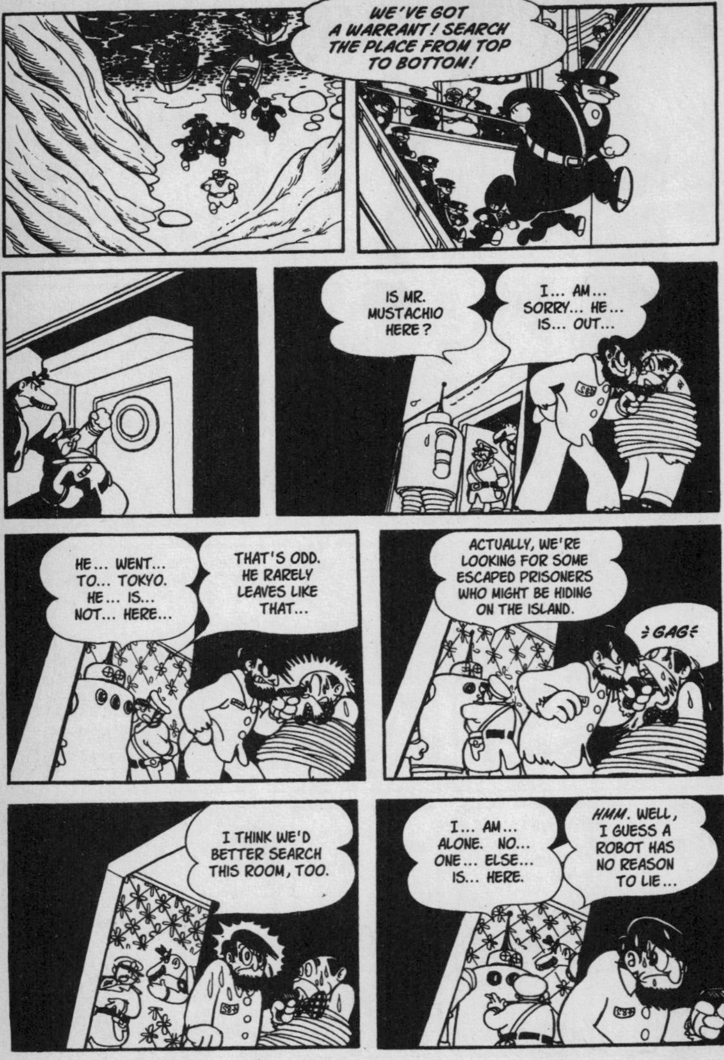
WE'VE GOT A WARRANT! SEARCH THE PLACE FROM TOP TO BOTTOM!
IS MR. MUSTACHIO HERE?
I... AM... SORRY... HE... IS... OUT...
HE... WENT... TO... TOKYO. HE... IS... NOT... HERE...
THAT'S ODD. HE RARELY LEAVES LIKE THAT...
ACTUALLY, WE'RE LOOKING FOR SOME ESCAPED PRISONERS WHO MIGHT BE HIDING ON THE ISLAND.
GAG
I THINK WE'D BETTER SEARCH THIS ROOM, TOO.
I... AM... ALONE. NO... ONE... ELSE... IS... HERE.
HMM. WELL, I GUESS A ROBOT HAS NO REASON TO LIE...

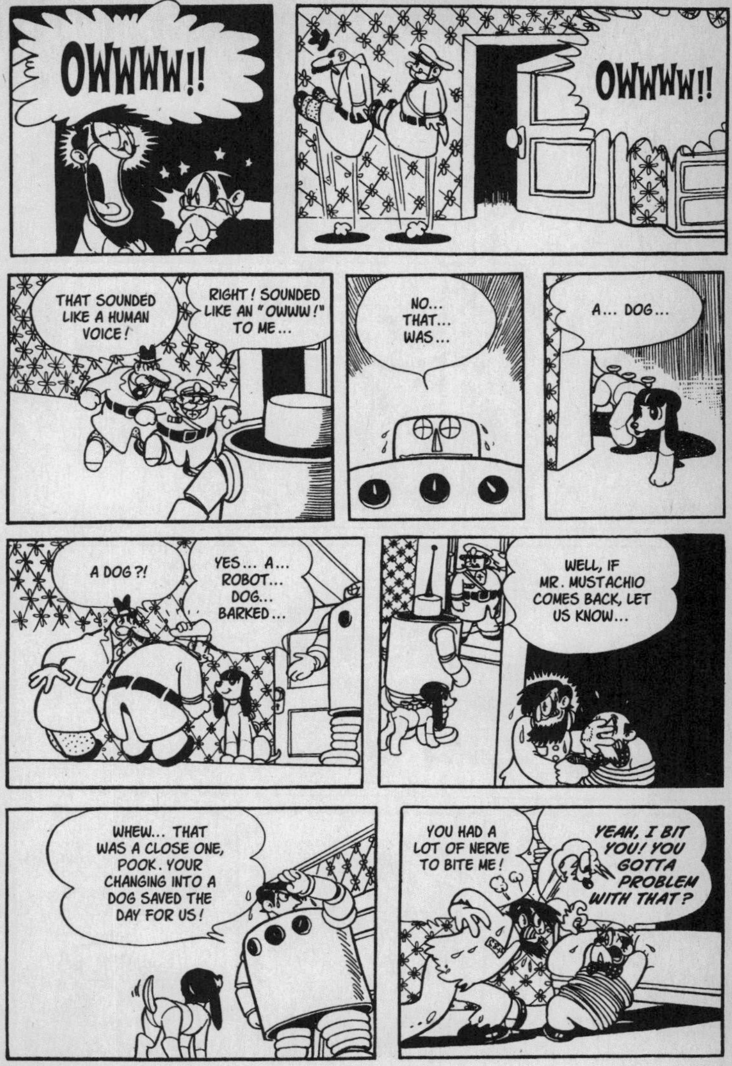
OWWWW!!
OWWWW!!
THAT SOUNDED LIKE A HUMAN VOICE!
RIGHT! SOUNDED LIKE AN "OWWW!" TO ME...
NO... THAT... WAS...
A... DOG...
A DOG?!
YES... A... ROBOT... DOG... BARKED...
WELL, IF MR. MUSTACHIO COMES BACK, LET US KNOW...
WHEW... THAT WAS A CLOSE ONE, POOK. YOUR CHANGING INTO A DOG SAVED THE DAY FOR US!
YOU HAD A LOT OF NERVE TO BITE ME!
YEAH, I BIT YOU! YOU GOTTA PROBLEM WITH THAT?

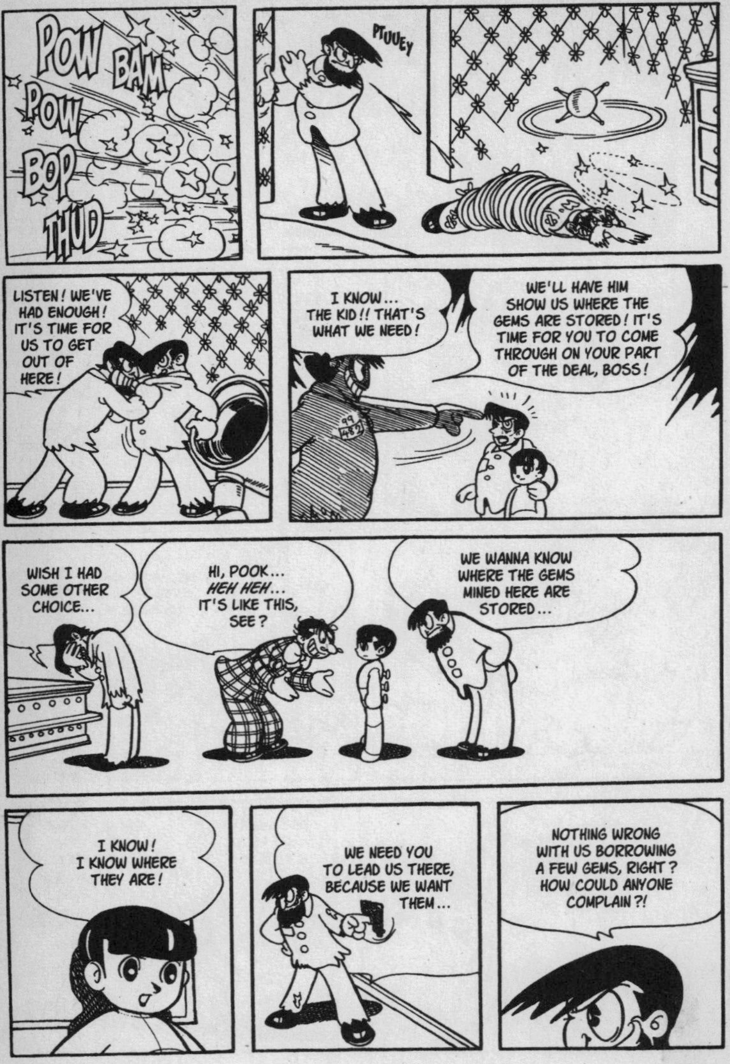
POW
BAM
POW
BOP
THUD
PTUUEY
LISTEN! WE'VE HAD ENOUGH! IT'S TIME FOR US TO GET OUT OF HERE!
I KNOW... THE KID!! THAT'S WHAT WE NEED!
WE'LL HAVE HIM SHOW US WHERE THE GEMS ARE STORED! IT'S TIME FOR YOU TO COME THROUGH ON YOUR PART OF THE DEAL, BOSS!
WISH I HAD SOME OTHER CHOICE...
HI, POOK... *HEH HEH*... IT'S LIKE THIS, SEE?
WE WANNA KNOW WHERE THE GEMS MINED HERE ARE STORED...
I KNOW! I KNOW WHERE THEY ARE!
WE NEED YOU TO LEAD US THERE, BECAUSE WE WANT THEM...
NOTHING WRONG WITH US BORROWING A FEW GEMS, RIGHT? HOW COULD ANYONE COMPLAIN?!

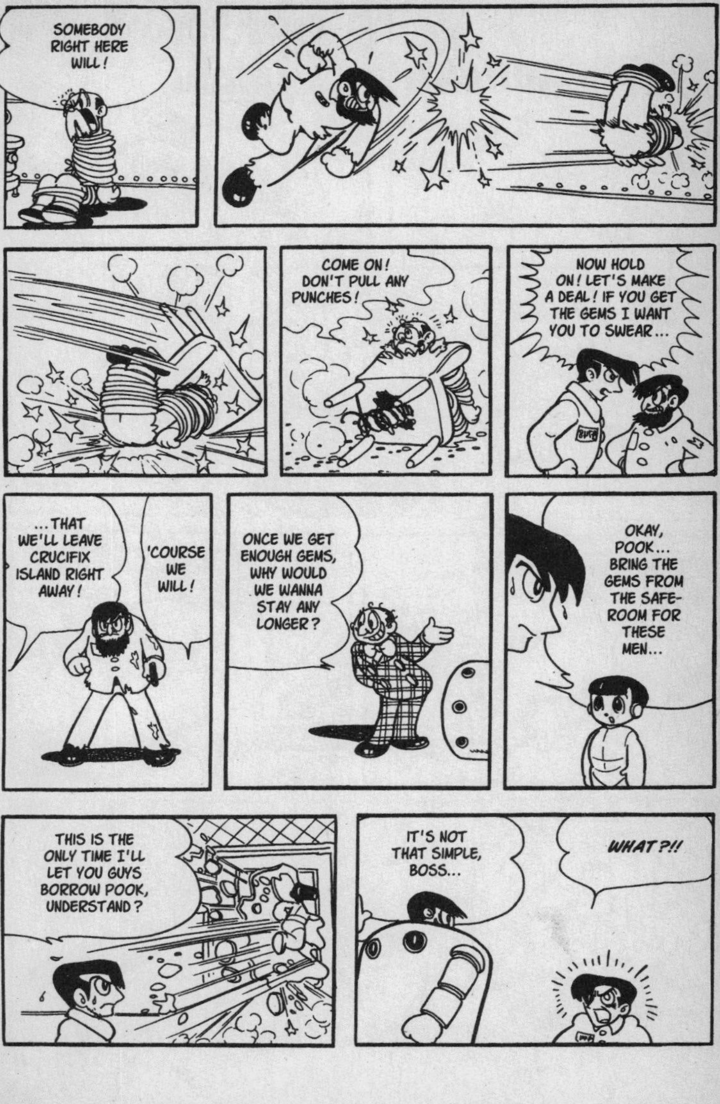
SOMEBODY RIGHT HERE WILL!
COME ON! DON'T PULL ANY PUNCHES!
NOW HOLD ON! LET'S MAKE A DEAL! IF YOU GET THE GEMS I WANT YOU TO SWEAR...
...THAT WE'LL LEAVE CRUCIFIX ISLAND RIGHT AWAY!
'COURSE WE WILL!
ONCE WE GET ENOUGH GEMS, WHY WOULD WE WANNA STAY ANY LONGER?
OKAY, POOK... BRING THE GEMS FROM THE SAFE-ROOM FOR THESE MEN...
THIS IS THE ONLY TIME I'LL LET YOU GUYS BORROW POOK, UNDERSTAND?
IT'S NOT THAT SIMPLE, BOSS...
WHAT?!!

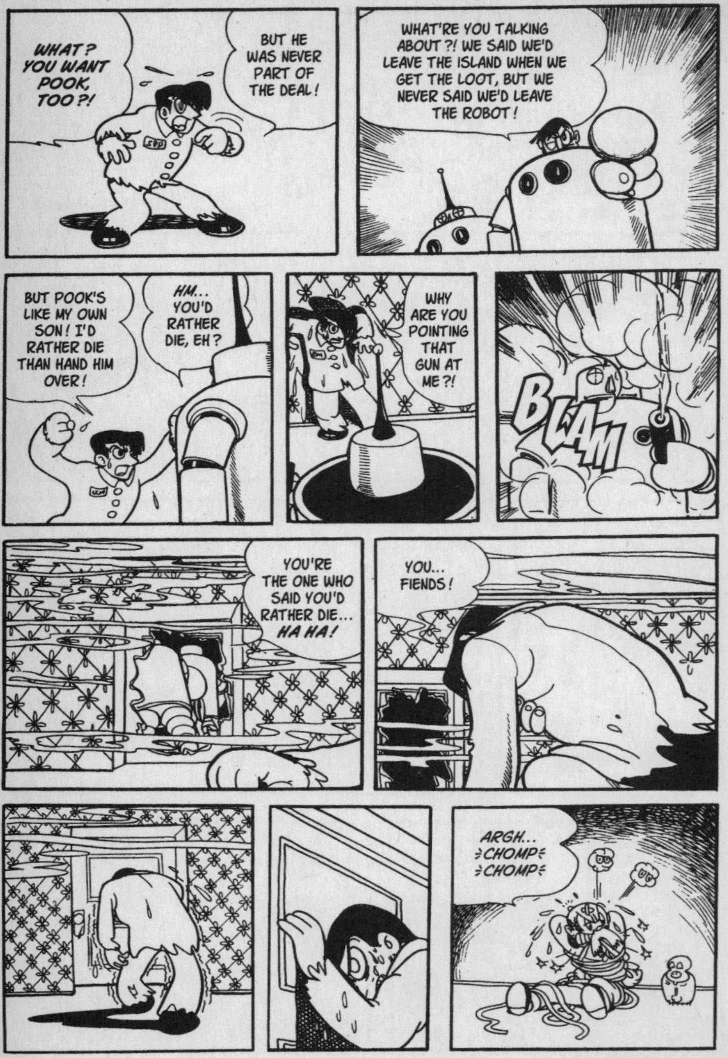
WHAT? YOU WANT POOK, TOO?!
BUT HE WAS NEVER PART OF THE DEAL!
WHAT'RE YOU TALKING ABOUT?! WE SAID WE'D LEAVE THE ISLAND WHEN WE GET THE LOOT, BUT WE NEVER SAID WE'D LEAVE THE ROBOT!
BUT POOK'S LIKE MY OWN SON! I'D RATHER DIE THAN HAND HIM OVER!
HM... YOU'D RATHER DIE, EH?
WHY ARE YOU POINTING THAT GUN AT ME?!
BLAM
YOU'RE THE ONE WHO SAID YOU'D RATHER DIE... HA HA!
YOU... FIENDS!
ARGH...
CHOMP
CHOMP

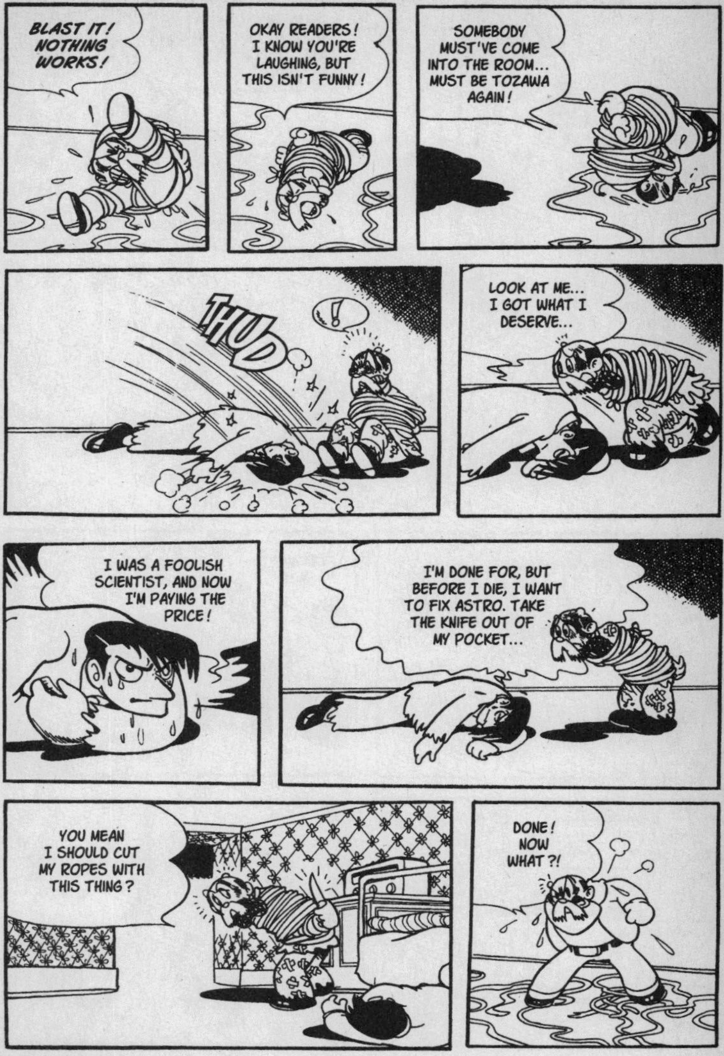
BLAST IT! NOTHING WORKS!
OKAY READERS! I KNOW YOU'RE LAUGHING, BUT THIS ISN'T FUNNY!
SOMEBODY MUST'VE COME INTO THE ROOM... MUST BE TOZAWA AGAIN!
THUD
!
LOOK AT ME... I GOT WHAT I DESERVE...
I WAS A FOOLISH SCIENTIST, AND NOW I'M PAYING THE PRICE!
I'M DONE FOR, BUT BEFORE I DIE, I WANT TO FIX ASTRO. TAKE THE KNIFE OUT OF MY POCKET...
YOU MEAN I SHOULD CUT MY ROPES WITH THIS THING?
DONE! NOW WHAT?!

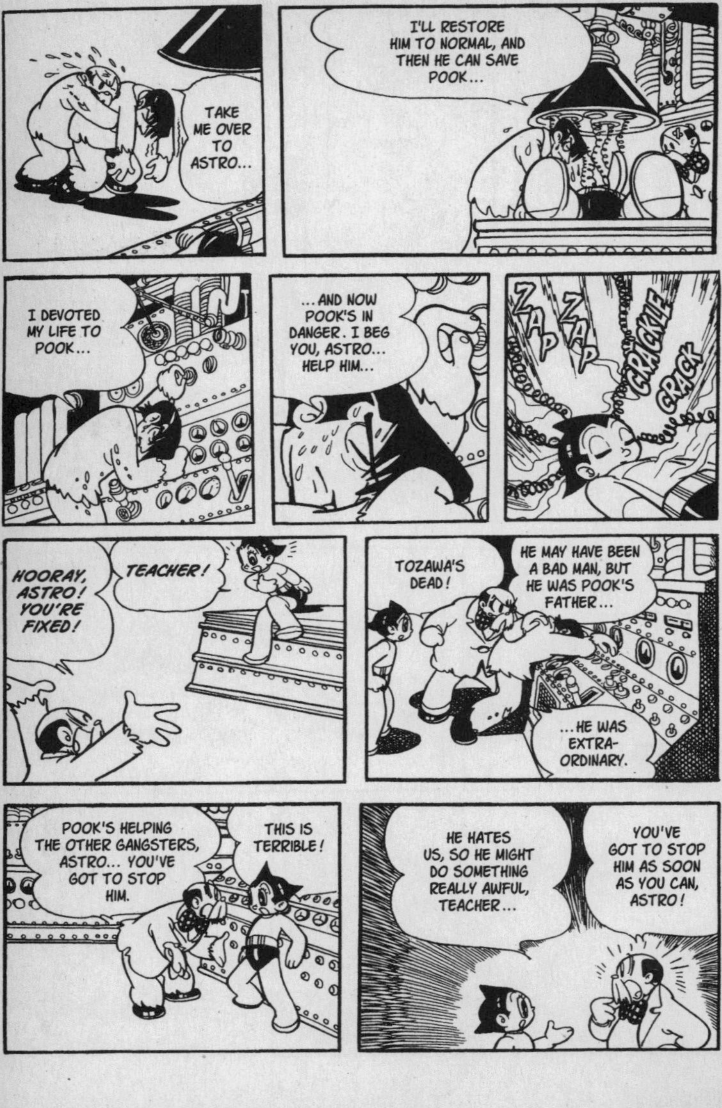
TAKE ME OVER TO ASTRO...
I'LL RESTORE HIM TO NORMAL, AND THEN HE CAN SAVE POOK...
I DEVOTED MY LIFE TO POOK...
...AND NOW POOK'S IN DANGER. I BEG YOU, ASTRO... HELP HIM...
ZAP
ZAP
CRACKLE
CRACK
HOORAY, ASTRO! YOU'RE FIXED!
TEACHER!
TOZAWA'S DEAD!
HE MAY HAVE BEEN A BAD MAN, BUT HE WAS POOK'S FATHER...
...HE WAS EXTRA-ORDINARY.
POOK'S HELPING THE OTHER GANGSTERS, ASTRO... YOU'VE GOT TO STOP HIM.
THIS IS TERRIBLE!
HE HATES US, SO HE MIGHT DO SOMETHING REALLY AWFUL, TEACHER...
YOU'VE GOT TO STOP HIM AS SOON AS YOU CAN, ASTRO!

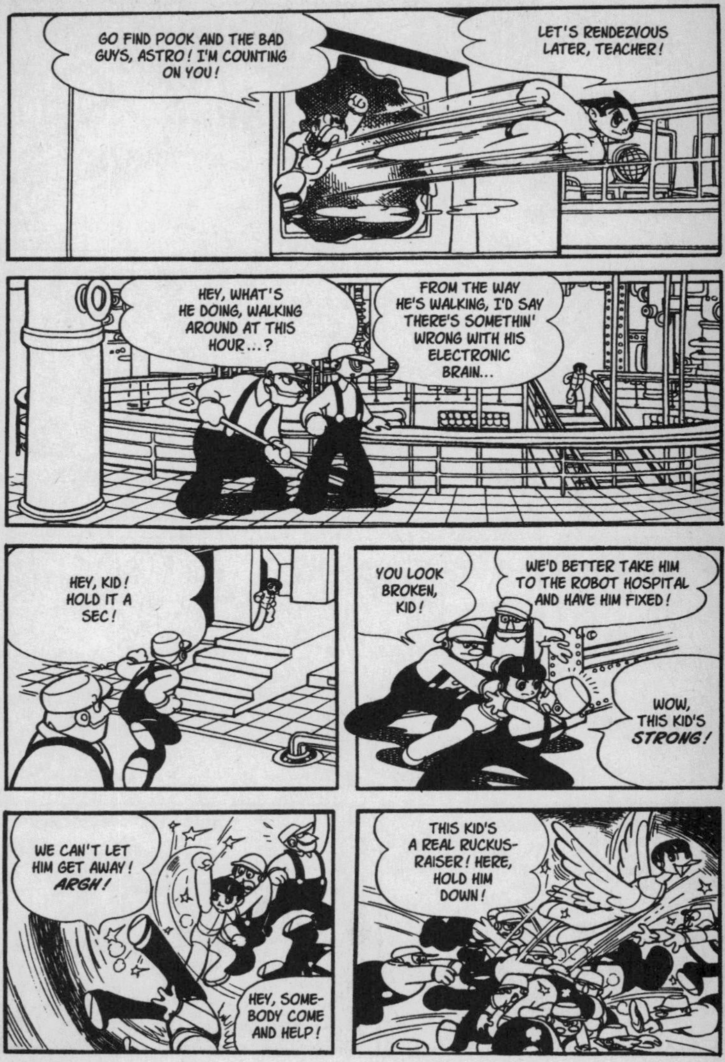
GO FIND POOK AND THE BAD GUYS, ASTRO! I'M COUNTING ON YOU!
LET'S RENDEZVOUS LATER, TEACHER!
HEY, WHAT'S HE DOING, WALKING AROUND AT THIS HOUR...?
FROM THE WAY HE'S WALKING, I'D SAY THERE'S SOMETHIN' WRONG WITH HIS ELECTRONIC BRAIN...
HEY, KID! HOLD IT A SEC!
YOU LOOK BROKEN, KID!
WE'D BETTER TAKE HIM TO THE ROBOT HOSPITAL AND HAVE HIM FIXED!
WOW, THIS KID'S STRONG!
WE CAN'T LET HIM GET AWAY! ARGH!
HEY, SOME-BODY COME AND HELP!
THIS KID'S A REAL RUCKUS-RAISER! HERE, HOLD HIM DOWN!

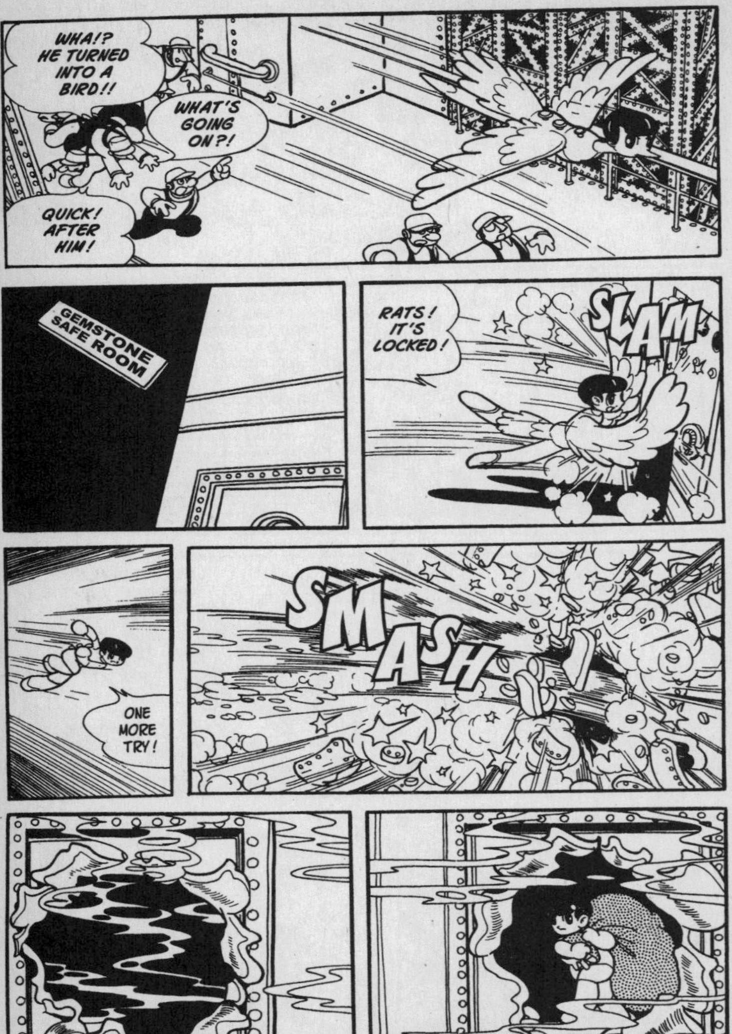
WHA!? HE TURNED INTO A BIRD!!
WHAT'S GOING ON?!
QUICK! AFTER HIM!
GEMSTONE SAFE ROOM
RATS! IT'S LOCKED!
SLAM
ONE MORE TRY!
SMASH

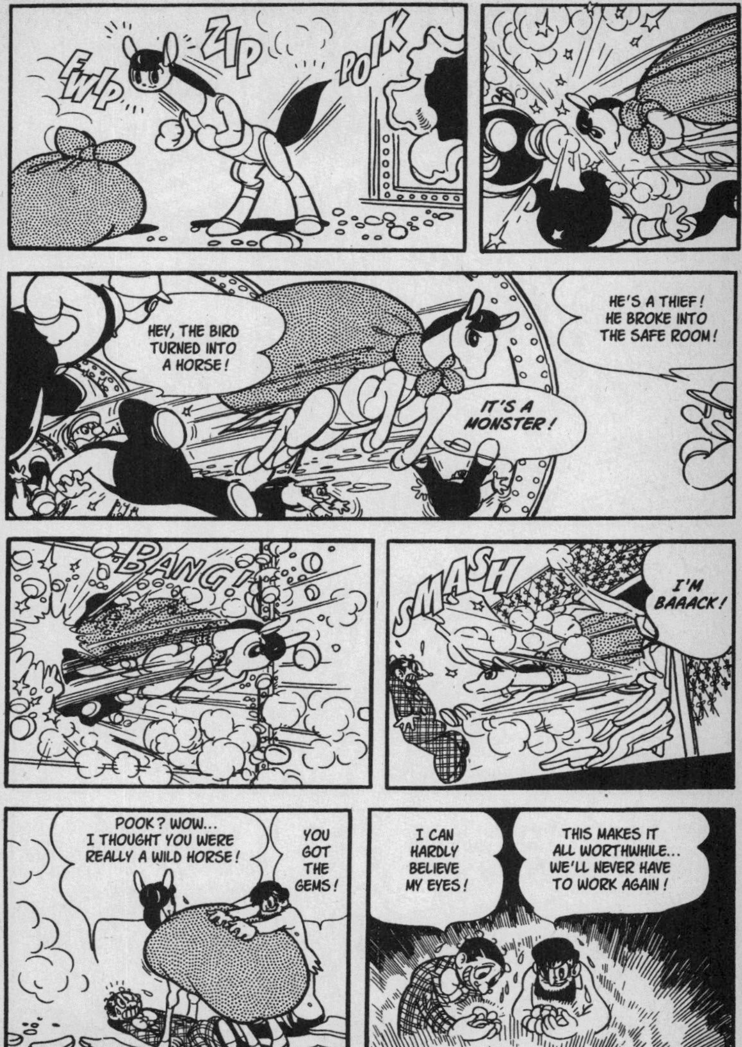
FWIP
ZIP
POIK
HEY, THE BIRD TURNED INTO A HORSE!
HE'S A THIEF! HE BROKE INTO THE SAFE ROOM!
IT'S A MONSTER!
BANG!
SMASH
I'M BAAACK!
POOK? WOW... I THOUGHT YOU WERE REALLY A WILD HORSE!
YOU GOT THE GEMS!
I CAN HARDLY BELIEVE MY EYES!
THIS MAKES IT ALL WORTHWHILE... WE'LL NEVER HAVE TO WORK AGAIN!

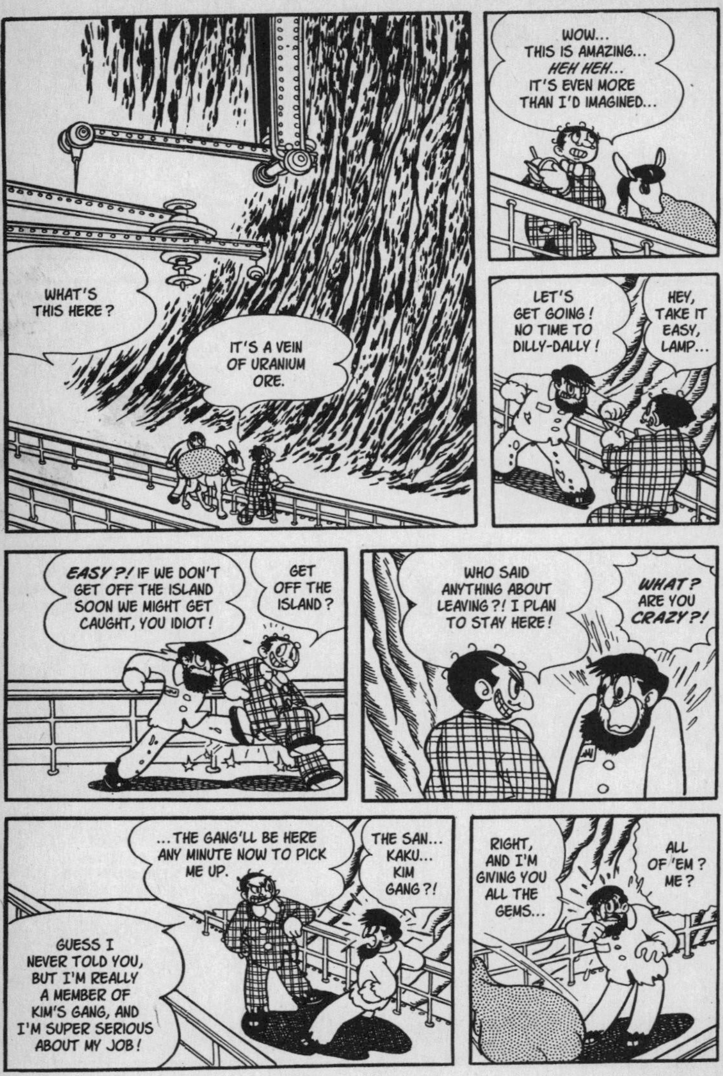
WHAT'S THIS HERE?
IT'S A VEIN OF URANIUM ORE.
WOW... THIS IS AMAZING... HEH HEH... IT'S EVEN MORE THAN I'D IMAGINED...
LET'S GET GOING! NO TIME TO DILLY-DALLY!
HEY, TAKE IT EASY, LAMP...
EASY?! IF WE DON'T GET OFF THE ISLAND SOON WE MIGHT GET CAUGHT, YOU IDIOT!
GET OFF THE ISLAND?
WHO SAID ANYTHING ABOUT LEAVING?! I PLAN TO STAY HERE!
WHAT? ARE YOU CRAZY?!
GUESS I NEVER TOLD YOU, BUT I'M REALLY A MEMBER OF KIM'S GANG, AND I'M SUPER SERIOUS ABOUT MY JOB!
...THE GANG'LL BE HERE ANY MINUTE NOW TO PICK ME UP.
THE SAN... KAKU... KIM GANG?!
RIGHT, AND I'M GIVING YOU ALL THE GEMS...
ALL OF 'EM? ME?

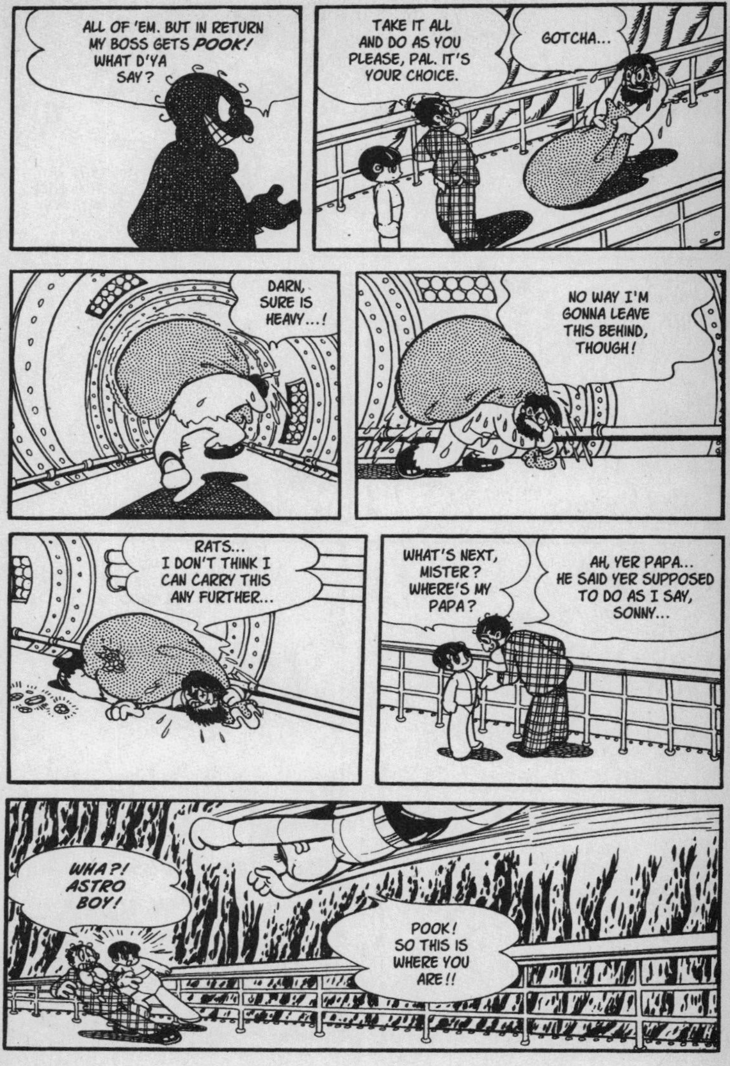
ALL OF 'EM. BUT IN RETURN MY BOSS GETS *POOK!* WHAT D'YA SAY?
TAKE IT ALL AND DO AS YOU PLEASE, PAL. IT'S YOUR CHOICE.
GOTCHA...
DARN, SURE IS HEAVY...!
NO WAY I'M GONNA LEAVE THIS BEHIND, THOUGH!
RATS... I DON'T THINK I CAN CARRY THIS ANY FURTHER...
WHAT'S NEXT, MISTER? WHERE'S MY PAPA?
AH, YER PAPA... HE SAID YER SUPPOSED TO DO AS I SAY, SONNY...
WHA?! ASTRO BOY!
POOK! SO THIS IS WHERE YOU ARE!!

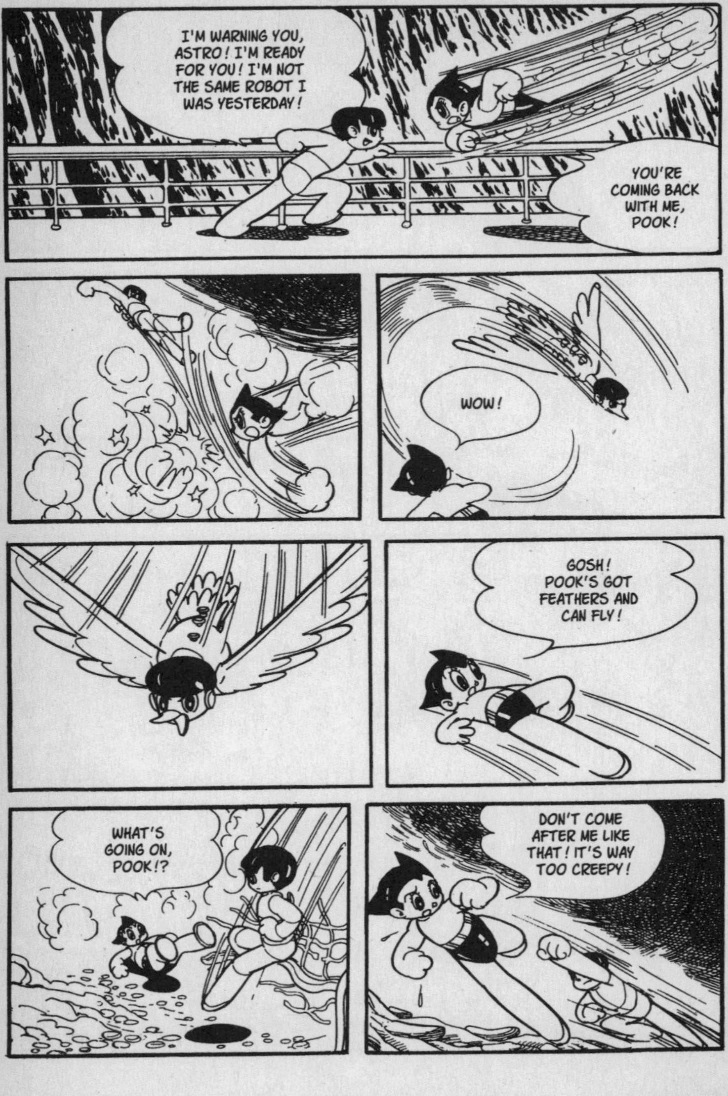
I'M WARNING YOU, ASTRO! I'M READY FOR YOU! I'M NOT THE SAME ROBOT I WAS YESTERDAY!
YOU'RE COMING BACK WITH ME, POOK!
WOW!
GOSH! POOK'S GOT FEATHERS AND CAN FLY!
WHAT'S GOING ON, POOK!?
DON'T COME AFTER ME LIKE THAT! IT'S WAY TOO CREEPY!

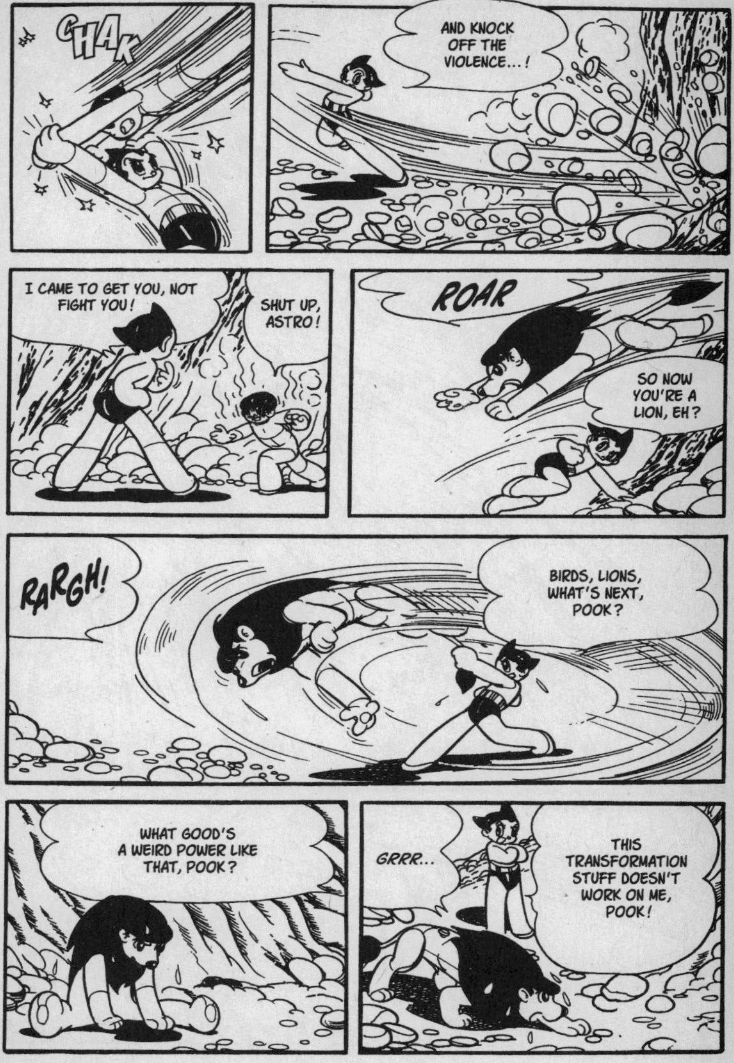
CHAK
AND KNOCK OFF THE VIOLENCE...!
I CAME TO GET YOU, NOT FIGHT YOU!
SHUT UP, ASTRO!
ROAR
SO NOW YOU'RE A LION, EH?
RARGH!
BIRDS, LIONS, WHAT'S NEXT, POOK?
WHAT GOOD'S A WEIRD POWER LIKE THAT, POOK?
GRRR...
THIS TRANSFORMATION STUFF DOESN'T WORK ON ME, POOK!

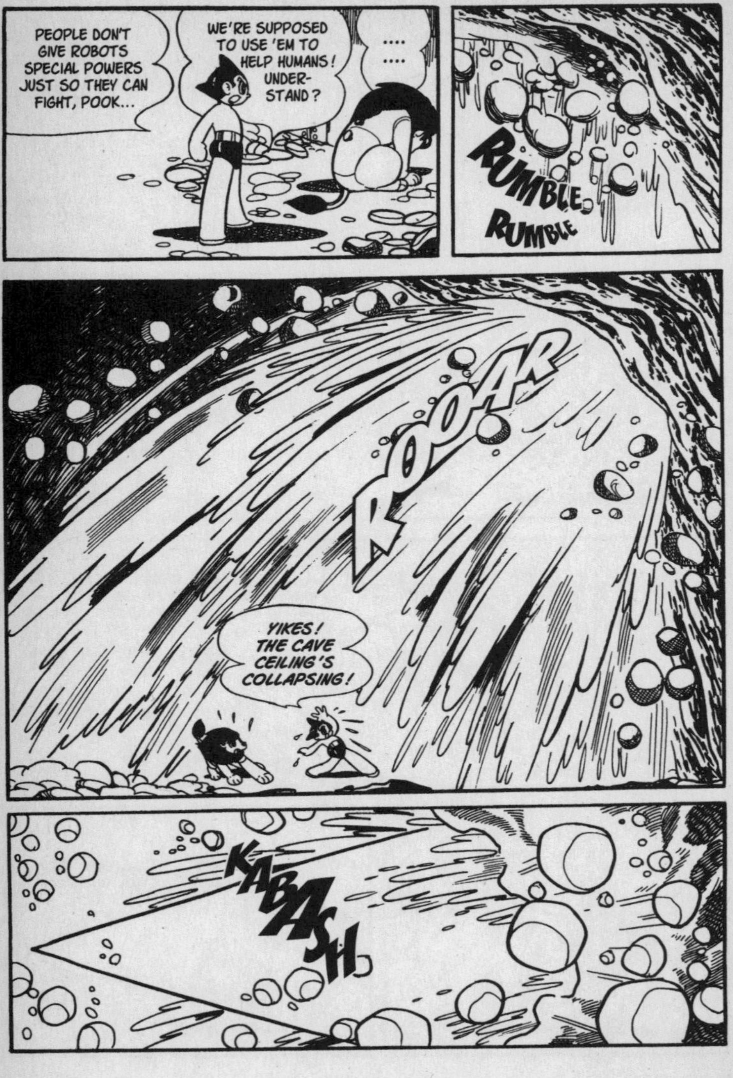
PEOPLE DON'T GIVE ROBOTS SPECIAL POWERS JUST SO THEY CAN FIGHT, POOK...
WE'RE SUPPOSED TO USE 'EM TO HELP HUMANS! UNDER-STAND?
....
....
RUMBLE
RUMBLE
ROOOAR
YIKES! THE CAVE CEILING'S COLLAPSING!
KABASH

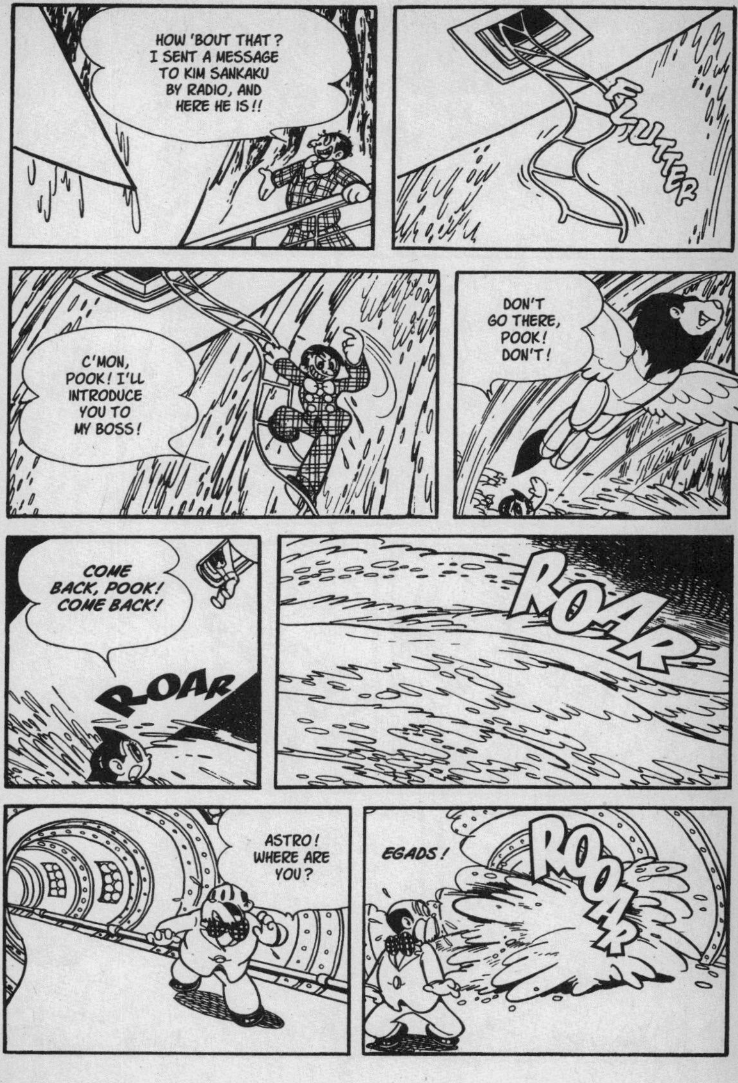

HOW 'BOUT THAT? I SENT A MESSAGE TO KIM SANKAKU BY RADIO, AND HERE HE IS!!
FLUTTER
C'MON, POOK! I'LL INTRODUCE YOU TO MY BOSS!
DON'T GO THERE, POOK! DON'T!
COME BACK, POOK! COME BACK!
ROAR
ROAR
ASTRO! WHERE ARE YOU?
EGADS!
ROOOAR

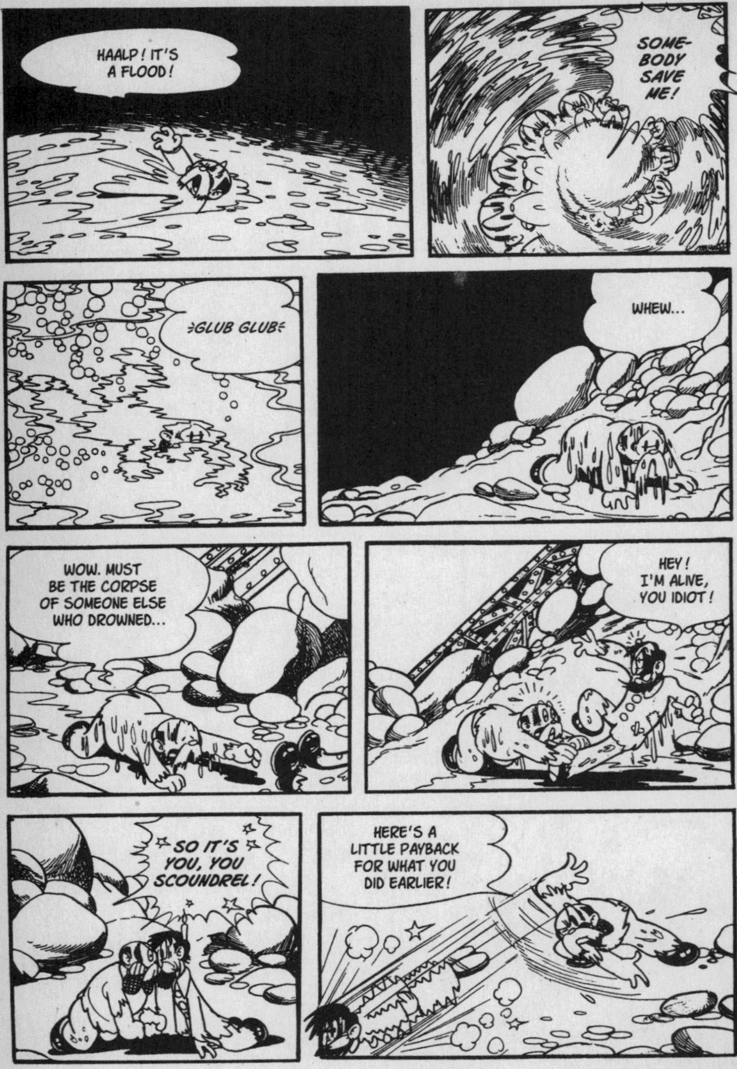
HAALP! IT'S A FLOOD!
SOME-BODY SAVE ME!
GLUB GLUB
WHEW...
WOW. MUST BE THE CORPSE OF SOMEONE ELSE WHO DROWNED...
HEY! I'M ALIVE, YOU IDIOT!
SO IT'S YOU, YOU SCOUNDREL!
HERE'S A LITTLE PAYBACK FOR WHAT YOU DID EARLIER!

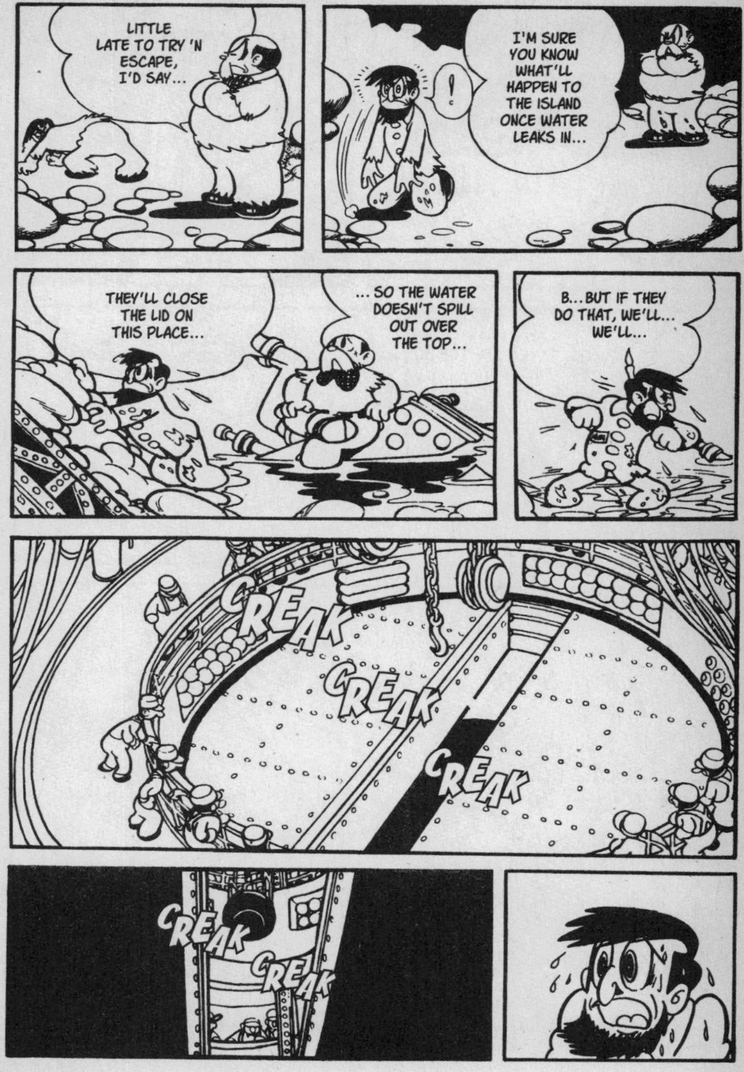
LITTLE LATE TO TRY 'N ESCAPE, I'D SAY...
!
I'M SURE YOU KNOW WHAT'LL HAPPEN TO THE ISLAND ONCE WATER LEAKS IN...
THEY'LL CLOSE THE LID ON THIS PLACE...
... SO THE WATER DOESN'T SPILL OUT OVER THE TOP...
B...BUT IF THEY DO THAT, WE'LL... WE'LL...
CREAK
CREAK
CREAK
CREAK
CREAK

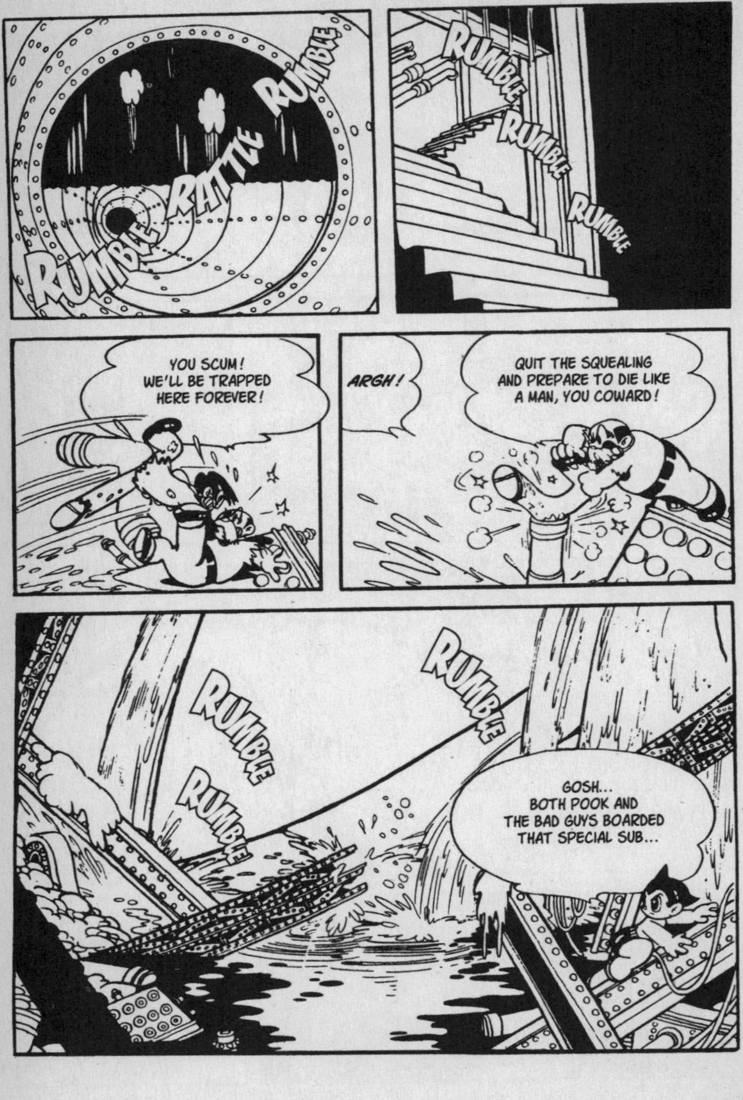
RUMBLE RATTLE RUMBLE
RUMBLE
RUMBLE
RUMBLE
YOU SCUM! WE'LL BE TRAPPED HERE FOREVER!
ARGH!
QUIT THE SQUEALING AND PREPARE TO DIE LIKE A MAN, YOU COWARD!
RUMBLE
RUMBLE
RUMBLE
GOSH... BOTH POOK AND THE BAD GUYS BOARDED THAT SPECIAL SUB...

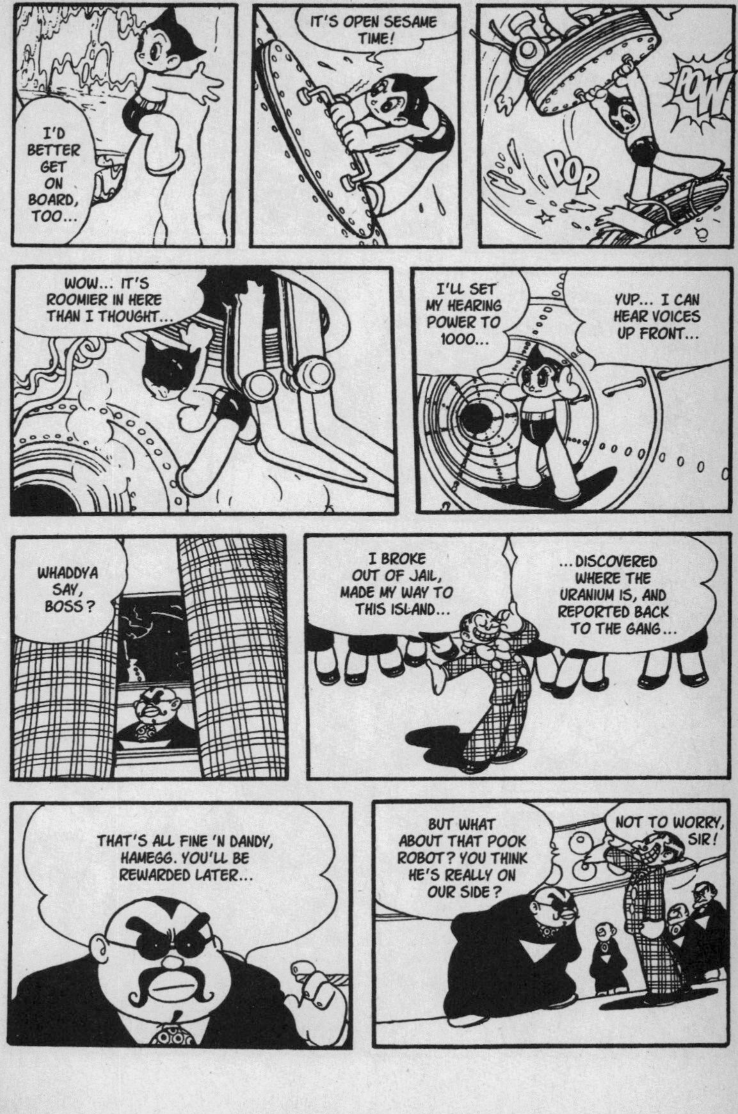

I'D BETTER GET ON BOARD, TOO...
IT'S OPEN SESAME TIME!
POW
POP
WOW... IT'S ROOMIER IN HERE THAN I THOUGHT...
I'LL SET MY HEARING POWER TO 1000...
YUP... I CAN HEAR VOICES UP FRONT...
WHADDYA SAY, BOSS?
I BROKE OUT OF JAIL, MADE MY WAY TO THIS ISLAND...
...DISCOVERED WHERE THE URANIUM IS, AND REPORTED BACK TO THE GANG...
THAT'S ALL FINE 'N DANDY, HAMEGG. YOU'LL BE REWARDED LATER...
BUT WHAT ABOUT THAT POOK ROBOT? YOU THINK HE'S REALLY ON OUR SIDE?
NOT TO WORRY, SIR!

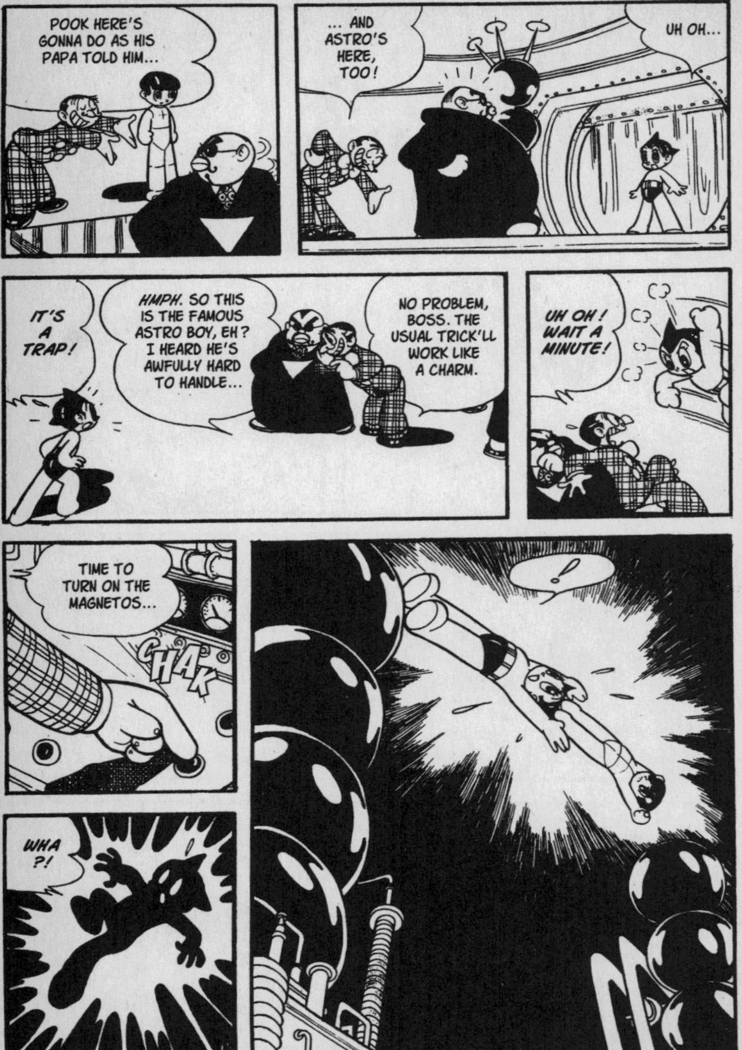
POOK HERE'S GONNA DO AS HIS PAPA TOLD HIM...
... AND ASTRO'S HERE, TOO!
UH OH...
IT'S A TRAP!
HMPH. SO THIS IS THE FAMOUS ASTRO BOY, EH? I HEARD HE'S AWFULLY HARD TO HANDLE...
NO PROBLEM, BOSS. THE USUAL TRICK'LL WORK LIKE A CHARM.
UH OH! WAIT A MINUTE!
TIME TO TURN ON THE MAGNETOS...
CHAK
!
WHA ?!

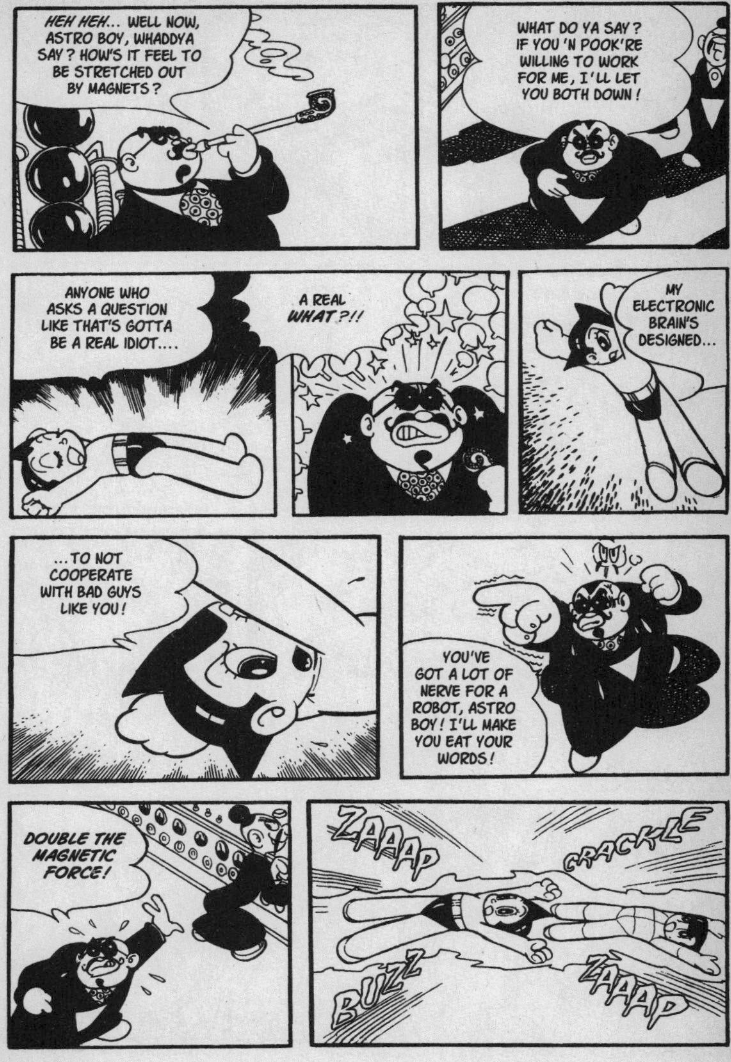
HEH HEH... WELL NOW, ASTRO BOY, WHADDYA SAY? HOW'S IT FEEL TO BE STRETCHED OUT BY MAGNETS?
WHAT DO YA SAY? IF YOU 'N POOK'RE WILLING TO WORK FOR ME, I'LL LET YOU BOTH DOWN!
ANYONE WHO ASKS A QUESTION LIKE THAT'S GOTTA BE A REAL IDIOT....
A REAL WHAT?!!
MY ELECTRONIC BRAIN'S DESIGNED...
...TO NOT COOPERATE WITH BAD GUYS LIKE YOU!
YOU'VE GOT A LOT OF NERVE FOR A ROBOT, ASTRO BOY! I'LL MAKE YOU EAT YOUR WORDS!
DOUBLE THE MAGNETIC FORCE!
ZAAAAP
CRACKLE
BUZZ
ZAAAAP

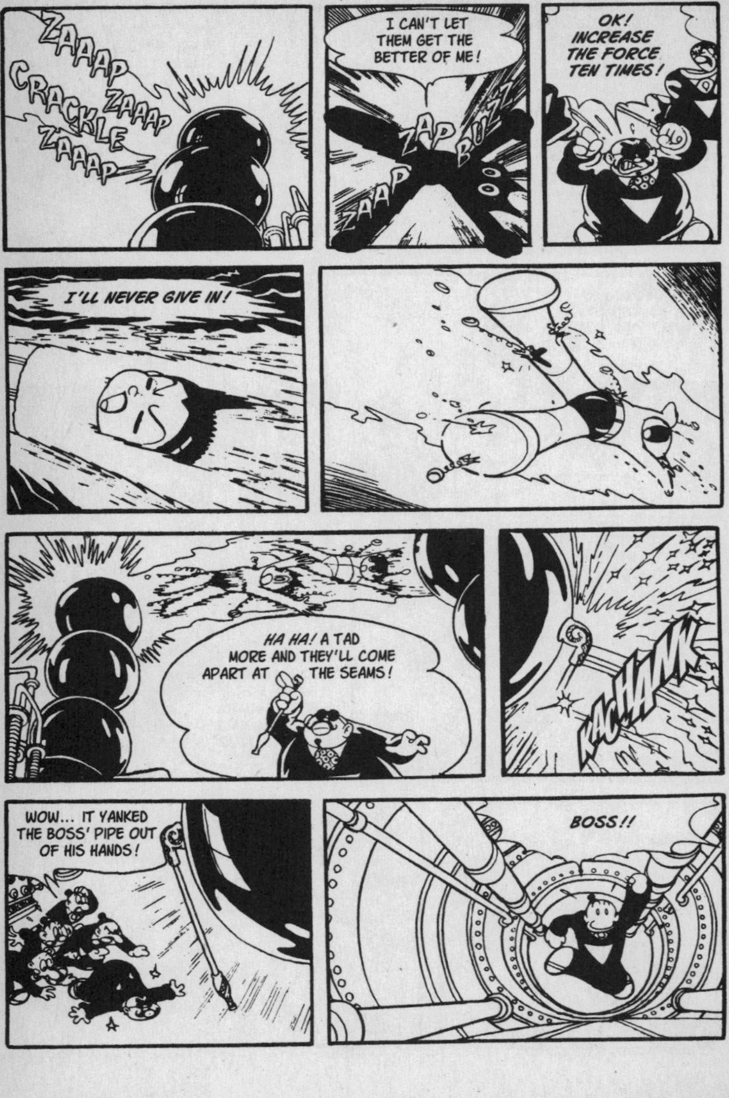
ZAAAAP
CRACKLE
ZAAAAP
ZAAAAP
I CAN'T LET THEM GET THE BETTER OF ME!
ZAP BUZZ
ZAAP
OK! INCREASE THE FORCE TEN TIMES!
I'LL NEVER GIVE IN!
HA HA! A TAD MORE AND THEY'LL COME APART AT THE SEAMS!
KACHANK
WOW... IT YANKED THE BOSS' PIPE OUT OF HIS HANDS!
BOSS!!

WE'VE GOT A PROBLEM, BOSS! HUNDREDS OF ROBOTS ARE CHECKING TO SEE WHERE THE WATER'S LEAKING INTO THE ISLAND!

WHAT'LL WE DO IF WE'RE DETECTED?!

ROBOTS ARE ON THEIR WAY HERE?

HMPH. HE'S RIGHT...

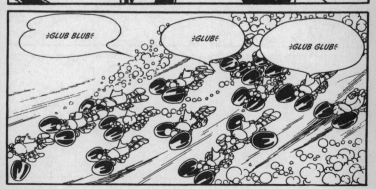

≋GLUB BLUB≋

≋GLUB≋

≋GLUB GLUB≋

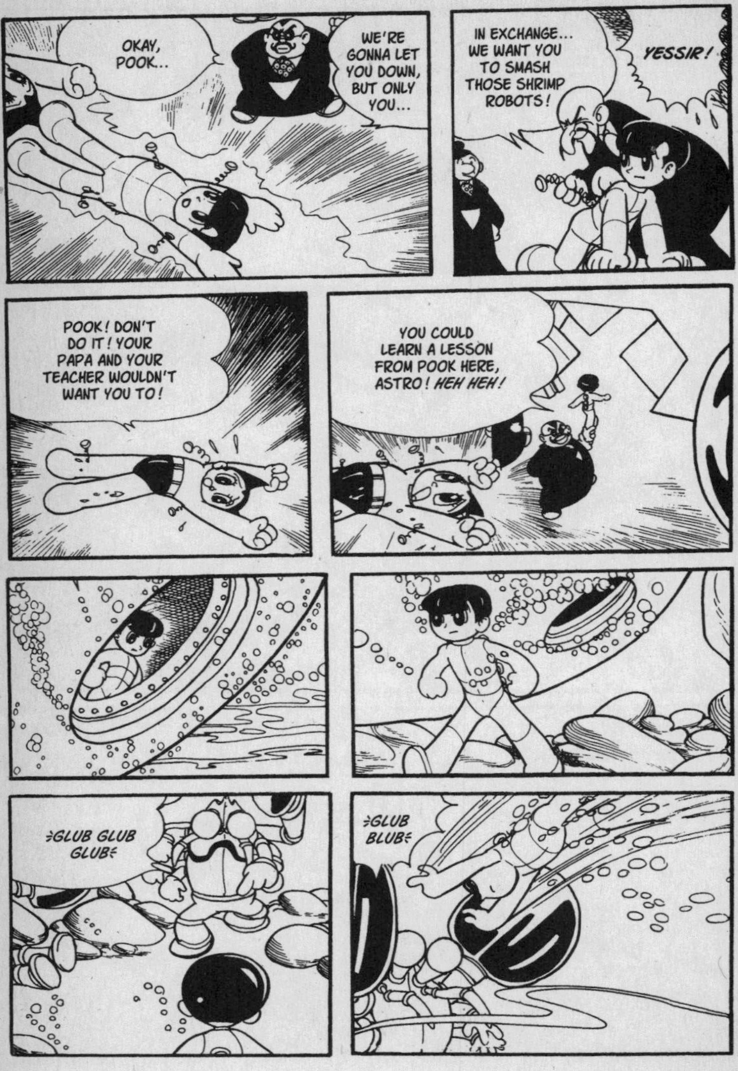
OKAY, POOK...
WE'RE GONNA LET YOU DOWN, BUT ONLY YOU...
IN EXCHANGE... WE WANT YOU TO SMASH THOSE SHRIMP ROBOTS!
YESSIR!
POOK! DON'T DO IT! YOUR PAPA AND YOUR TEACHER WOULDN'T WANT YOU TO!
YOU COULD LEARN A LESSON FROM POOK HERE, ASTRO! HEH HEH!
GLUB GLUB GLUB
GLUB BLUB

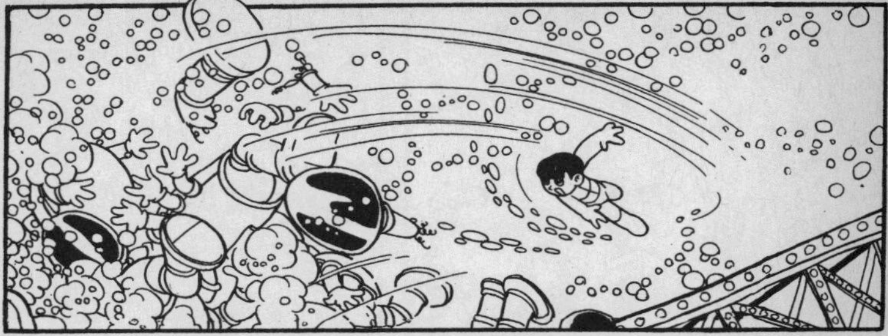

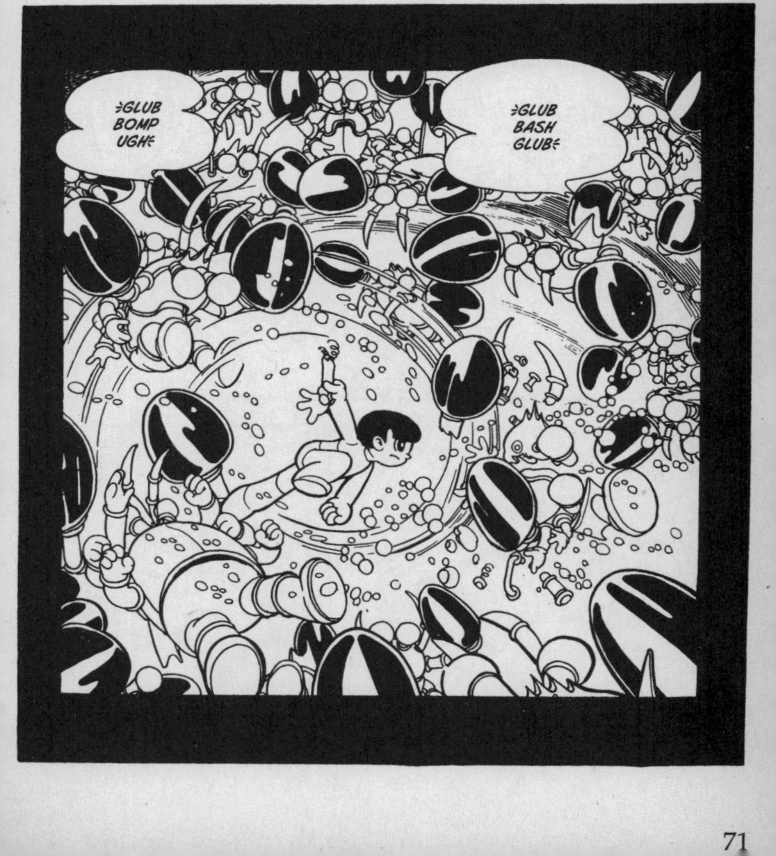
GLUB BOMP UGH
GLUB BASH GLUB

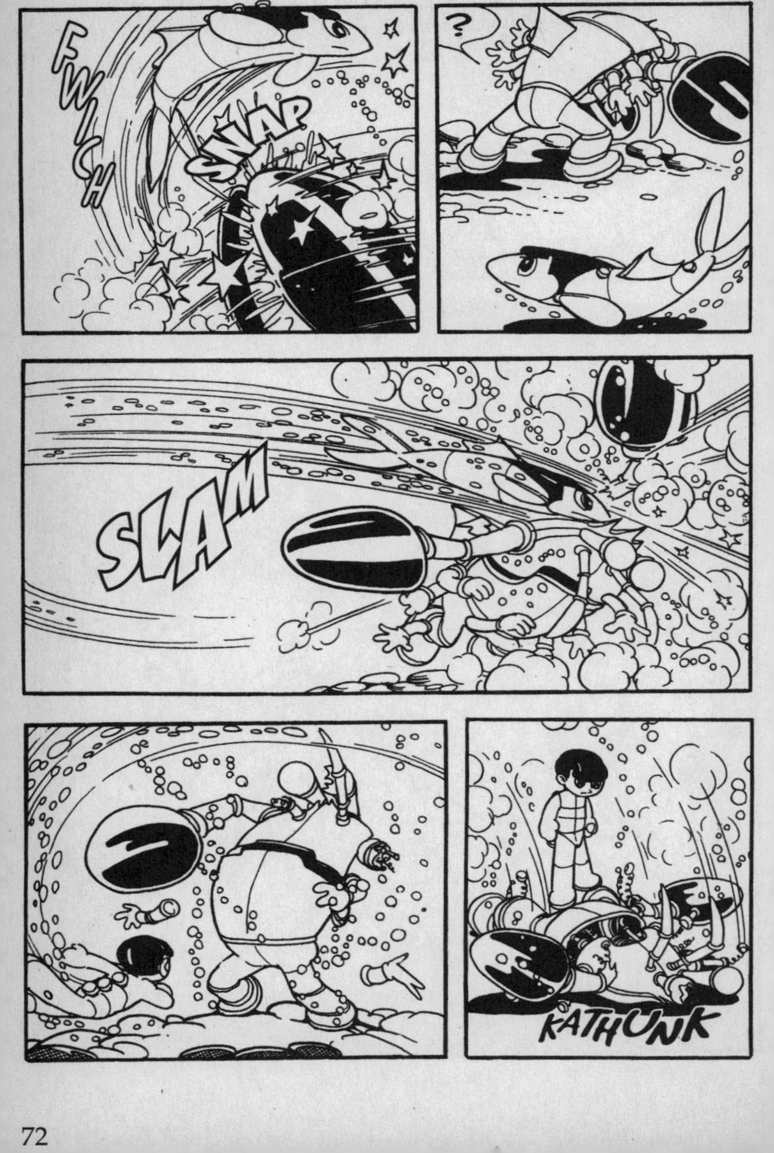
FWICH
SNAP
?
SLAM
KATHUNK

SEE THAT, BOSS? HE WIPED OUT THE SHRIMP ROBOTS!

WAY TO GO, POOK!

NOW'S THE TIME FOR US TO DIG UP THE URANIUM!

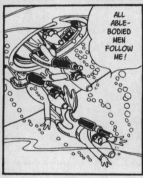

ALL ABLE-BODIED MEN FOLLOW ME!

HURRY IT UP!

WHO GOES THERE?!

WHO GOES THERE YOURSELF?

IT'S YOU!

HI! NICE WEATHER!?

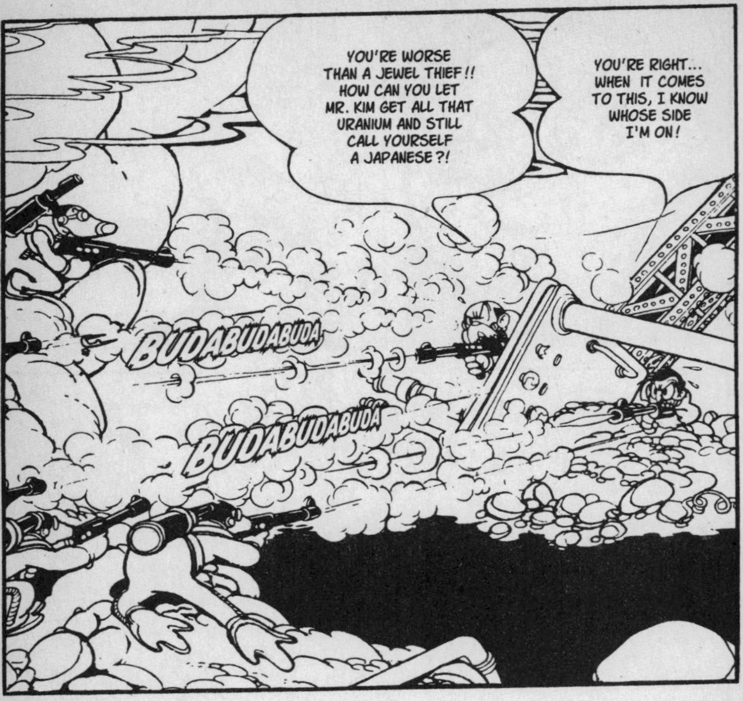
YOU'RE WORSE THAN A JEWEL THIEF!! HOW CAN YOU LET MR. KIM GET ALL THAT URANIUM AND STILL CALL YOURSELF A JAPANESE?!
YOU'RE RIGHT... WHEN IT COMES TO THIS, I KNOW WHOSE SIDE I'M ON!
BUDABUDABUDA
BUDABUDABUDA

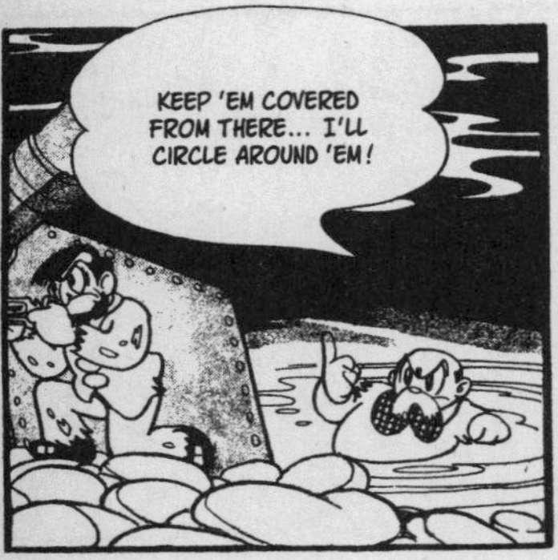
KEEP 'EM COVERED FROM THERE... I'LL CIRCLE AROUND 'EM!

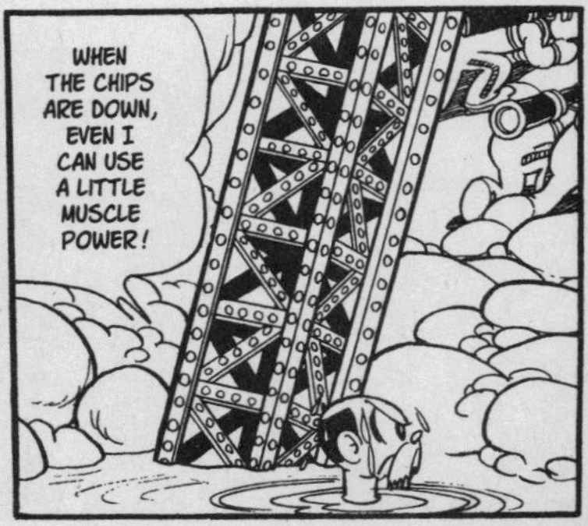
WHEN THE CHIPS ARE DOWN, EVEN I CAN USE A LITTLE MUSCLE POWER!

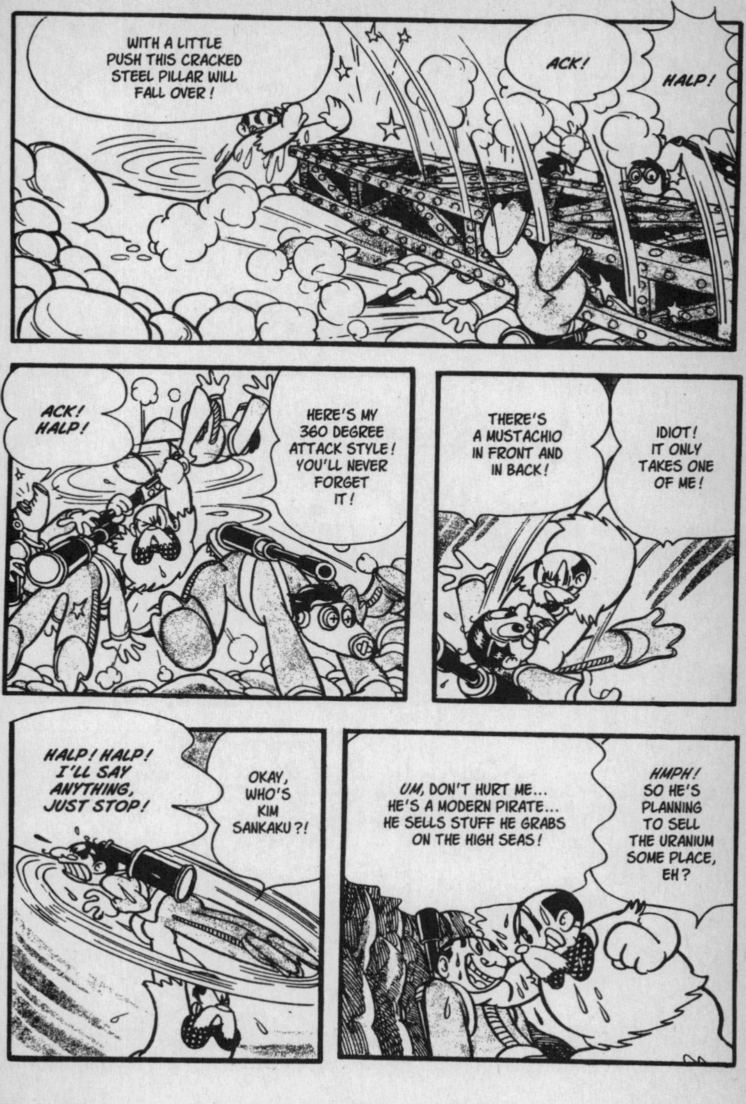
WITH A LITTLE PUSH THIS CRACKED STEEL PILLAR WILL FALL OVER!
ACK!
HALP!
ACK! HALP!
HERE'S MY 360 DEGREE ATTACK STYLE! YOU'LL NEVER FORGET IT!
THERE'S A MUSTACHIO IN FRONT AND IN BACK!
IDIOT! IT ONLY TAKES ONE OF ME!
HALP! HALP! I'LL SAY ANYTHING, JUST STOP!
OKAY, WHO'S KIM SANKAKU?!
UM, DON'T HURT ME... HE'S A MODERN PIRATE... HE SELLS STUFF HE GRABS ON THE HIGH SEAS!
HMPH! SO HE'S PLANNING TO SELL THE URANIUM SOME PLACE, EH?

EXACTLY! HE'S GOT CUSTOMERS IN COUNTRIES 'ROUND THE WORLD!

HEH HEH... AND HE'S TAKEN ASTRO BOY HOSTAGE AND SUSPENDED HIM IN THE AIR BY MAGNETS!

LISTEN, MR. JEWELRY THIEF... I'VE GOTTA GO SAVE ASTRO! ARE YOU COMING WITH ME OR NOT?

COUNT ME IN, PAL! I'VE GOT A SCORE TA SETTLE!

GOOD! LET'S GO, THEN!

IF THAT MAGNETISM THROWS ASTRO OUT OF WHACK, WE'RE DOOMED!

WE'VE GOTTA RESCUE HIM BEFORE HE'S RUINED!

HANG IN THERE, ASTRO... WE'RE ON OUR WAY!

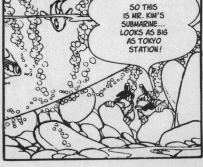

SO THIS IS MR. KIM'S SUBMARINE... LOOKS AS BIG AS TOKYO STATION!

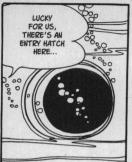

LUCKY FOR US, THERE'S AN ENTRY HATCH HERE...

HEAVEN MUST BE ON OUR SIDE! NO TIME TO LOSE, LET'S GO IN!

THIS MUST BE WHERE THEY CARRY IN THE URANIUM...

CLICK

TAP

CLICK

HMM... THIS MUST BE THE ATOMIC ENGINE....

HANG ON A SEC... LET'S MAKE SURE THEY CAN'T MOVE THIS THING...

BE CAREFUL WHAT YOU DO WITH THOSE DIALS!!

RELAX... I'M A SCHOOL TEACHER. I KNOW A THING OR TWO ABOUT ENGINES...

THERE! I FIXED IT!

...NOW THE SHIP'LL BLOW UP WHEN THEY START THE ENGINE!

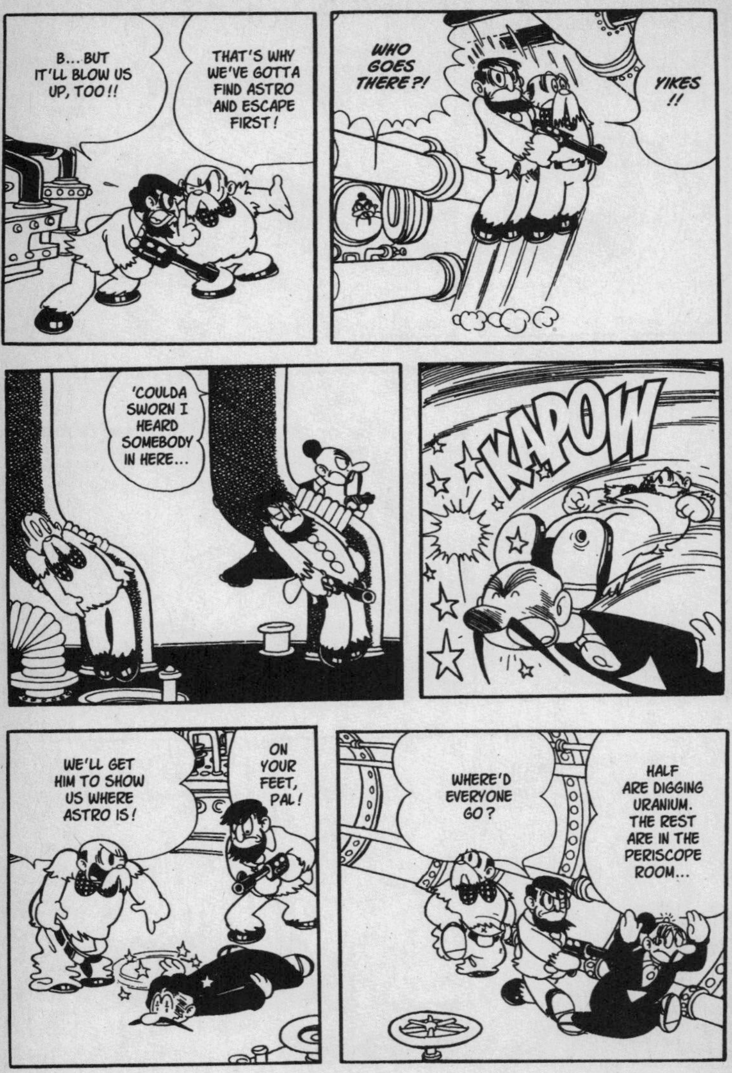
B... BUT IT'LL BLOW US UP, TOO!!
THAT'S WHY WE'VE GOTTA FIND ASTRO AND ESCAPE FIRST!
WHO GOES THERE?!
YIKES !!
'COULDA SWORN I HEARD SOMEBODY IN HERE...
KAPOW
WE'LL GET HIM TO SHOW US WHERE ASTRO IS!
ON YOUR FEET, PAL!
WHERE'D EVERYONE GO?
HALF ARE DIGGING URANIUM. THE REST ARE IN THE PERISCOPE ROOM...

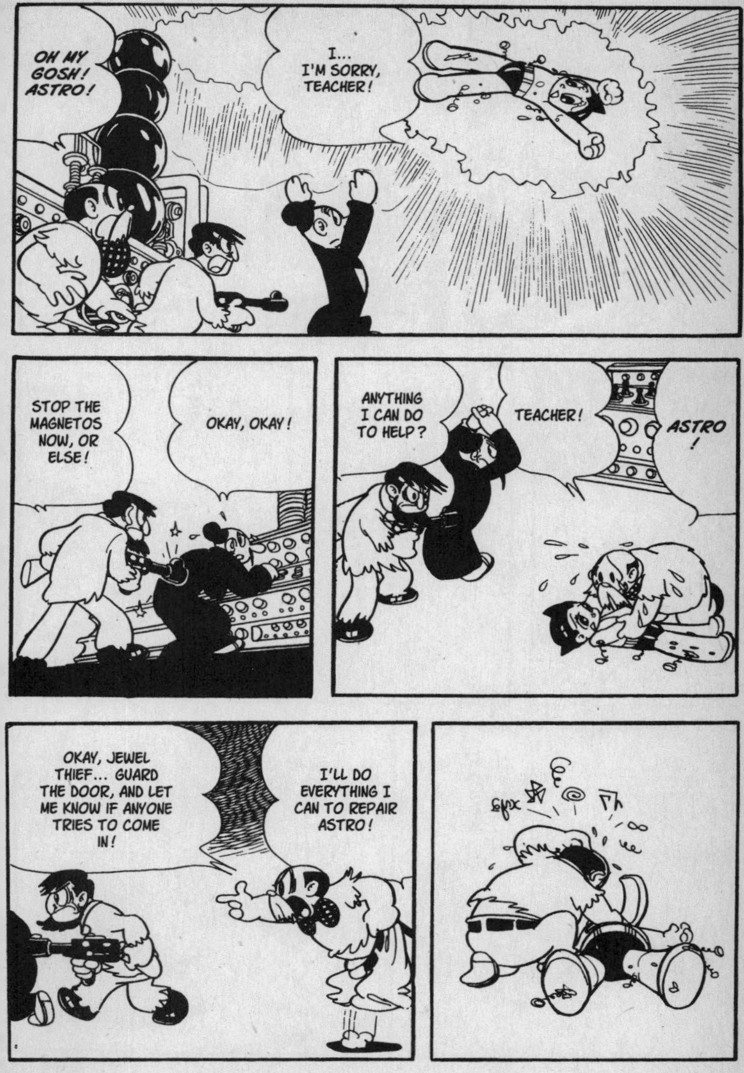
OH MY GOSH! ASTRO!
I... I'M SORRY, TEACHER!
STOP THE MAGNETOS NOW, OR ELSE!
OKAY, OKAY!
ANYTHING I CAN DO TO HELP?
TEACHER!
ASTRO!
OKAY, JEWEL THIEF... GUARD THE DOOR, AND LET ME KNOW IF ANYONE TRIES TO COME IN!
I'LL DO EVERYTHING I CAN TO REPAIR ASTRO!

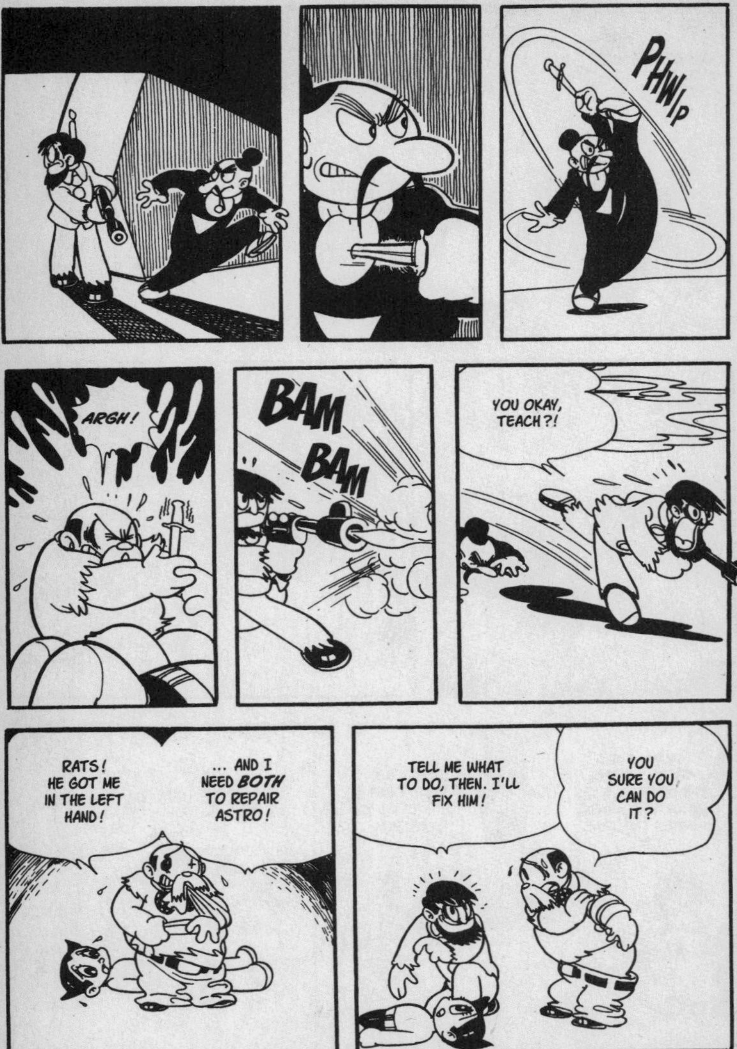

PHWIP
ARGH!
BAM
BAM
YOU OKAY, TEACH?!
RATS! HE GOT ME IN THE LEFT HAND!
... AND I NEED *BOTH* TO REPAIR ASTRO!
TELL ME WHAT TO DO, THEN. I'LL FIX HIM!
YOU SURE YOU CAN DO IT?

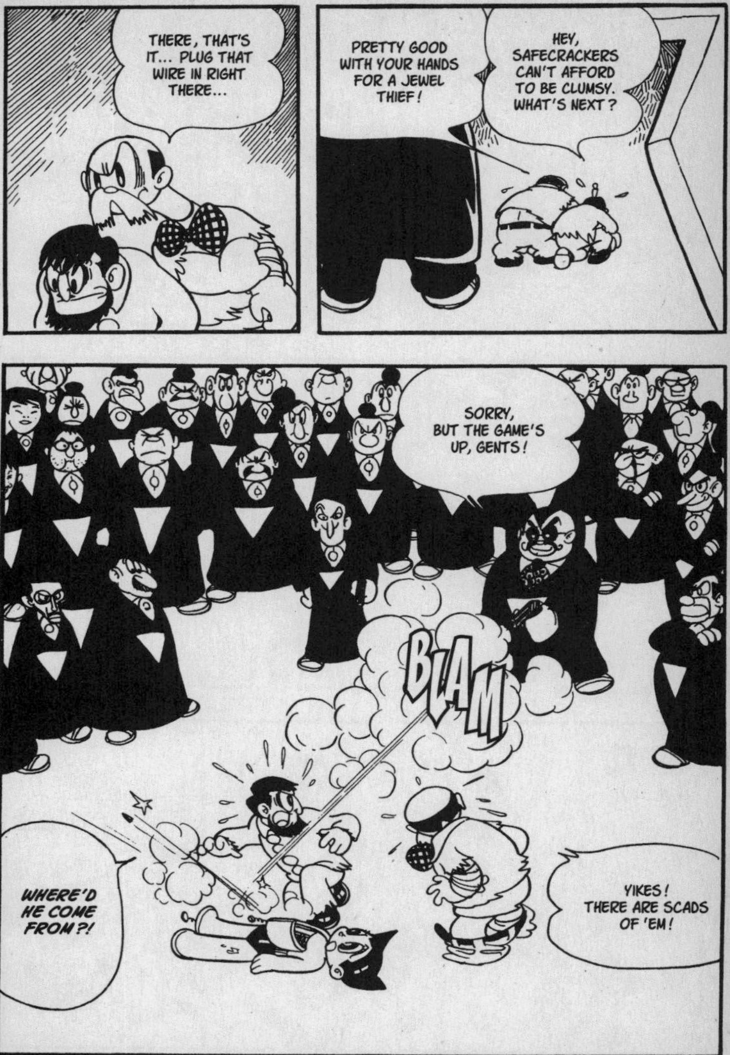
THERE, THAT'S IT... PLUG THAT WIRE IN RIGHT THERE...
PRETTY GOOD WITH YOUR HANDS FOR A JEWEL THIEF!
HEY, SAFECRACKERS CAN'T AFFORD TO BE CLUMSY. WHAT'S NEXT?
SORRY, BUT THE GAME'S UP, GENTS!
BLAM
WHERE'D HE COME FROM?!
YIKES! THERE ARE SCADS OF 'EM!

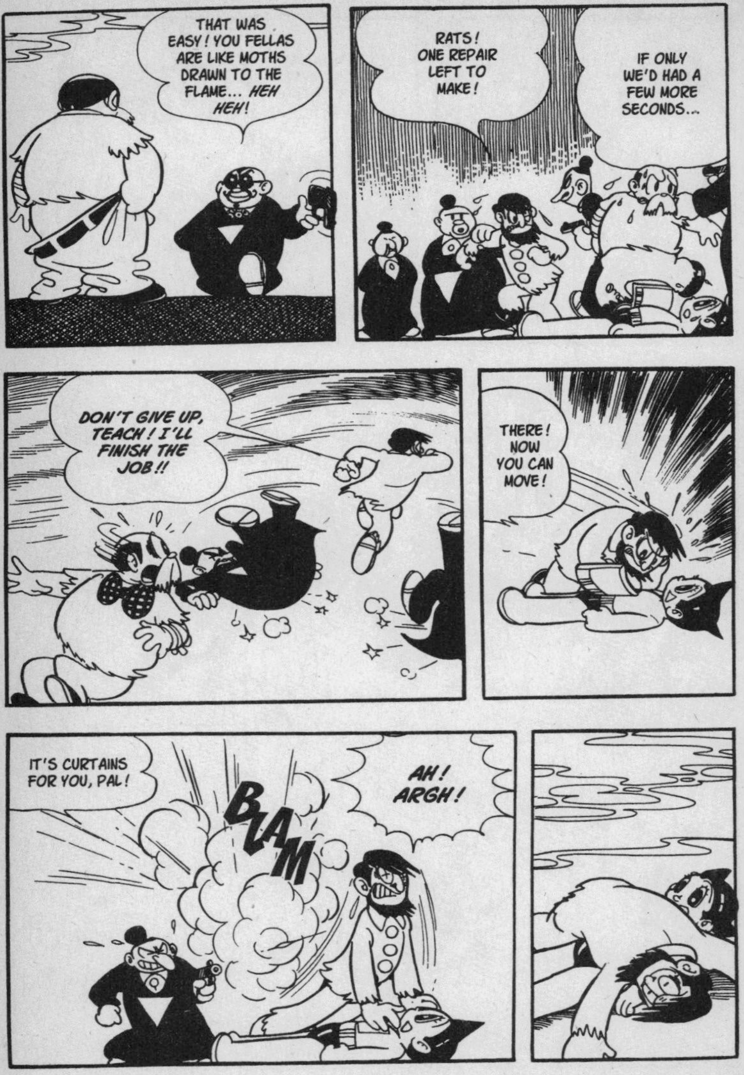
THAT WAS EASY! YOU FELLAS ARE LIKE MOTHS DRAWN TO THE FLAME... *HEH HEH*!
RATS! ONE REPAIR LEFT TO MAKE!
IF ONLY WE'D HAD A FEW MORE SECONDS...
DON'T GIVE UP, TEACH! I'LL FINISH THE JOB!!
THERE! NOW YOU CAN MOVE!
IT'S CURTAINS FOR YOU, PAL!
BLAM
AH! ARGH!

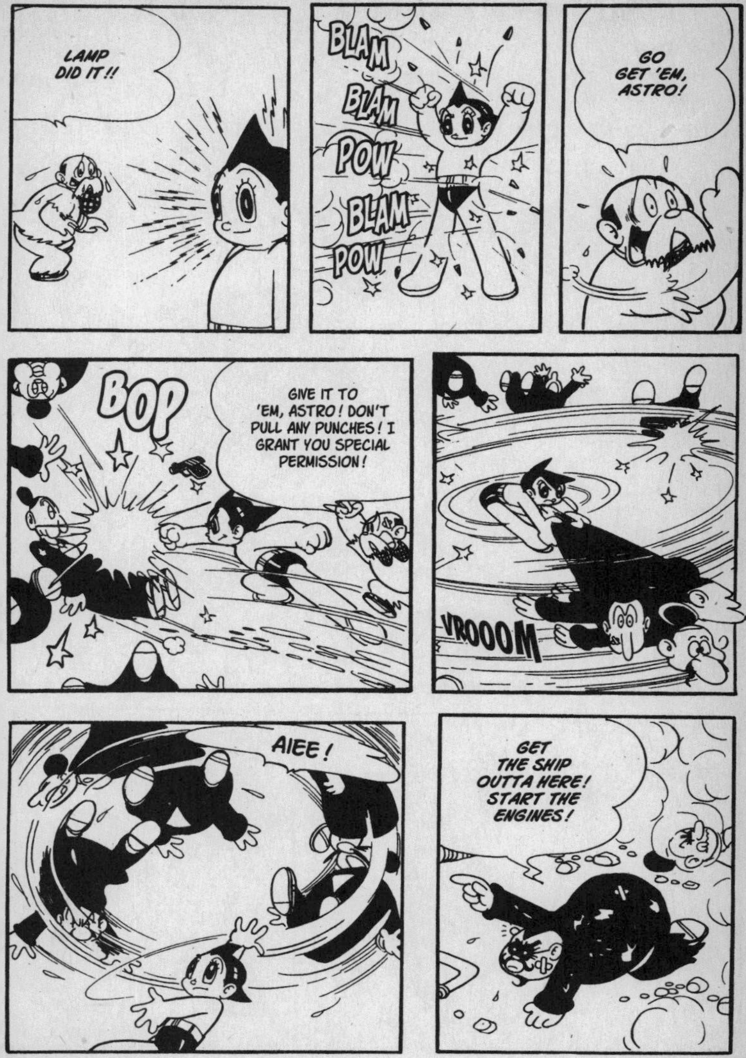
LAMP DID IT!!
BLAM
BLAM
POW
BLAM
POW
GO GET 'EM, ASTRO!
BOP
GIVE IT TO 'EM, ASTRO! DON'T PULL ANY PUNCHES! I GRANT YOU SPECIAL PERMISSION!
VROOOM
AIEE!
GET THE SHIP OUTTA HERE! START THE ENGINES!

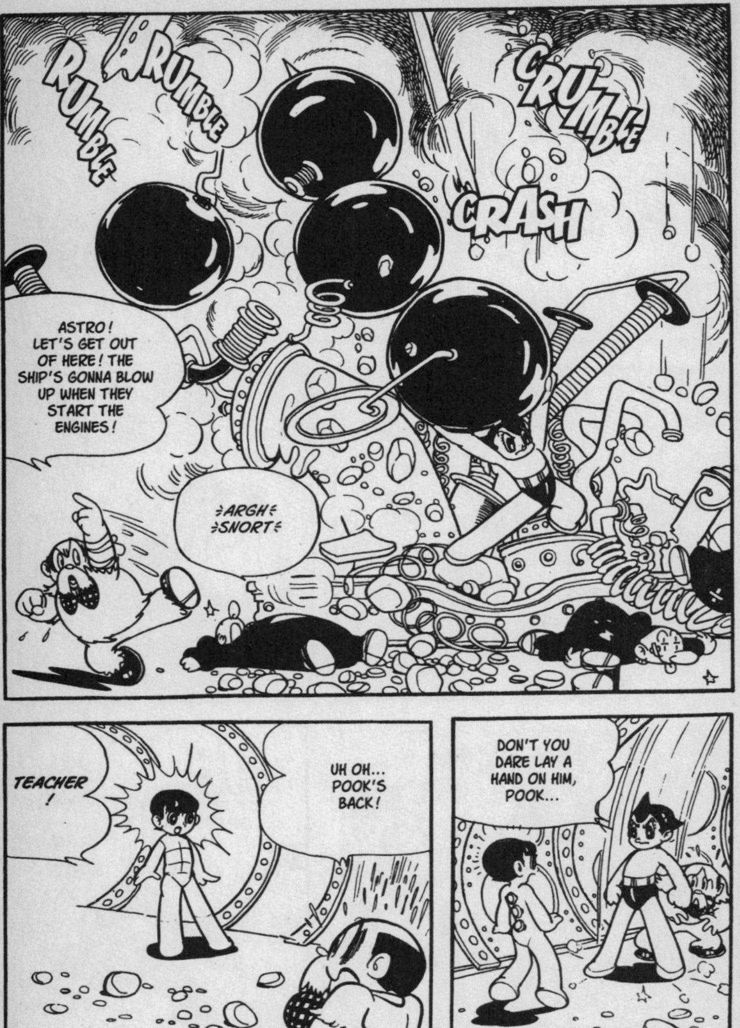
RUMBLE
RUMBLE
CRUMBLE
CRASH
ASTRO! LET'S GET OUT OF HERE! THE SHIP'S GONNA BLOW UP WHEN THEY START THE ENGINES!
ARGH SNORT
TEACHER!
UH OH... POOK'S BACK!
DON'T YOU DARE LAY A HAND ON HIM, POOK...

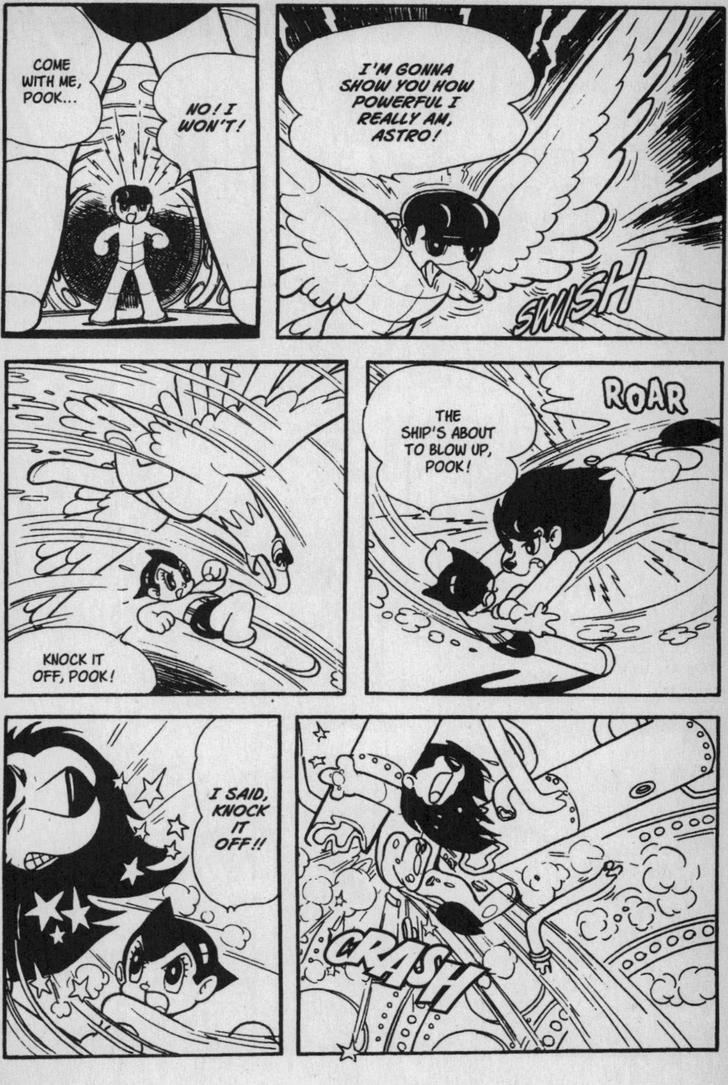
COME WITH ME, POOK...
NO! I WON'T!
I'M GONNA SHOW YOU HOW POWERFUL I REALLY AM, ASTRO!
SWISH
KNOCK IT OFF, POOK!
ROAR
THE SHIP'S ABOUT TO BLOW UP, POOK!
I SAID, KNOCK IT OFF!!
CRASH

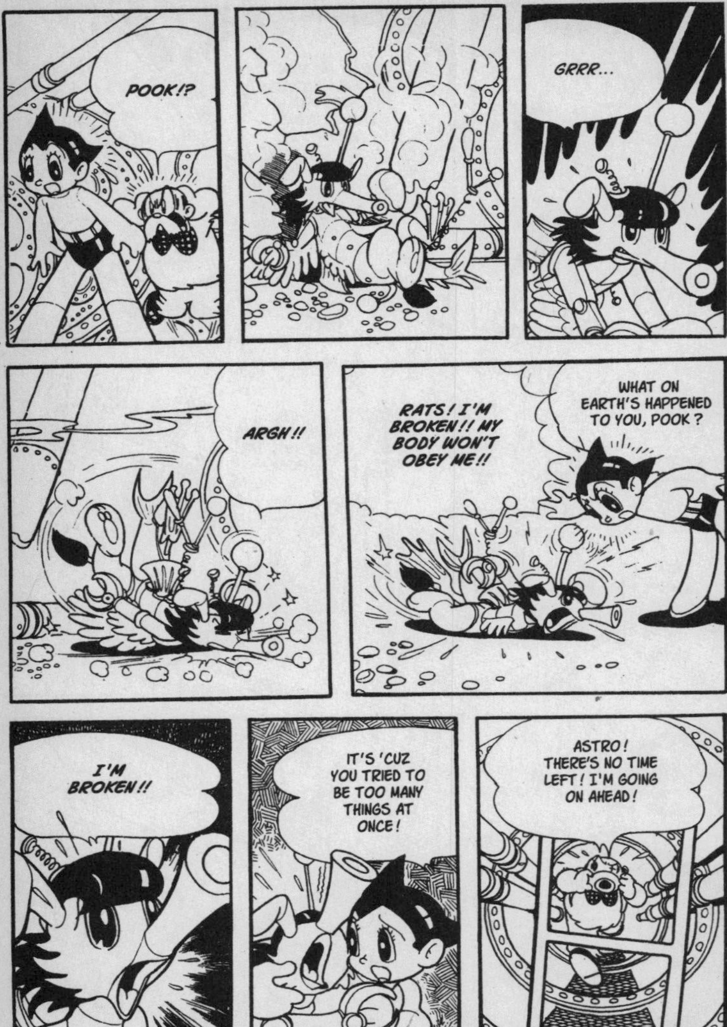
POOK!?
GRRR...
ARGH!!
RATS! I'M BROKEN!! MY BODY WON'T OBEY ME!!
WHAT ON EARTH'S HAPPENED TO YOU, POOK?
I'M BROKEN!!
IT'S 'CUZ YOU TRIED TO BE TOO MANY THINGS AT ONCE!
ASTRO! THERE'S NO TIME LEFT! I'M GOING ON AHEAD!

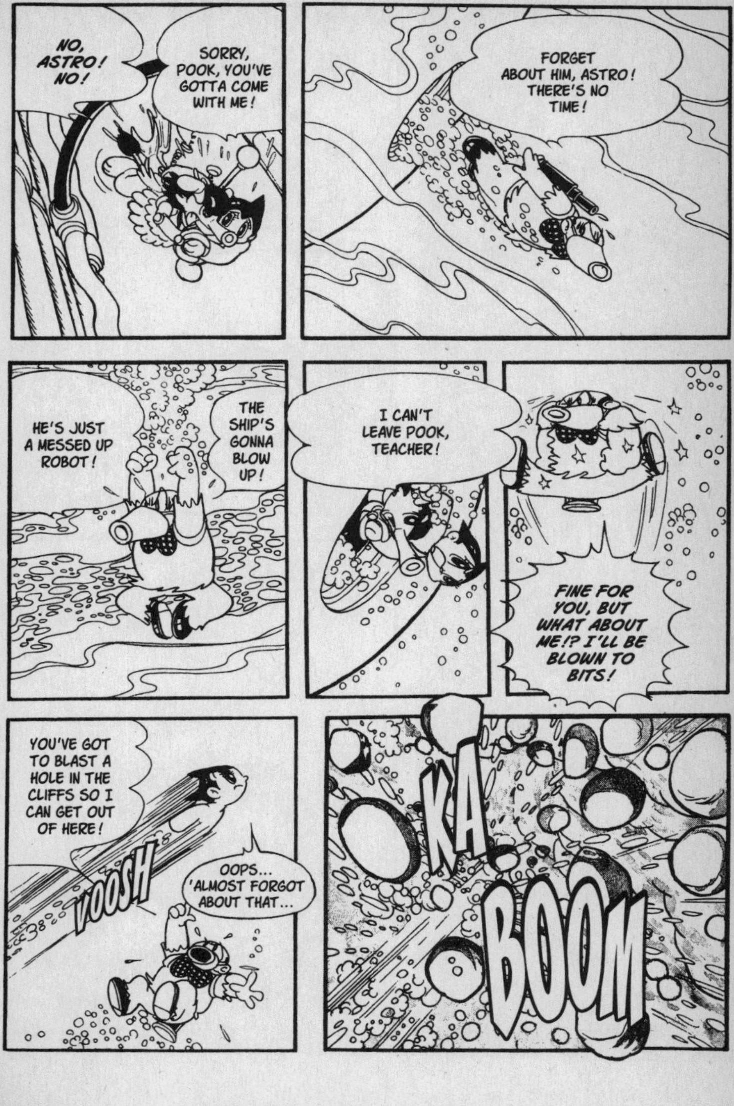
NO, ASTRO! NO!
SORRY, POOK, YOU'VE GOTTA COME WITH ME!
FORGET ABOUT HIM, ASTRO! THERE'S NO TIME!
HE'S JUST A MESSED UP ROBOT!
THE SHIP'S GONNA BLOW UP!
I CAN'T LEAVE POOK, TEACHER!
FINE FOR YOU, BUT WHAT ABOUT ME!? I'LL BE BLOWN TO BITS!
YOU'VE GOT TO BLAST A HOLE IN THE CLIFFS SO I CAN GET OUT OF HERE!
VOOSH
OOPS... 'ALMOST FORGOT ABOUT THAT...
KA
BOOM

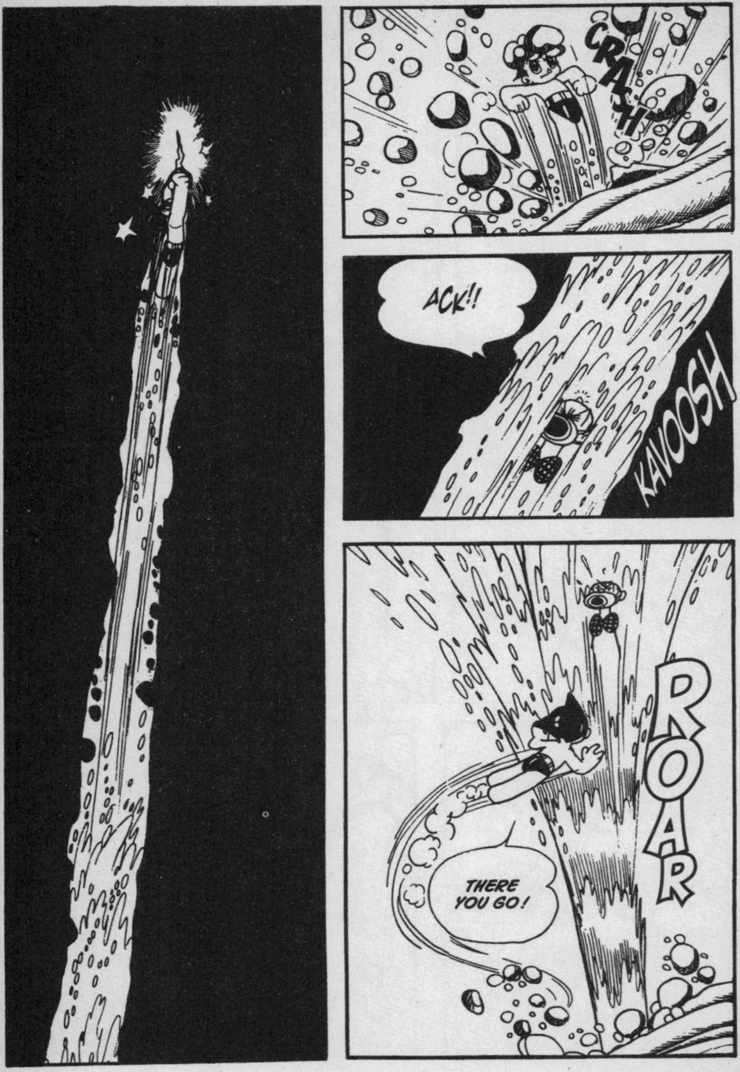
CRASH
ACK!!
KAVOOSH
ROAR
THERE YOU GO!

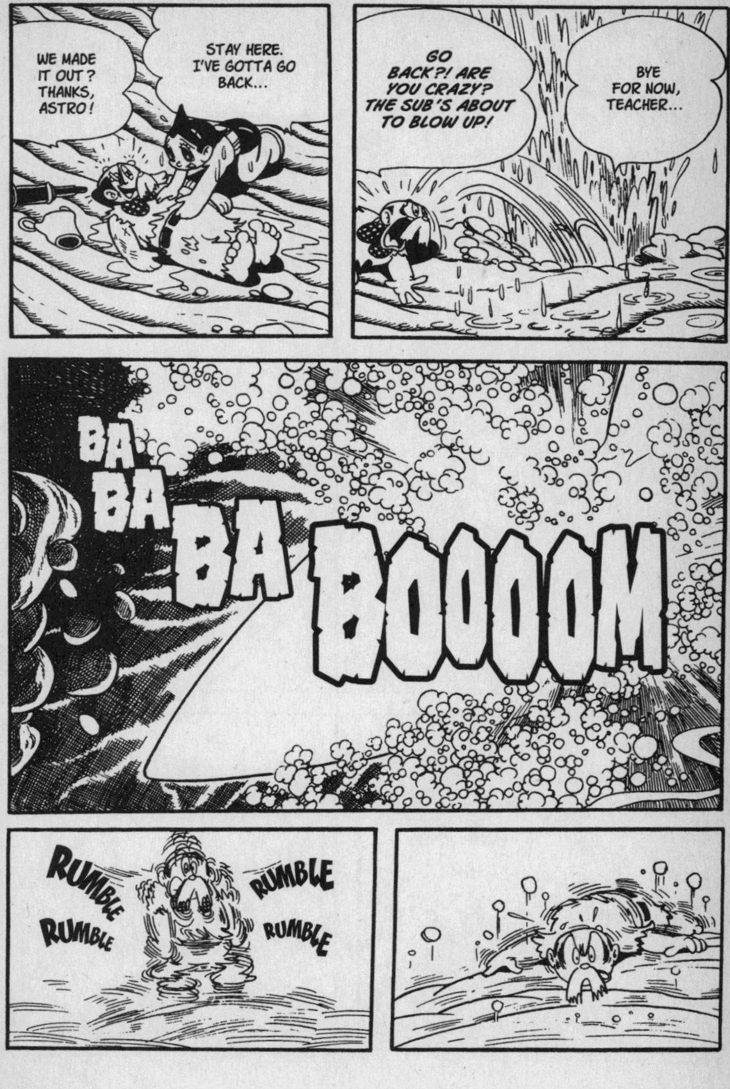
WE MADE IT OUT? THANKS, ASTRO!
STAY HERE. I'VE GOTTA GO BACK...
GO BACK?! ARE YOU CRAZY? THE SUB'S ABOUT TO BLOW UP!
BYE FOR NOW, TEACHER...
BA BA BA BA BOOOOM
RUMBLE
RUMBLE
RUMBLE
RUMBLE

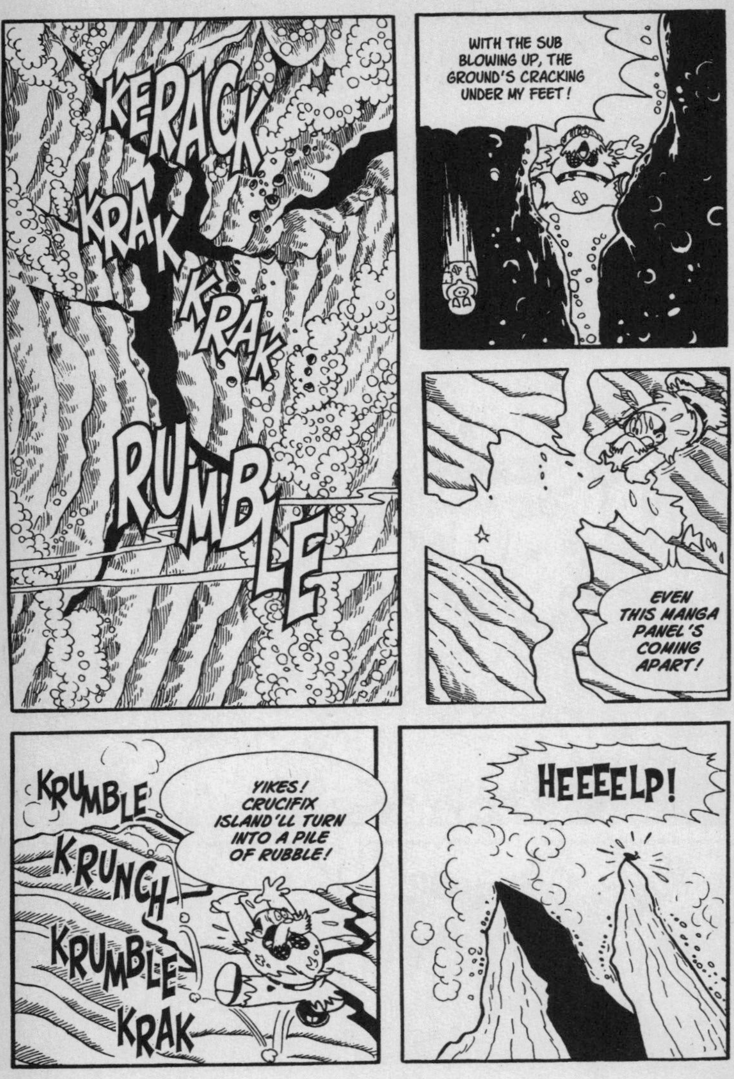
KERACK
KRAK
KRAK
RUMBLE
WITH THE SUB BLOWING UP, THE GROUND'S CRACKING UNDER MY FEET!
EVEN THIS MANGA PANEL'S COMING APART!
KRUMBLE
YIKES! CRUCIFIX ISLAND'LL TURN INTO A PILE OF RUBBLE!
KRUNCH
KRUMBLE
KRAK
HEEEELP!

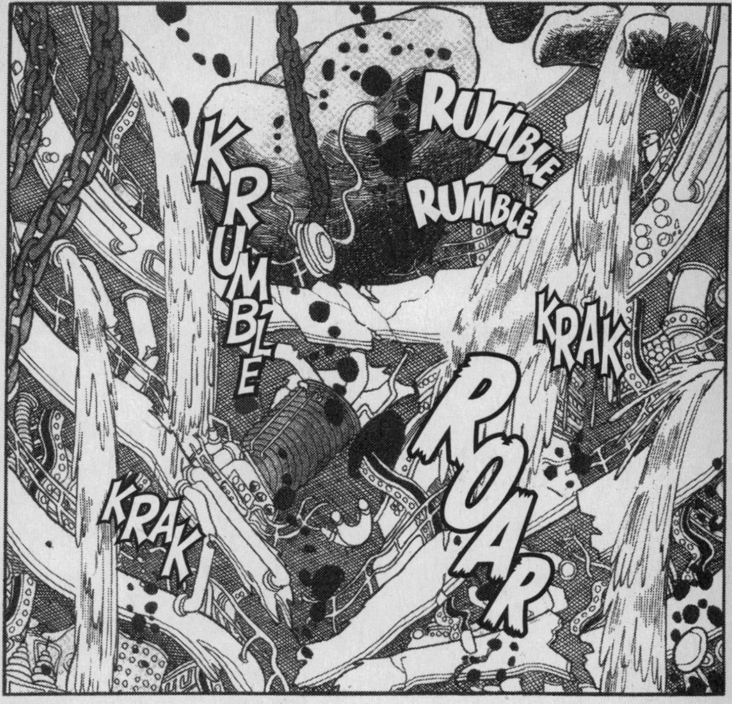
RUMBLE
RUMBLE
KRUMBLE
KRAK
ROAR
KRAK

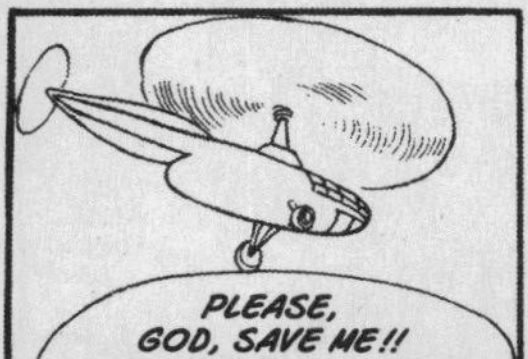
PLEASE, GOD, SAVE ME!! HELICOPTER! HALP!

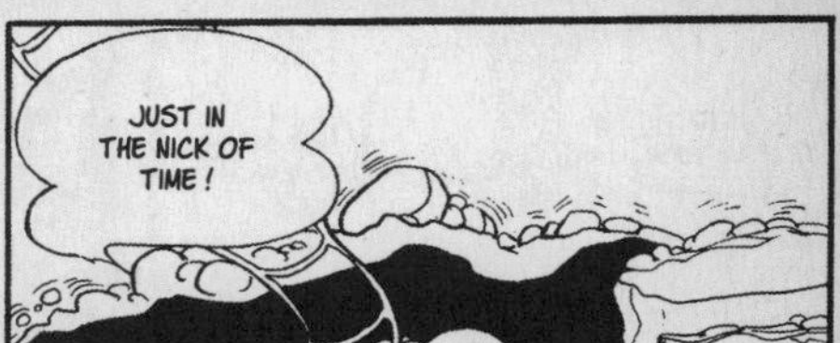
JUST IN THE NICK OF TIME!

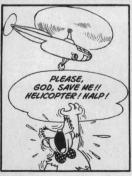

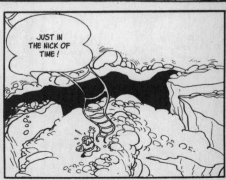

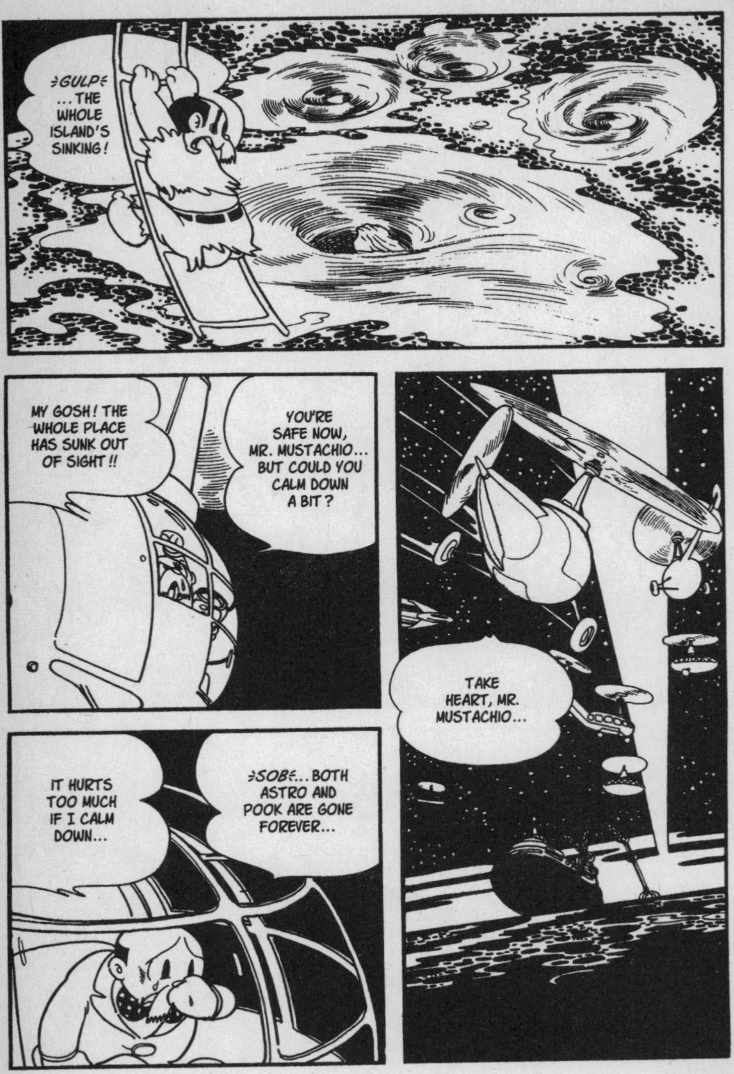
⸗GULP⸗ ...THE WHOLE ISLAND'S SINKING!
MY GOSH! THE WHOLE PLACE HAS SUNK OUT OF SIGHT!!
YOU'RE SAFE NOW, MR. MUSTACHIO... BUT COULD YOU CALM DOWN A BIT?
IT HURTS TOO MUCH IF I CALM DOWN...
⸗SOB⸗...BOTH ASTRO AND POOK ARE GONE FOREVER...
TAKE HEART, MR. MUSTACHIO...

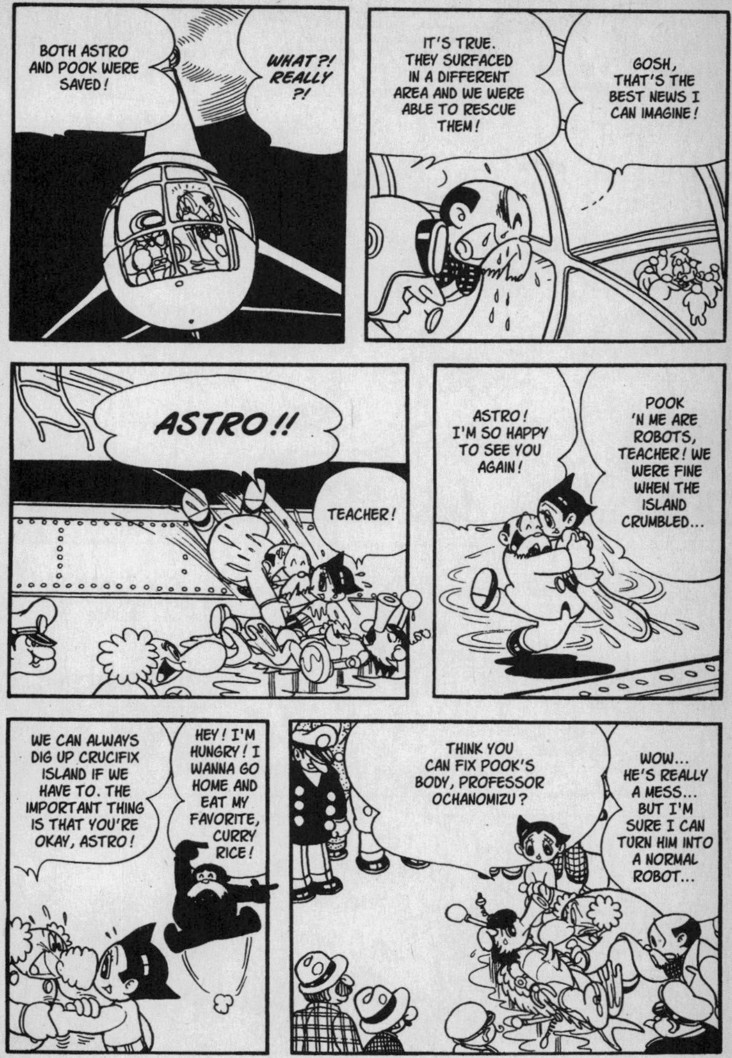
BOTH ASTRO AND POOK WERE SAVED!
WHAT?! REALLY?!
IT'S TRUE. THEY SURFACED IN A DIFFERENT AREA AND WE WERE ABLE TO RESCUE THEM!
GOSH, THAT'S THE BEST NEWS I CAN IMAGINE!
ASTRO!!
TEACHER!
ASTRO! I'M SO HAPPY TO SEE YOU AGAIN!
POOK 'N ME ARE ROBOTS, TEACHER! WE WERE FINE WHEN THE ISLAND CRUMBLED...
WE CAN ALWAYS DIG UP CRUCIFIX ISLAND IF WE HAVE TO. THE IMPORTANT THING IS THAT YOU'RE OKAY, ASTRO!
HEY! I'M HUNGRY! I WANNA GO HOME AND EAT MY FAVORITE, CURRY RICE!
THINK YOU CAN FIX POOK'S BODY, PROFESSOR OCHANOMIZU?
WOW... HE'S REALLY A MESS... BUT I'M SURE I CAN TURN HIM INTO A NORMAL ROBOT...

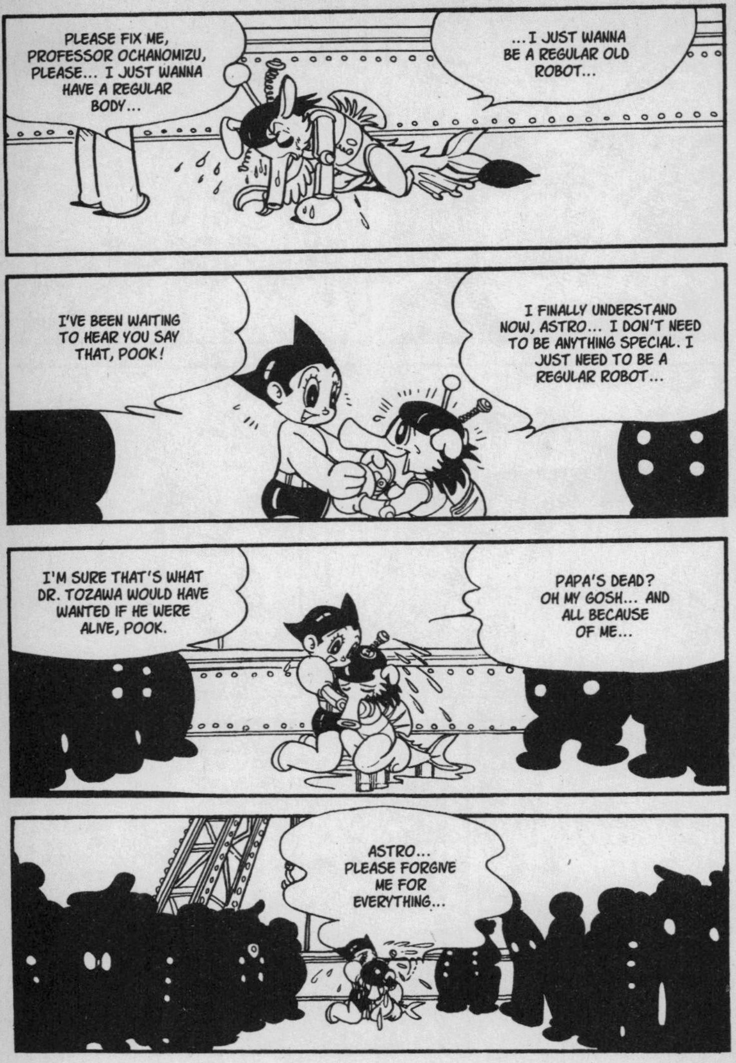
PLEASE FIX ME, PROFESSOR OCHANOMIZU, PLEASE... I JUST WANNA HAVE A REGULAR BODY...
...I JUST WANNA BE A REGULAR OLD ROBOT...
I'VE BEEN WAITING TO HEAR YOU SAY THAT, POOK!
I FINALLY UNDERSTAND NOW, ASTRO... I DON'T NEED TO BE ANYTHING SPECIAL. I JUST NEED TO BE A REGULAR ROBOT...
I'M SURE THAT'S WHAT DR. TOZAWA WOULD HAVE WANTED IF HE WERE ALIVE, POOK.
PAPA'S DEAD? OH MY GOSH... AND ALL BECAUSE OF ME...
ASTRO... PLEASE FORGIVE ME FOR EVERYTHING...

SPACE SNOW LEOPARD

First serialized between February and April
1960 in *Shonen* magazine.

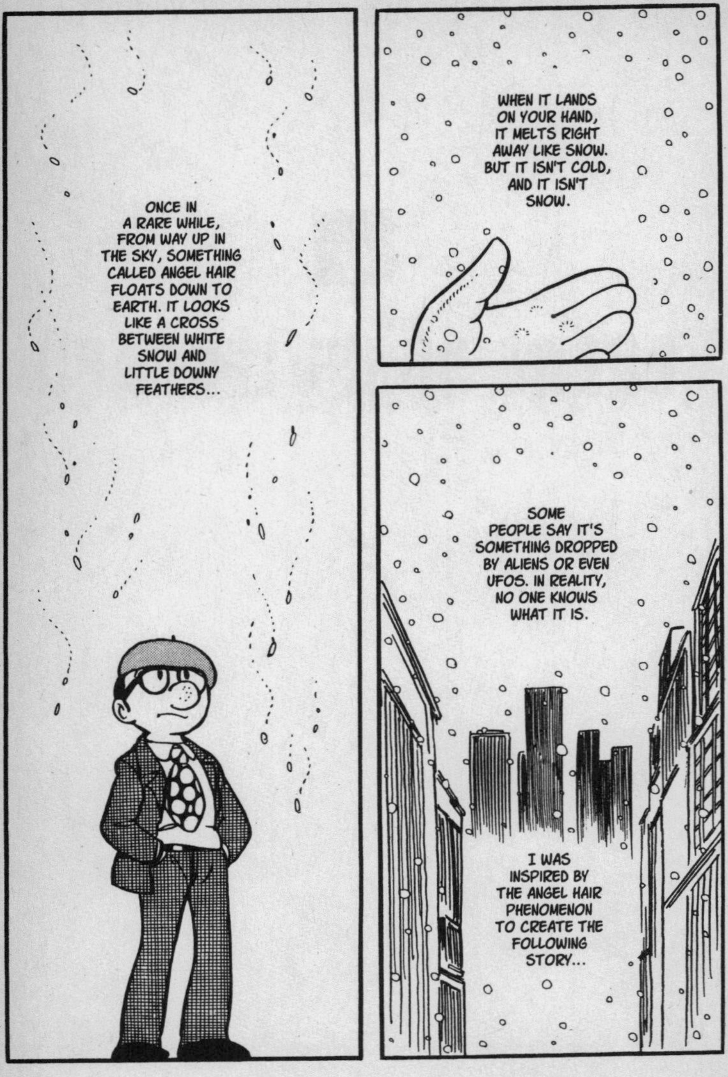
ONCE IN A RARE WHILE, FROM WAY UP IN THE SKY, SOMETHING CALLED ANGEL HAIR FLOATS DOWN TO EARTH. IT LOOKS LIKE A CROSS BETWEEN WHITE SNOW AND LITTLE DOWNY FEATHERS...
WHEN IT LANDS ON YOUR HAND, IT MELTS RIGHT AWAY LIKE SNOW. BUT IT ISN'T COLD, AND IT ISN'T SNOW.
SOME PEOPLE SAY IT'S SOMETHING DROPPED BY ALIENS OR EVEN UFOS. IN REALITY, NO ONE KNOWS WHAT IT IS.
I WAS INSPIRED BY THE ANGEL HAIR PHENOMENON TO CREATE THE FOLLOWING STORY...

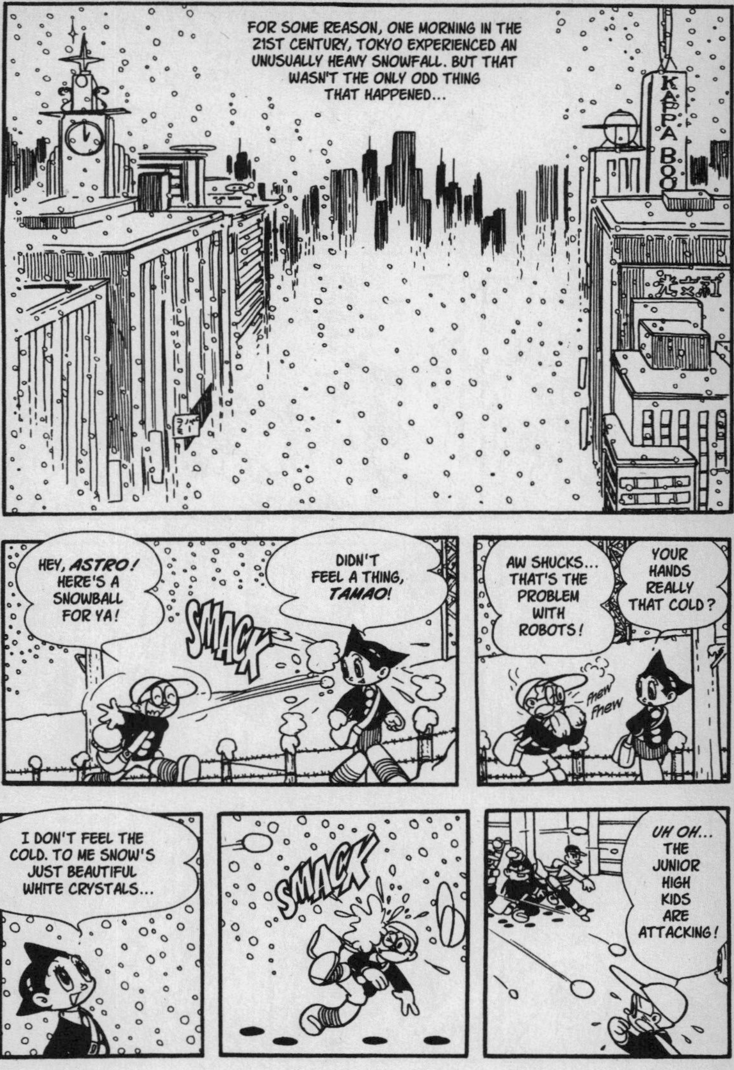
FOR SOME REASON, ONE MORNING IN THE 21ST CENTURY, TOKYO EXPERIENCED AN UNUSUALLY HEAVY SNOWFALL. BUT THAT WASN'T THE ONLY ODD THING THAT HAPPENED...
KAPPA BOO
HEY, ASTRO! HERE'S A SNOWBALL FOR YA!
SMACK
DIDN'T FEEL A THING, TAMAO!
AW SHUCKS... THAT'S THE PROBLEM WITH ROBOTS!
fhew fhew
YOUR HANDS REALLY THAT COLD?
I DON'T FEEL THE COLD. TO ME SNOW'S JUST BEAUTIFUL WHITE CRYSTALS...
SMACK
UH OH... THE JUNIOR HIGH KIDS ARE ATTACKING!

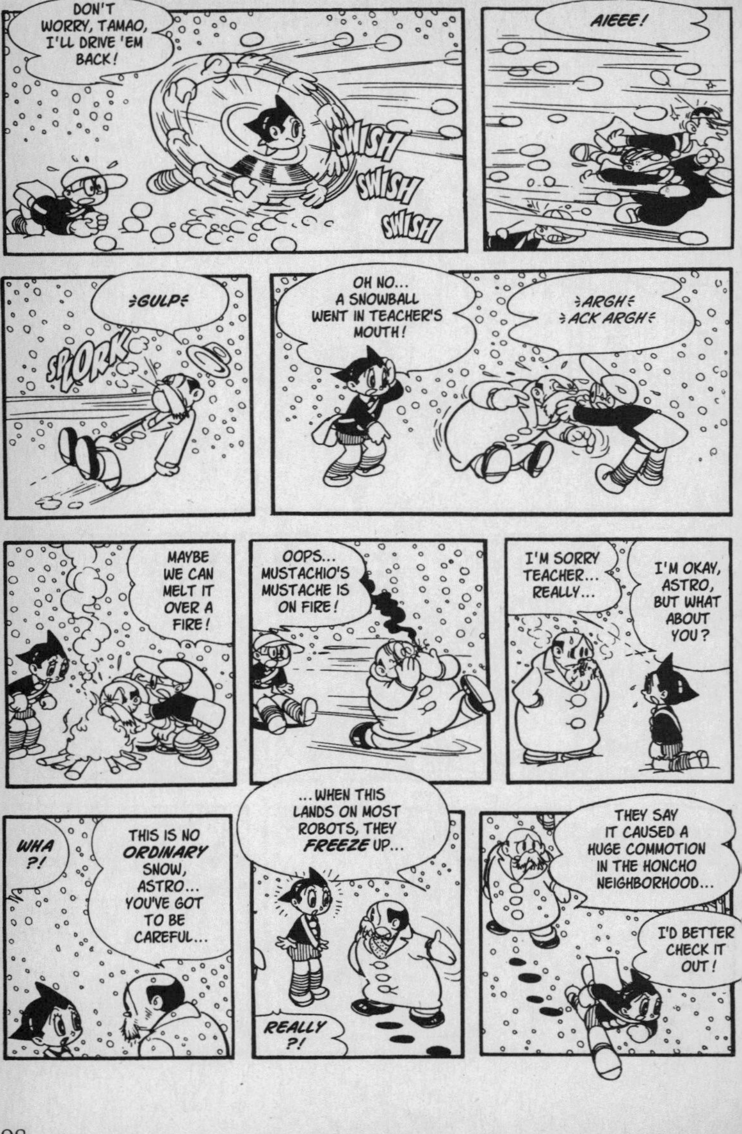
DON'T WORRY, TAMAO, I'LL DRIVE 'EM BACK!
SWISH
SWISH
SWISH
AIEEE!
GULP
SPLORK
OH NO... A SNOWBALL WENT IN TEACHER'S MOUTH!
ARGH
ACK ARGH
MAYBE WE CAN MELT IT OVER A FIRE!
OOPS... MUSTACHIO'S MUSTACHE IS ON FIRE!
I'M SORRY TEACHER... REALLY...
I'M OKAY, ASTRO, BUT WHAT ABOUT YOU?
WHA ?!
THIS IS NO ORDINARY SNOW, ASTRO... YOU'VE GOT TO BE CAREFUL...
...WHEN THIS LANDS ON MOST ROBOTS, THEY FREEZE UP...
REALLY ?!
THEY SAY IT CAUSED A HUGE COMMOTION IN THE HONCHO NEIGHBORHOOD...
I'D BETTER CHECK IT OUT!

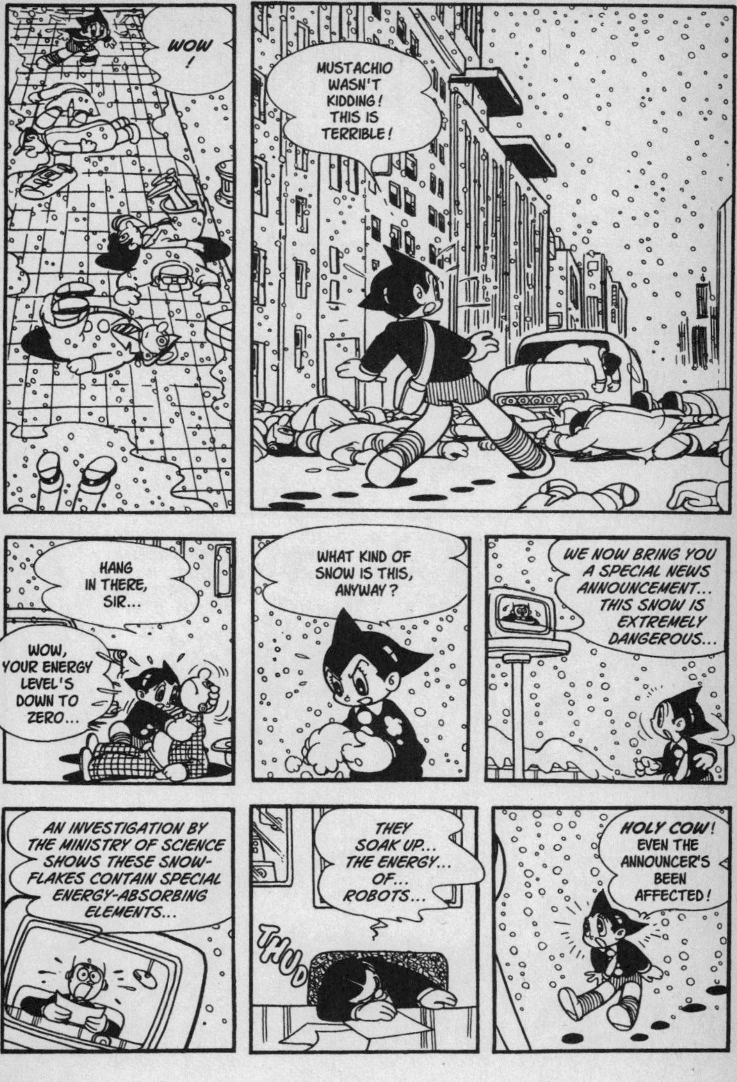
WOW!
MUSTACHIO WASN'T KIDDING! THIS IS TERRIBLE!
HANG IN THERE, SIR...
WOW, YOUR ENERGY LEVEL'S DOWN TO ZERO...
WHAT KIND OF SNOW IS THIS, ANYWAY?
WE NOW BRING YOU A SPECIAL NEWS ANNOUNCEMENT... THIS SNOW IS EXTREMELY DANGEROUS...
AN INVESTIGATION BY THE MINISTRY OF SCIENCE SHOWS THESE SNOW-FLAKES CONTAIN SPECIAL ENERGY-ABSORBING ELEMENTS...
THEY SOAK UP... THE ENERGY... OF... ROBOTS...
THUD
HOLY COW! EVEN THE ANNOUNCER'S BEEN AFFECTED!

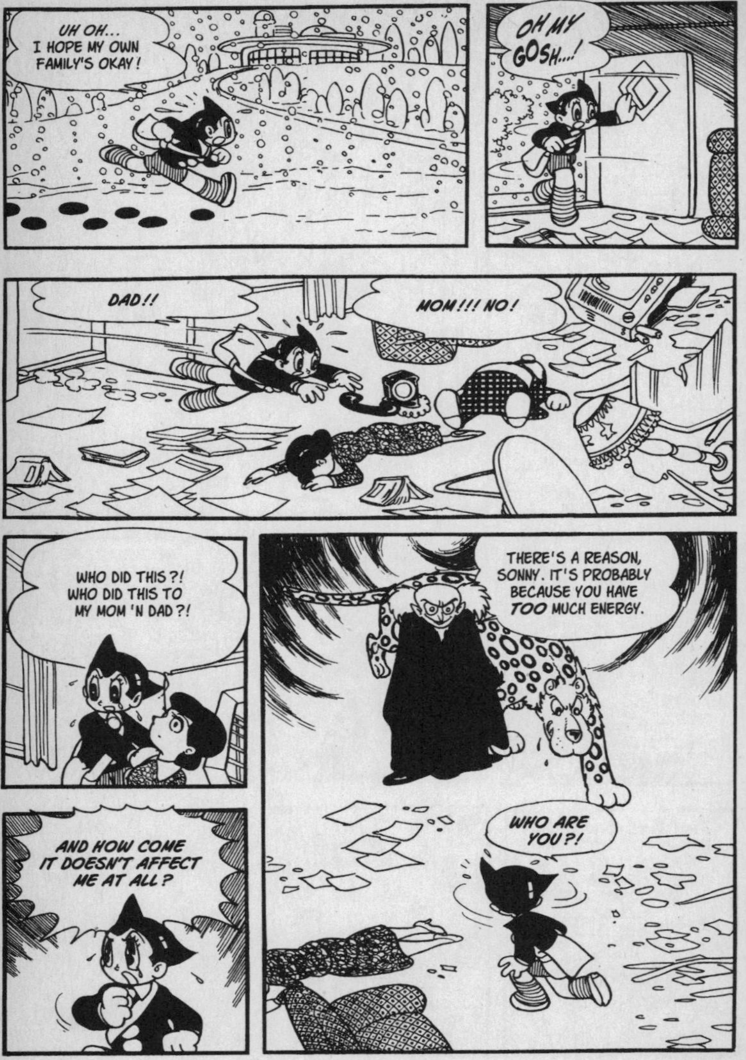
UH OH...
I HOPE MY OWN FAMILY'S OKAY!
OH MY GOSH...!
DAD!!
MOM!!! NO!
WHO DID THIS?! WHO DID THIS TO MY MOM 'N DAD?!
AND HOW COME IT DOESN'T AFFECT ME AT ALL?
THERE'S A REASON, SONNY. IT'S PROBABLY BECAUSE YOU HAVE TOO MUCH ENERGY.
WHO ARE YOU?!

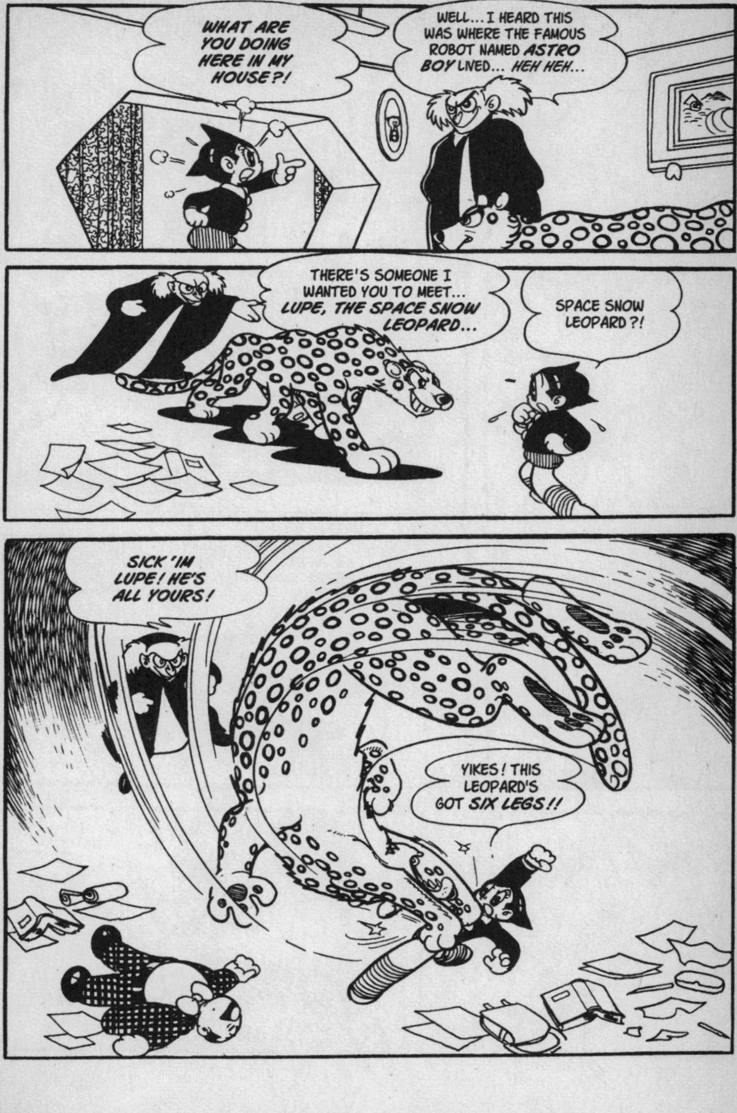
WHAT ARE YOU DOING HERE IN MY HOUSE?!
WELL... I HEARD THIS WAS WHERE THE FAMOUS ROBOT NAMED ASTRO BOY LIVED... HEH HEH...
THERE'S SOMEONE I WANTED YOU TO MEET... LUPE, THE SPACE SNOW LEOPARD...
SPACE SNOW LEOPARD?!
SICK 'IM LUPE! HE'S ALL YOURS!
YIKES! THIS LEOPARD'S GOT SIX LEGS!!

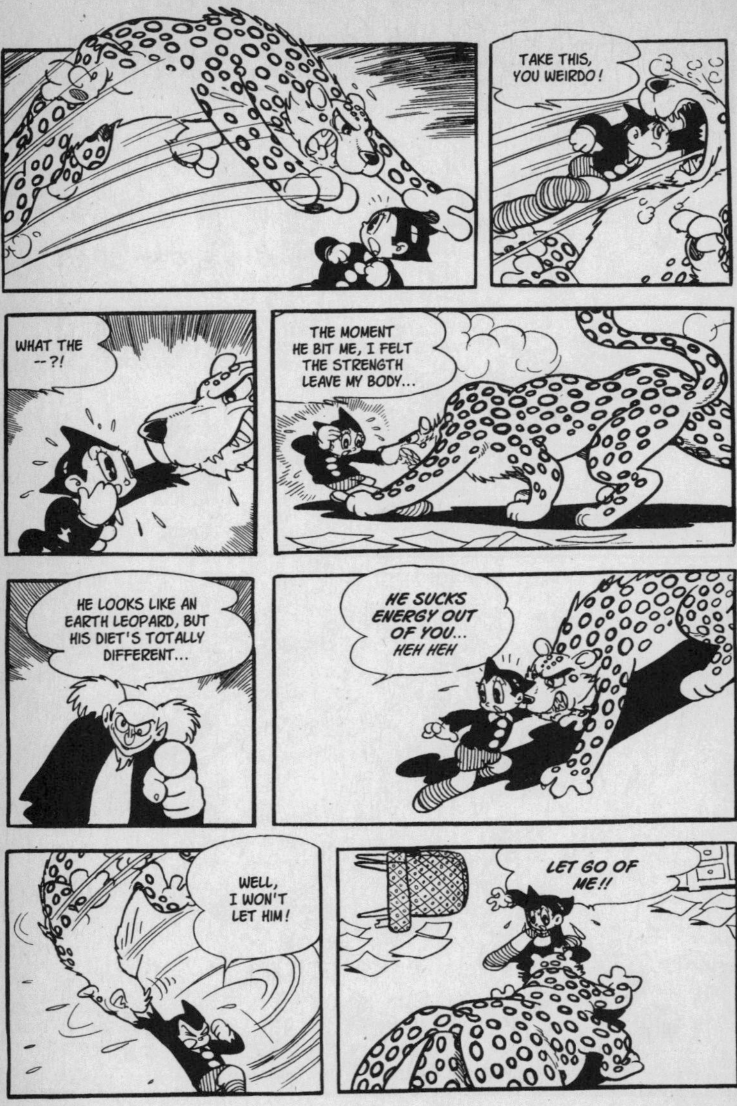
TAKE THIS, YOU WEIRDO!
WHAT THE --?!
THE MOMENT HE BIT ME, I FELT THE STRENGTH LEAVE MY BODY...
HE LOOKS LIKE AN EARTH LEOPARD, BUT HIS DIET'S TOTALLY DIFFERENT...
HE SUCKS ENERGY OUT OF YOU... HEH HEH
WELL, I WON'T LET HIM!
LET GO OF ME!!

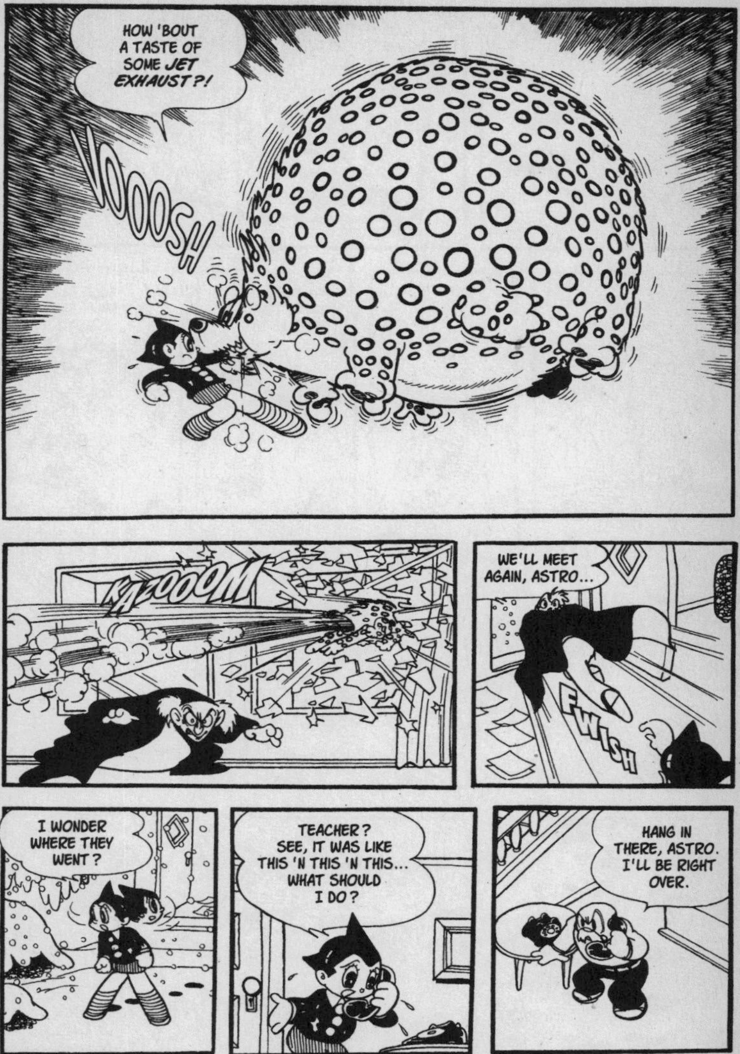
HOW 'BOUT A TASTE OF SOME *JET EXHAUST*?!
VOOOSH
KAZOOOM
WE'LL MEET AGAIN, ASTRO...
FWISH
I WONDER WHERE THEY WENT?
TEACHER? SEE, IT WAS LIKE THIS 'N THIS 'N THIS... WHAT SHOULD I DO?
HANG IN THERE, ASTRO. I'LL BE RIGHT OVER.

HUHN--? MY CAR ENGINE'S GONE DEAD ON ME!

MUST BE CAUSED BY THIS WEIRD SNOW...

I'LL HAVE TO FIND A TAXI...

WHAT THE ?!

WH-WHAT ARE THESE *TRACKS* DOING HERE ?!

MUST BE A HUGE, WILD BEAST...

MAYBE IT'S AN ABOMINABLE SNOWMAN...

CHOMP

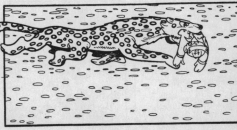

104

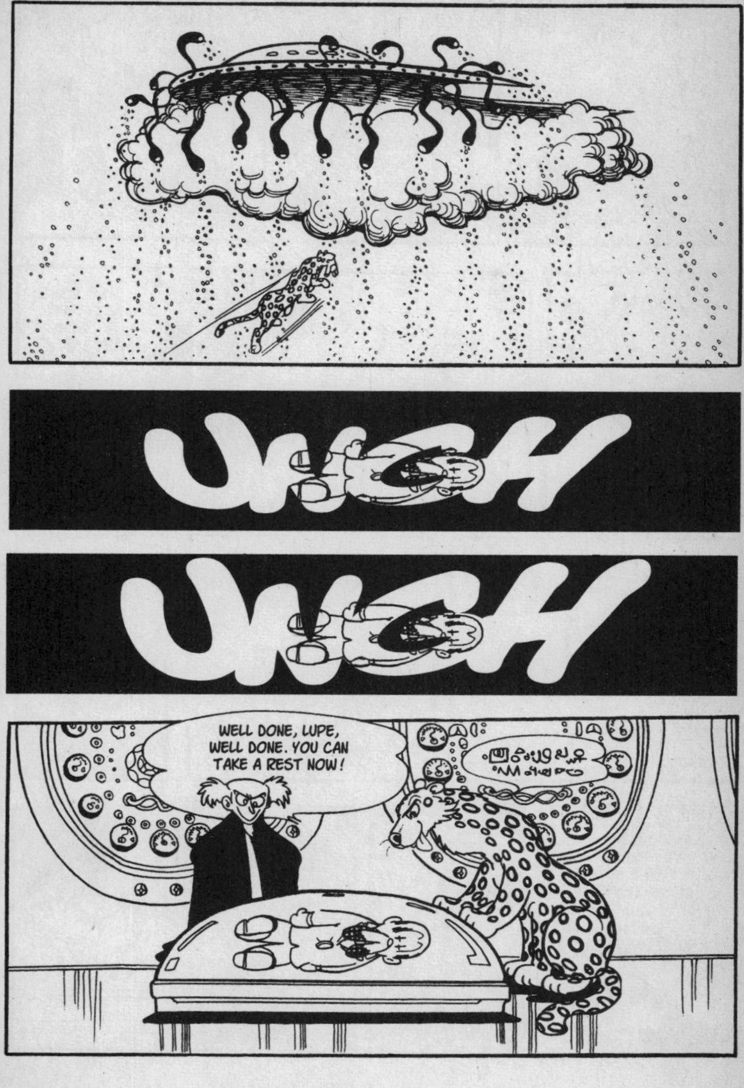
WELL DONE, LUPE, WELL DONE. YOU CAN TAKE A REST NOW!

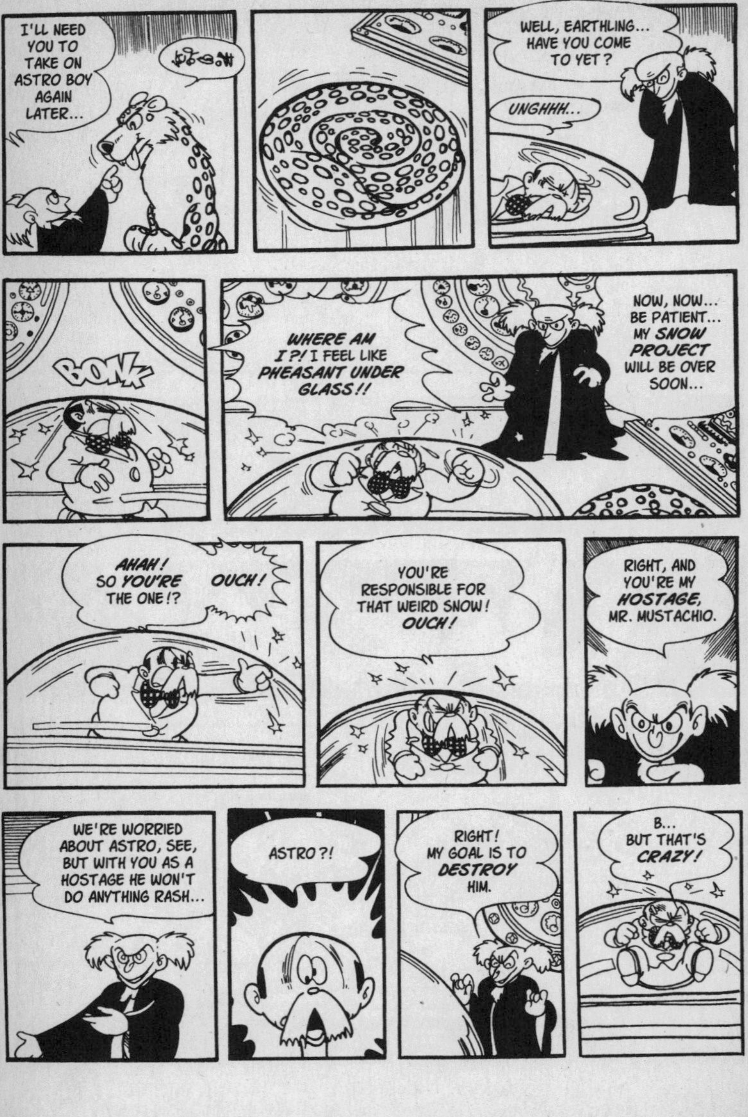

I'LL NEED YOU TO TAKE ON ASTRO BOY AGAIN LATER...
WELL, EARTHLING... HAVE YOU COME TO YET?
UNGHHH...
BONK
WHERE AM I?! I FEEL LIKE PHEASANT UNDER GLASS!!
NOW, NOW... BE PATIENT... MY SNOW PROJECT WILL BE OVER SOON...
AHAH! SO YOU'RE THE ONE!? OUCH!
YOU'RE RESPONSIBLE FOR THAT WEIRD SNOW! OUCH!
RIGHT, AND YOU'RE MY HOSTAGE, MR. MUSTACHIO.
WE'RE WORRIED ABOUT ASTRO, SEE, BUT WITH YOU AS A HOSTAGE HE WON'T DO ANYTHING RASH...
ASTRO?!
RIGHT! MY GOAL IS TO DESTROY HIM.
B... BUT THAT'S CRAZY!

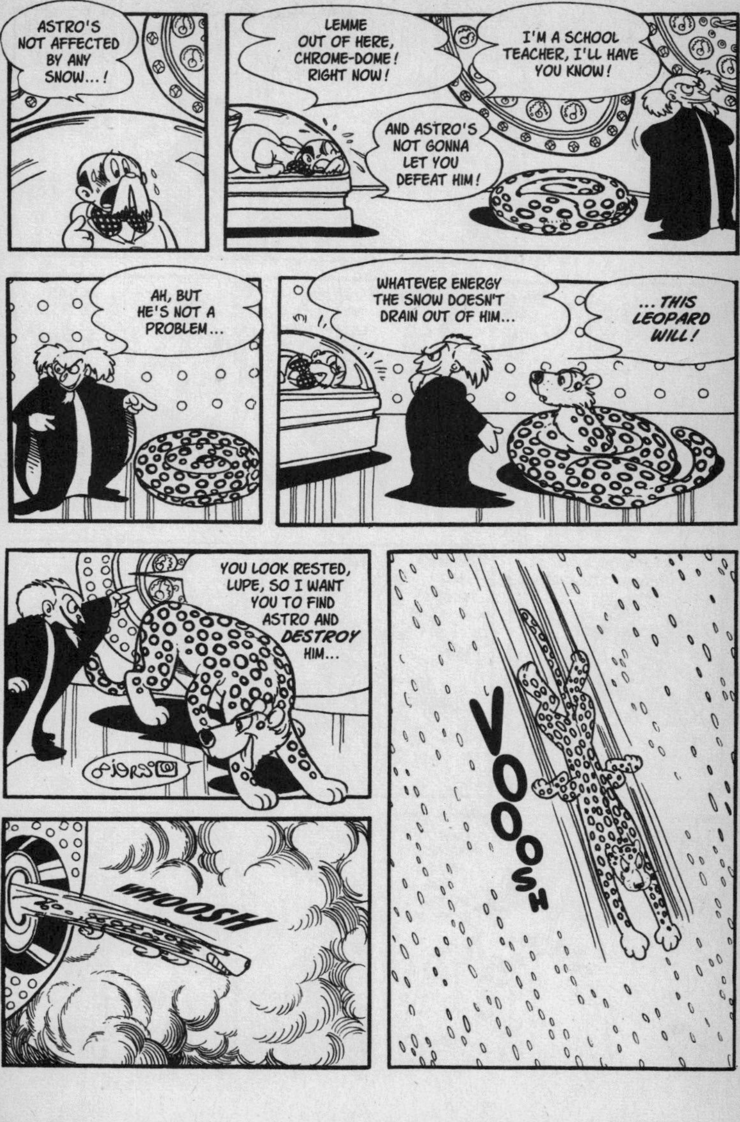
ASTRO'S NOT AFFECTED BY ANY SNOW...!
LEMME OUT OF HERE, CHROME-DOME! RIGHT NOW!
I'M A SCHOOL TEACHER, I'LL HAVE YOU KNOW!
AND ASTRO'S NOT GONNA LET YOU DEFEAT HIM!
AH, BUT HE'S NOT A PROBLEM...
WHATEVER ENERGY THE SNOW DOESN'T DRAIN OUT OF HIM...
...THIS LEOPARD WILL!
YOU LOOK RESTED, LUPE, SO I WANT YOU TO FIND ASTRO AND DESTROY HIM...
VOOOOSH
WHOOSH

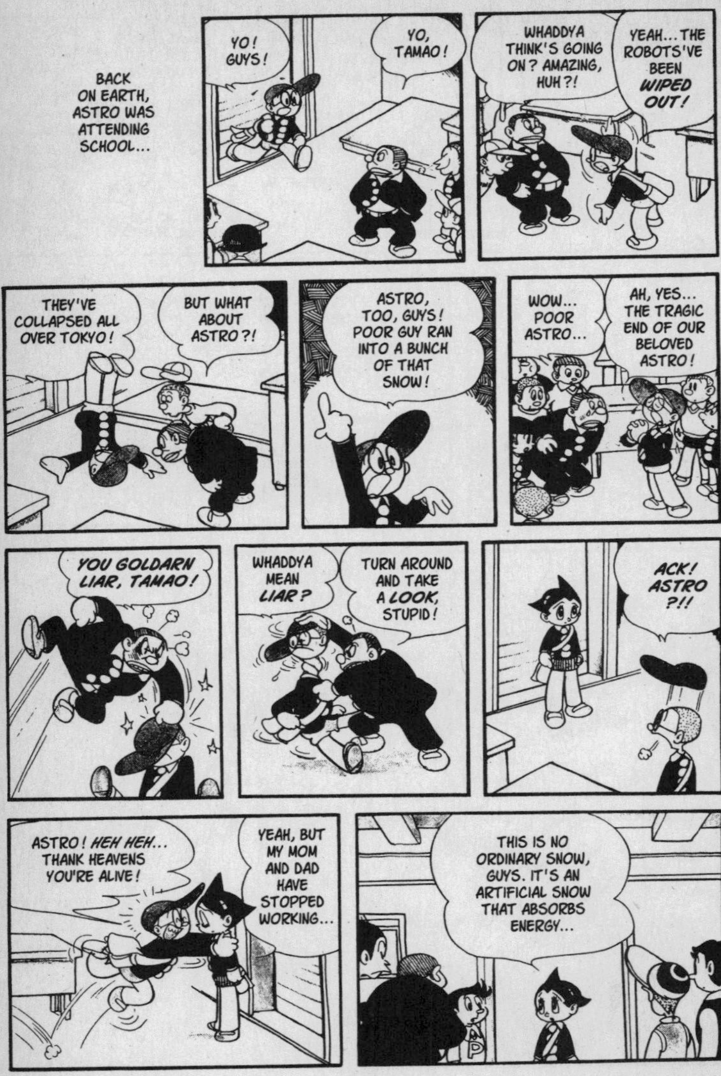
BACK ON EARTH, ASTRO WAS ATTENDING SCHOOL...
YO! GUYS!
YO, TAMAO!
WHADDYA THINK'S GOING ON? AMAZING, HUH?!
YEAH... THE ROBOTS'VE BEEN *WIPED OUT!*
THEY'VE COLLAPSED ALL OVER TOKYO!
BUT WHAT ABOUT ASTRO?!
ASTRO, TOO, GUYS! POOR GUY RAN INTO A BUNCH OF THAT SNOW!
WOW... POOR ASTRO...
AH, YES... THE TRAGIC END OF OUR BELOVED ASTRO!
YOU GOLDARN LIAR, TAMAO!
WHADDYA MEAN *LIAR?*
TURN AROUND AND TAKE A *LOOK,* STUPID!
ACK! ASTRO ?!!
ASTRO! *HEH HEH...* THANK HEAVENS YOU'RE ALIVE!
YEAH, BUT MY MOM AND DAD HAVE STOPPED WORKING...
THIS IS NO ORDINARY SNOW, GUYS. IT'S AN ARTIFICIAL SNOW THAT ABSORBS ENERGY...

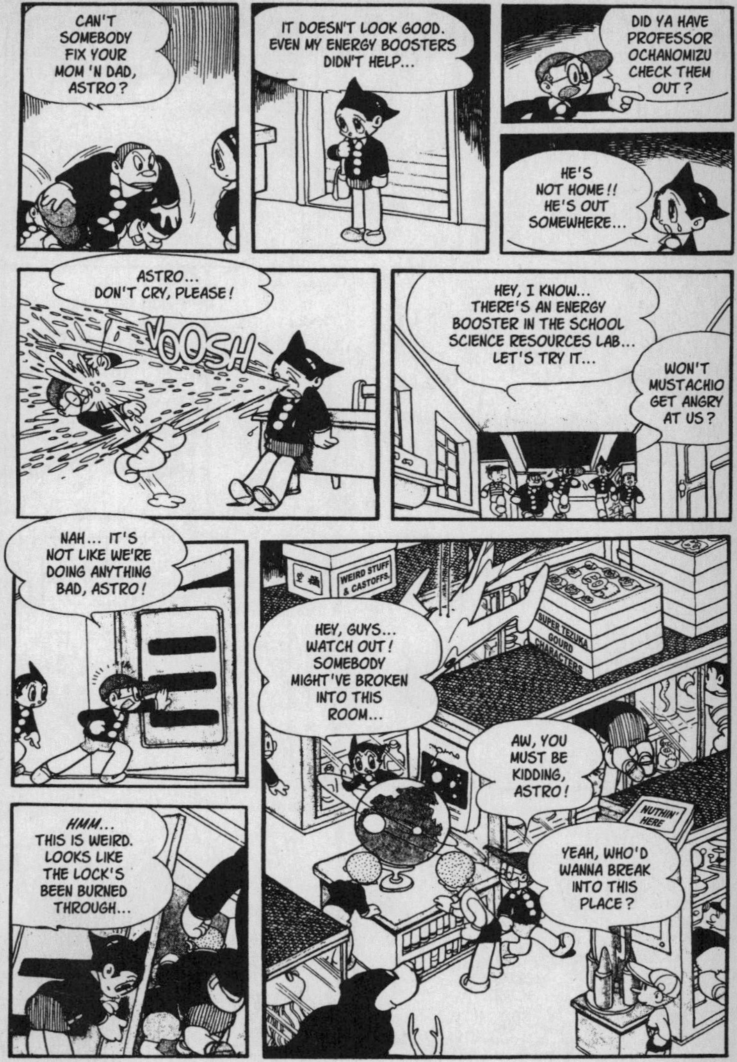
CAN'T SOMEBODY FIX YOUR MOM 'N DAD, ASTRO?
IT DOESN'T LOOK GOOD. EVEN MY ENERGY BOOSTERS DIDN'T HELP...
DID YA HAVE PROFESSOR OCHANOMIZU CHECK THEM OUT?
HE'S NOT HOME!! HE'S OUT SOMEWHERE...
ASTRO... DON'T CRY, PLEASE!
VOOSH
HEY, I KNOW... THERE'S AN ENERGY BOOSTER IN THE SCHOOL SCIENCE RESOURCES LAB... LET'S TRY IT...
WON'T MUSTACHIO GET ANGRY AT US?
NAH... IT'S NOT LIKE WE'RE DOING ANYTHING BAD, ASTRO!
HMM... THIS IS WEIRD. LOOKS LIKE THE LOCK'S BEEN BURNED THROUGH...
WEIRD STUFF & CASTOFFS
SUPER TEZUKA GOURD CHARACTERS
HEY, GUYS... WATCH OUT! SOMEBODY MIGHT'VE BROKEN INTO THIS ROOM...
AW, YOU MUST BE KIDDING, ASTRO!
NUTHIN' HERE
YEAH, WHO'D WANNA BREAK INTO THIS PLACE?

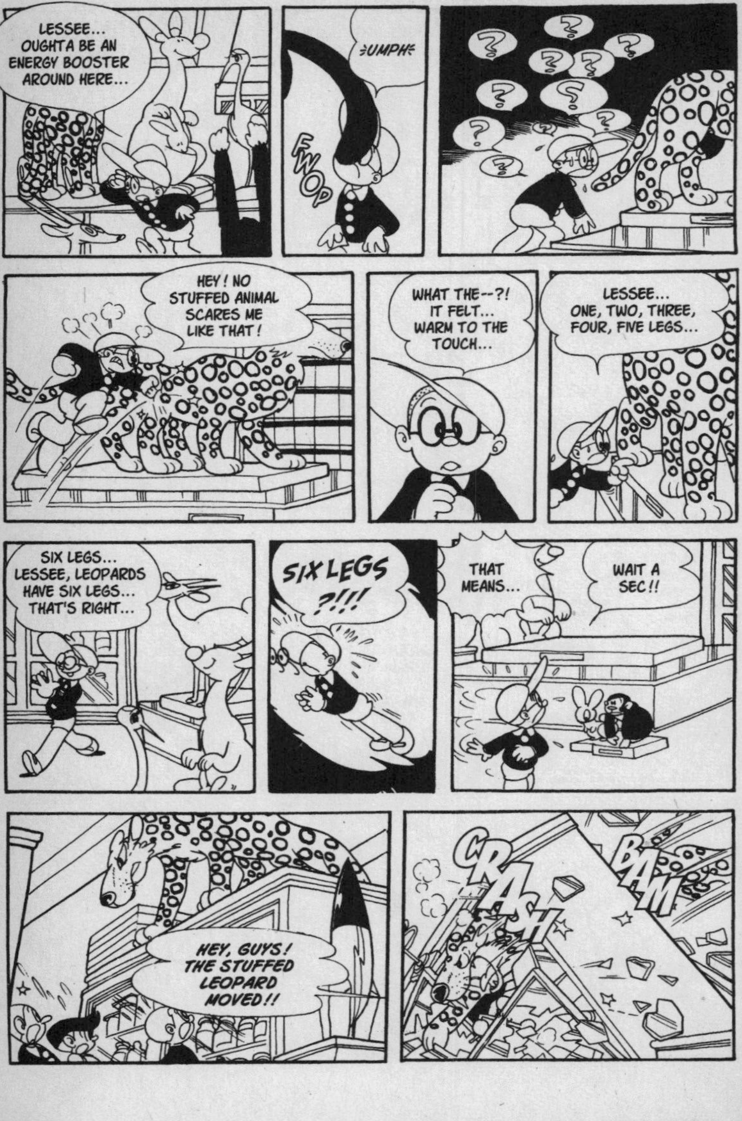
LESSEE... OUGHTA BE AN ENERGY BOOSTER AROUND HERE...
UMPH
FWOP
HEY! NO STUFFED ANIMAL SCARES ME LIKE THAT!
WHAT THE--?! IT FELT... WARM TO THE TOUCH...
LESSEE... ONE, TWO, THREE, FOUR, FIVE LEGS...
SIX LEGS... LESSEE, LEOPARDS HAVE SIX LEGS... THAT'S RIGHT...
SIX LEGS ?!!!
THAT MEANS...
WAIT A SEC!!
HEY, GUYS! THE STUFFED LEOPARD MOVED!!
CRASH
BAM

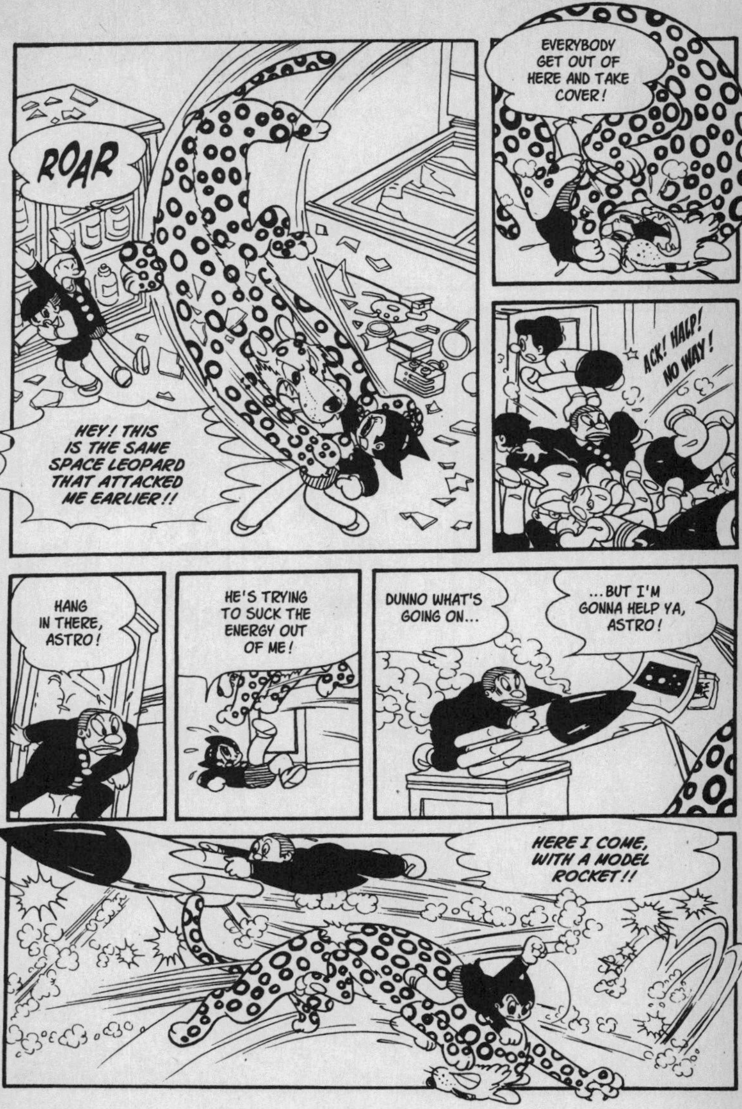
ROAR
HEY! THIS IS THE SAME SPACE LEOPARD THAT ATTACKED ME EARLIER!!
EVERYBODY GET OUT OF HERE AND TAKE COVER!
ACK! HALP! NO WAY!
HANG IN THERE, ASTRO!
HE'S TRYING TO SUCK THE ENERGY OUT OF ME!
DUNNO WHAT'S GOING ON...
...BUT I'M GONNA HELP YA, ASTRO!
HERE I COME, WITH A MODEL ROCKET!!

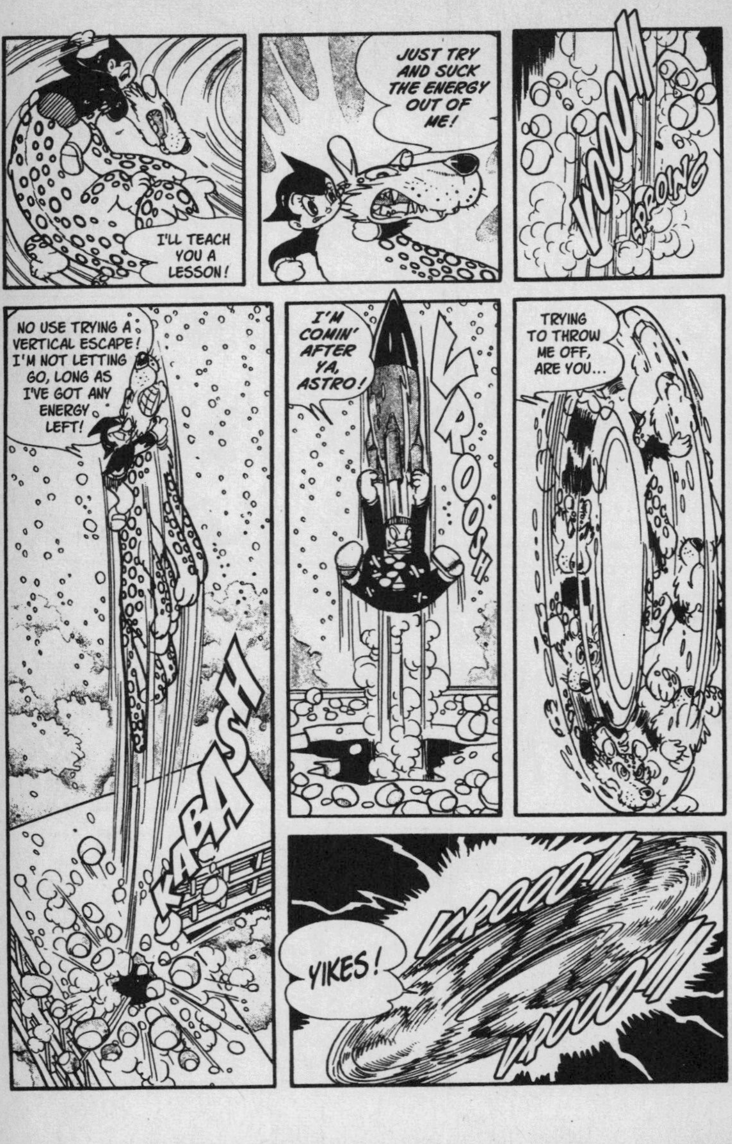
I'LL TEACH YOU A LESSON!
JUST TRY AND SUCK THE ENERGY OUT OF ME!
VOOOOM
SPROING
NO USE TRYING A VERTICAL ESCAPE! I'M NOT LETTING GO, LONG AS I'VE GOT ANY ENERGY LEFT!
KABASH
I'M COMIN' AFTER YA, ASTRO!
VROOOSH
TRYING TO THROW ME OFF, ARE YOU...
YIKES!
VROOOOM
VROOOOM

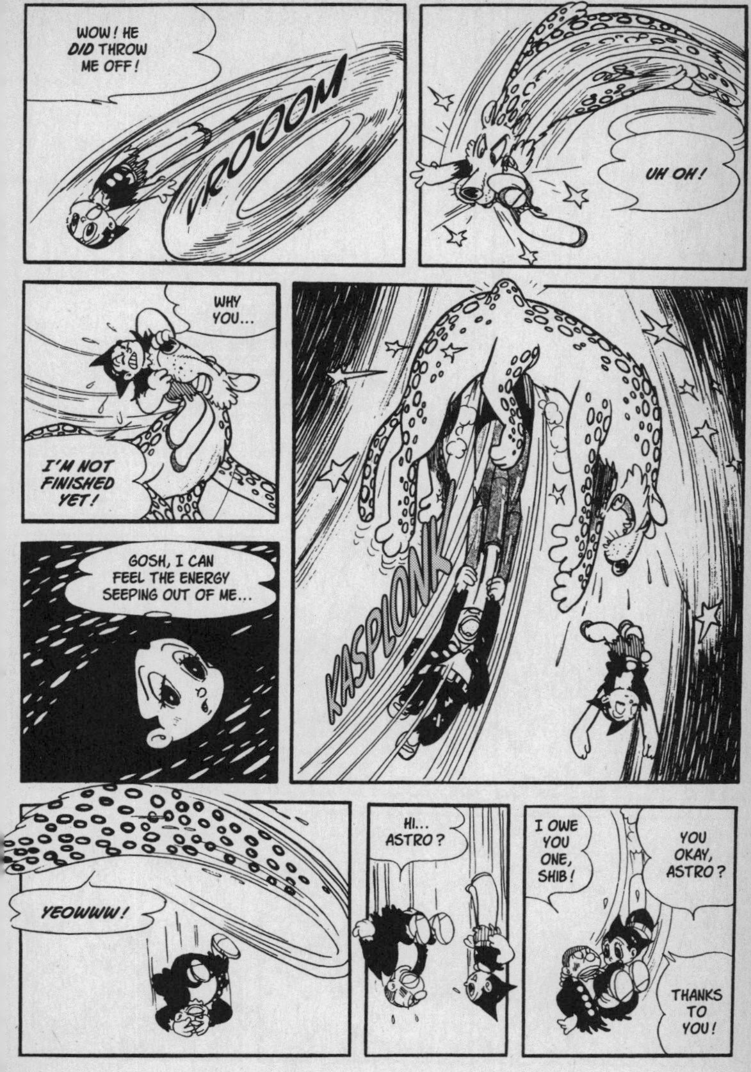
WOW! HE DID THROW ME OFF!
VROOOM
UH OH!
WHY YOU...
I'M NOT FINISHED YET!
GOSH, I CAN FEEL THE ENERGY SEEPING OUT OF ME...
KASPLONK
YEOWWW!
HI... ASTRO?
I OWE YOU ONE, SHIB!
YOU OKAY, ASTRO?
THANKS TO YOU!

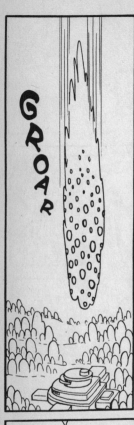

GROAR

SMASH

OCHANOMIZU RESEARCH LABORATORY

OWWWW! W...W... WHAT'S GOING ON?!

WHAT HAPPENED, PROFESSOR?

HAPPENED, SCHMAPPENED! I'M IN *PAIN!!*

LOOK, PROFESSOR, WHAT'S THIS?

STOP! DON'T TOUCH THAT STUFF!!

114

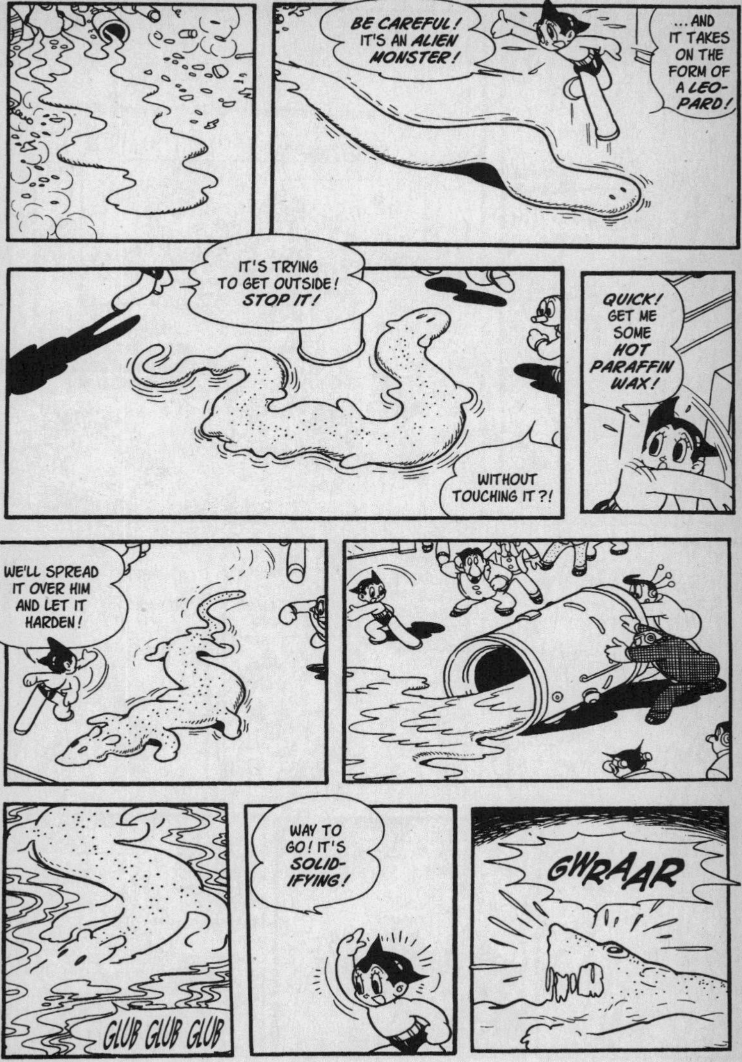
BE CAREFUL! IT'S AN ALIEN MONSTER!
...AND IT TAKES ON THE FORM OF A LEOPARD!
IT'S TRYING TO GET OUTSIDE! STOP IT!
WITHOUT TOUCHING IT?!
QUICK! GET ME SOME HOT PARAFFIN WAX!
WE'LL SPREAD IT OVER HIM AND LET IT HARDEN!
GLUB GLUB GLUB
WAY TO GO! IT'S SOLIDIFYING!
GWRAAR

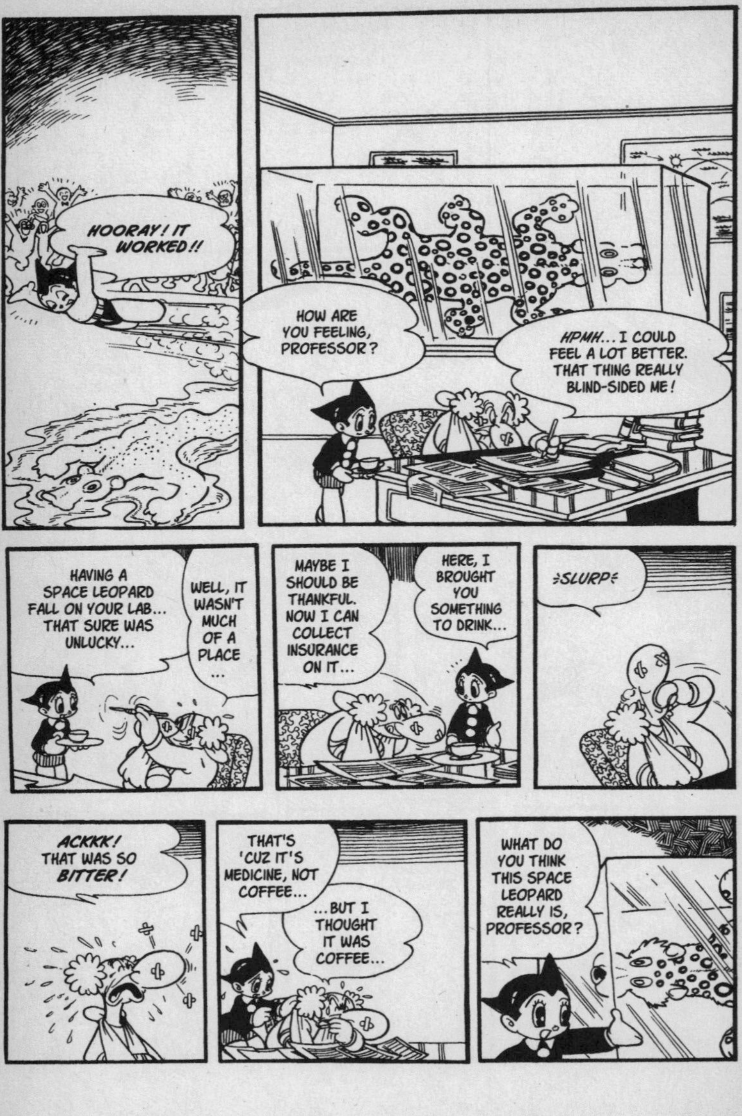
HOORAY! IT WORKED!!
HOW ARE YOU FEELING, PROFESSOR?
HPMH... I COULD FEEL A LOT BETTER. THAT THING REALLY BLIND-SIDED ME!
HAVING A SPACE LEOPARD FALL ON YOUR LAB... THAT SURE WAS UNLUCKY...
WELL, IT WASN'T MUCH OF A PLACE ...
MAYBE I SHOULD BE THANKFUL. NOW I CAN COLLECT INSURANCE ON IT...
HERE, I BROUGHT YOU SOMETHING TO DRINK...
SLURP
ACKKK! THAT WAS SO BITTER!
THAT'S 'CUZ IT'S MEDICINE, NOT COFFEE...
...BUT I THOUGHT IT WAS COFFEE...
WHAT DO YOU THINK THIS SPACE LEOPARD REALLY IS, PROFESSOR?

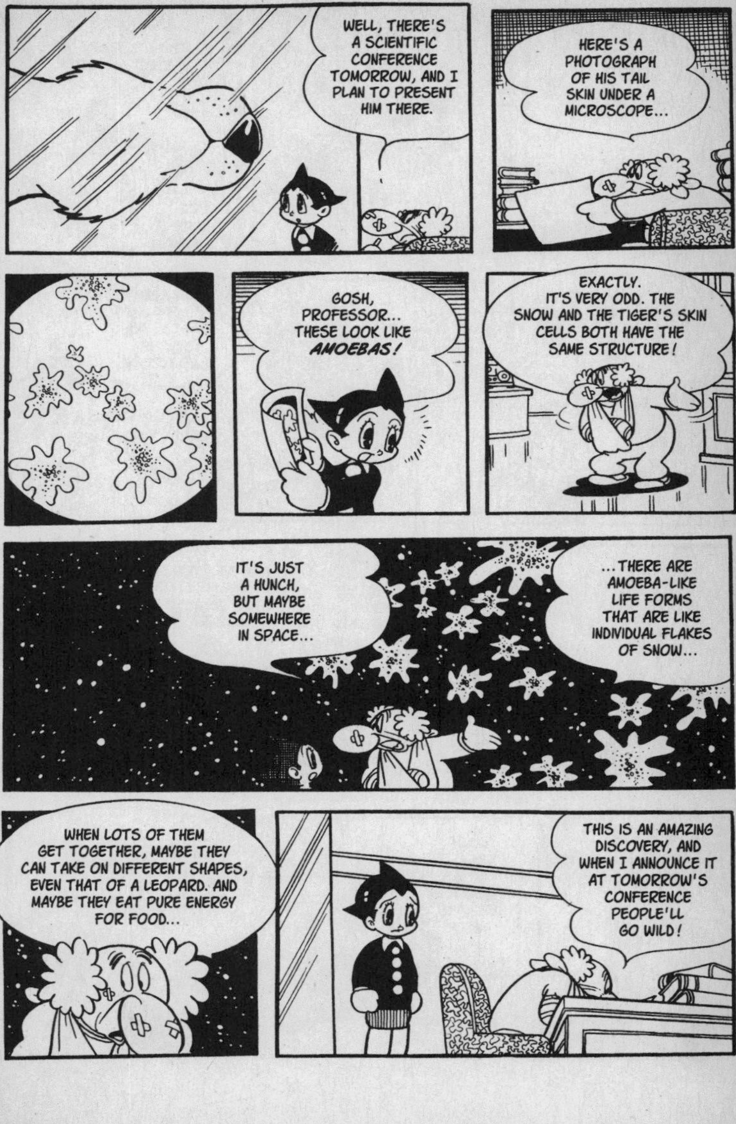
WELL, THERE'S A SCIENTIFIC CONFERENCE TOMORROW, AND I PLAN TO PRESENT HIM THERE.
HERE'S A PHOTOGRAPH OF HIS TAIL SKIN UNDER A MICROSCOPE...
GOSH, PROFESSOR... THESE LOOK LIKE *AMOEBAS!*
EXACTLY. IT'S VERY ODD. THE SNOW AND THE TIGER'S SKIN CELLS BOTH HAVE THE SAME STRUCTURE!
IT'S JUST A HUNCH, BUT MAYBE SOMEWHERE IN SPACE...
...THERE ARE AMOEBA-LIKE LIFE FORMS THAT ARE LIKE INDIVIDUAL FLAKES OF SNOW...
WHEN LOTS OF THEM GET TOGETHER, MAYBE THEY CAN TAKE ON DIFFERENT SHAPES, EVEN THAT OF A LEOPARD. AND MAYBE THEY EAT PURE ENERGY FOR FOOD...
THIS IS AN AMAZING DISCOVERY, AND WHEN I ANNOUNCE IT AT TOMORROW'S CONFERENCE PEOPLE'LL GO WILD!

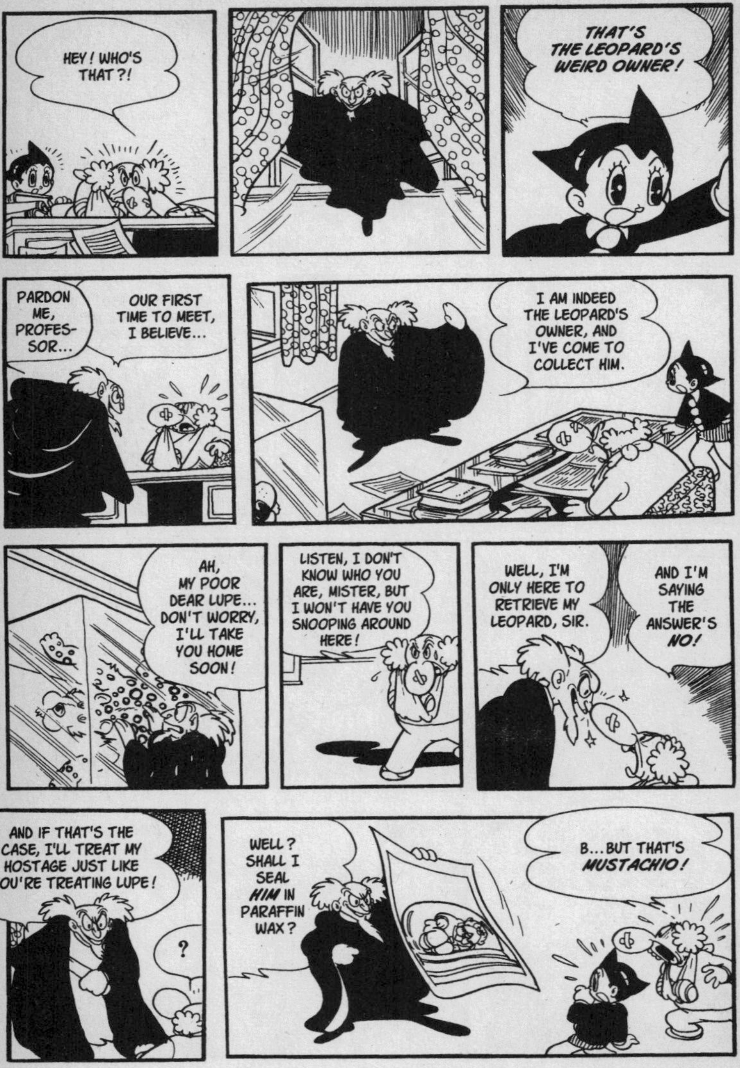
HEY! WHO'S THAT?!
THAT'S THE LEOPARD'S WEIRD OWNER!
PARDON ME, PROFES- SOR...
OUR FIRST TIME TO MEET, I BELIEVE...
I AM INDEED THE LEOPARD'S OWNER, AND I'VE COME TO COLLECT HIM.
AH, MY POOR DEAR LUPE... DON'T WORRY, I'LL TAKE YOU HOME SOON!
LISTEN, I DON'T KNOW WHO YOU ARE, MISTER, BUT I WON'T HAVE YOU SNOOPING AROUND HERE!
WELL, I'M ONLY HERE TO RETRIEVE MY LEOPARD, SIR.
AND I'M SAYING THE ANSWER'S NO!
AND IF THAT'S THE CASE, I'LL TREAT MY HOSTAGE JUST LIKE YOU'RE TREATING LUPE!
?
WELL? SHALL I SEAL HIM IN PARAFFIN WAX?
B...BUT THAT'S MUSTACHIO!

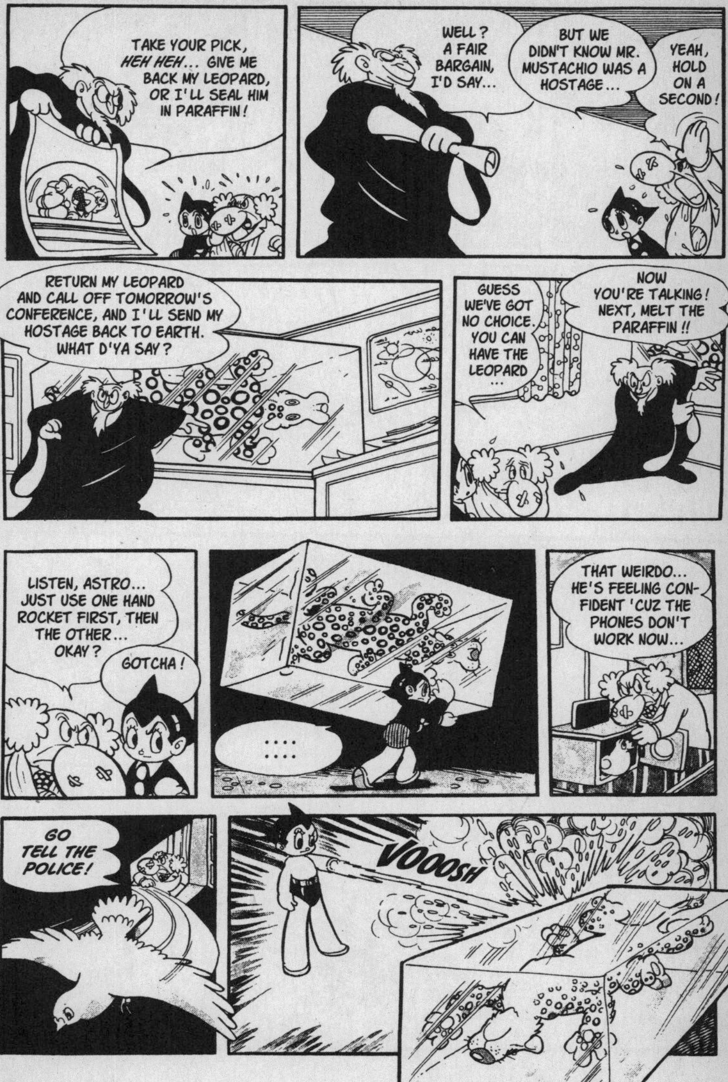
TAKE YOUR PICK, HEH HEH... GIVE ME BACK MY LEOPARD, OR I'LL SEAL HIM IN PARAFFIN!
WELL? A FAIR BARGAIN, I'D SAY...
BUT WE DIDN'T KNOW MR. MUSTACHIO WAS A HOSTAGE...
YEAH, HOLD ON A SECOND!
RETURN MY LEOPARD AND CALL OFF TOMORROW'S CONFERENCE, AND I'LL SEND MY HOSTAGE BACK TO EARTH. WHAT D'YA SAY?
GUESS WE'VE GOT NO CHOICE. YOU CAN HAVE THE LEOPARD ...
NOW YOU'RE TALKING! NEXT, MELT THE PARAFFIN!!
LISTEN, ASTRO... JUST USE ONE HAND ROCKET FIRST, THEN THE OTHER... OKAY?
GOTCHA!
....
....
THAT WEIRDO... HE'S FEELING CON-FIDENT 'CUZ THE PHONES DON'T WORK NOW...
GO TELL THE POLICE!
VOOOSH

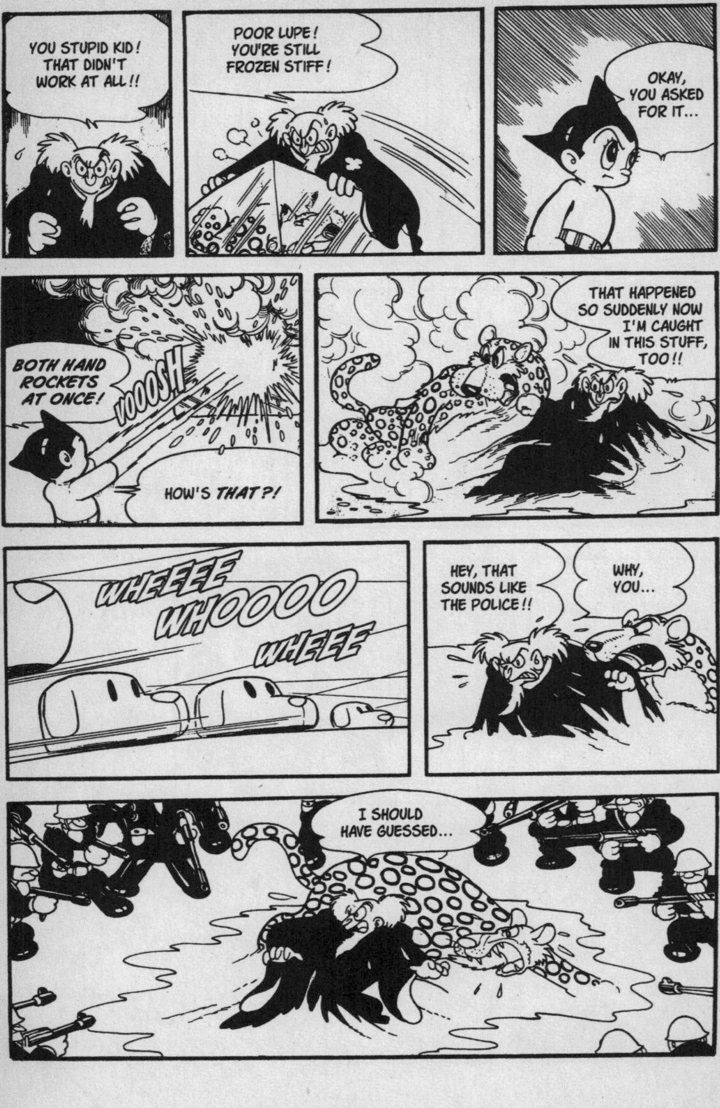
YOU STUPID KID! THAT DIDN'T WORK AT ALL!!
POOR LUPE! YOU'RE STILL FROZEN STIFF!
OKAY, YOU ASKED FOR IT...
BOTH HAND ROCKETS AT ONCE!
VOOOSH
HOW'S THAT?!
THAT HAPPENED SO SUDDENLY NOW I'M CAUGHT IN THIS STUFF, TOO!!
WHEEEE
WHOOOOO
WHEEE
HEY, THAT SOUNDS LIKE THE POLICE!!
WHY, YOU...
I SHOULD HAVE GUESSED...

IT'S NO USE RESISTING, MONSTER MAN. ONE WRONG MOVE AND WE BLAST YOU WITH OUR THERMAL RAY GUNS!

DOESN'T SCARE ME! *HEE HEE...* GO RIGHT AHEAD!

OKAY, MEN, SHOOT THE LEOPARD! LET 'IM HAVE IT!

ZAP ZAP

BZAP

ZAP ZAP ZAP ZAP BZAP

WOW! HE JUST *ABSORBS* THE ENERGY!!

BZAP ZAP ZAP

HOLD IT, *INSPECTOR NAKAMURA!* IT'S NO USE!!

?

THEY'LL JUST SUCK UP YOUR RAY GUN ENERGY AND BECOME MORE POWERFUL!

ZAP BZAP ZAP

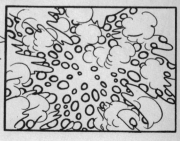

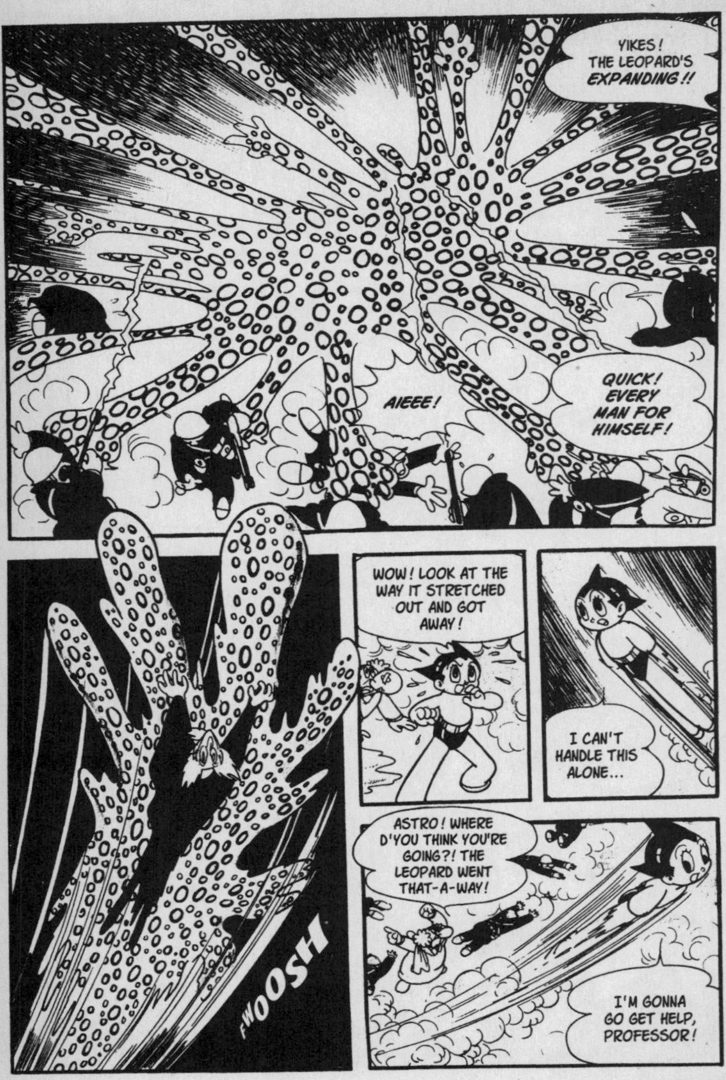
YIKES! THE LEOPARD'S EXPANDING!!
AIEEE!
QUICK! EVERY MAN FOR HIMSELF!
FWOOSH
WOW! LOOK AT THE WAY IT STRETCHED OUT AND GOT AWAY!
I CAN'T HANDLE THIS ALONE...
ASTRO! WHERE D'YOU THINK YOU'RE GOING?! THE LEOPARD WENT THAT-A-WAY!
I'M GONNA GO GET HELP, PROFESSOR!

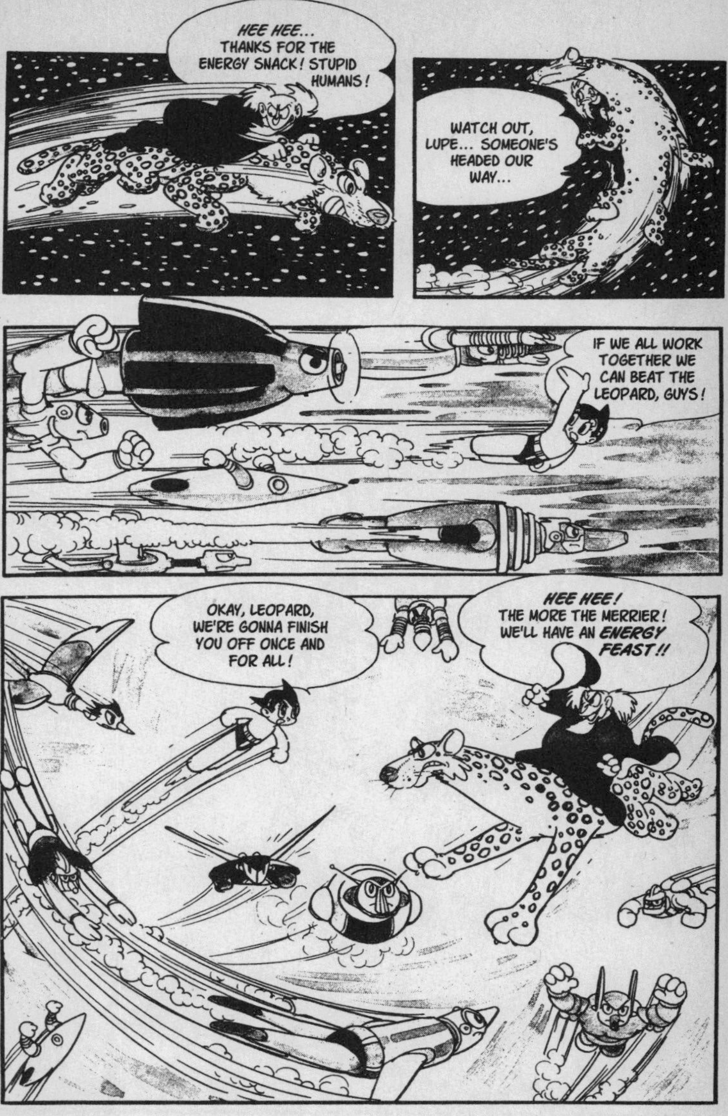
HEE HEE... THANKS FOR THE ENERGY SNACK! STUPID HUMANS!
WATCH OUT, LUPE... SOMEONE'S HEADED OUR WAY...
IF WE ALL WORK TOGETHER WE CAN BEAT THE LEOPARD, GUYS!
OKAY, LEOPARD, WE'RE GONNA FINISH YOU OFF ONCE AND FOR ALL!
HEE HEE! THE MORE THE MERRIER! WE'LL HAVE AN ENERGY FEAST!!

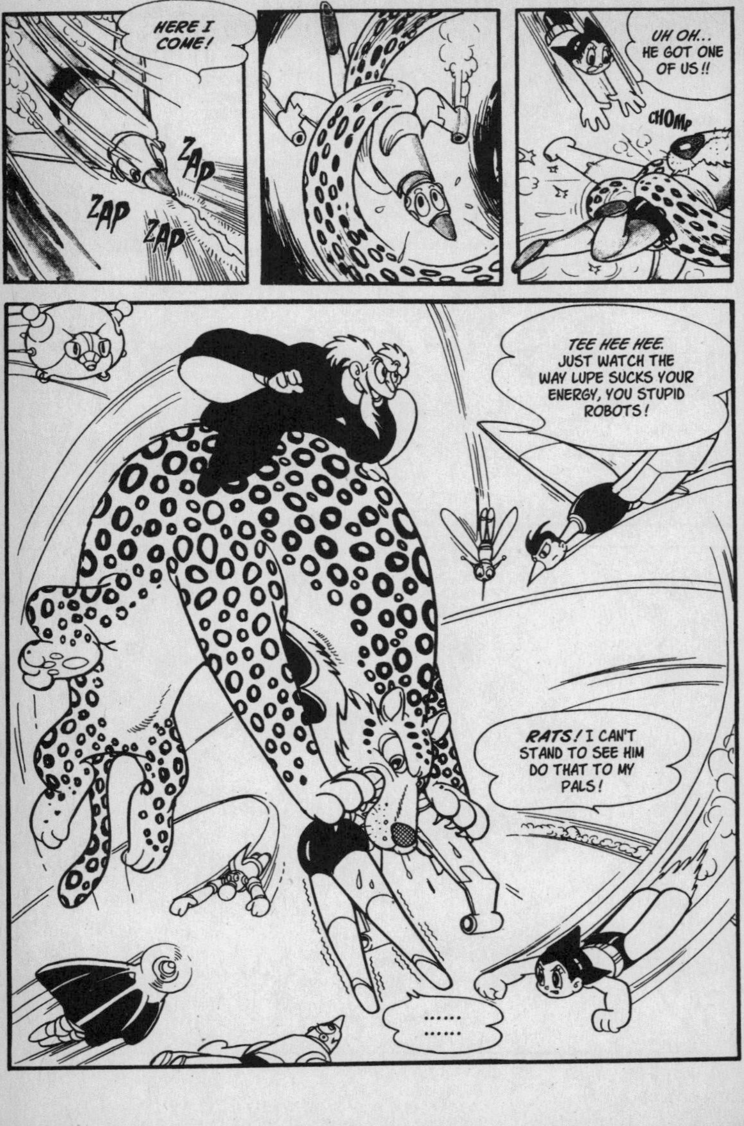
HERE I COME!
ZAP
ZAP
ZAP
UH OH... HE GOT ONE OF US!!
CHOMP
TEE HEE HEE. JUST WATCH THE WAY LUPE SUCKS YOUR ENERGY, YOU STUPID ROBOTS!
RATS! I CAN'T STAND TO SEE HIM DO THAT TO MY PALS!
......
......

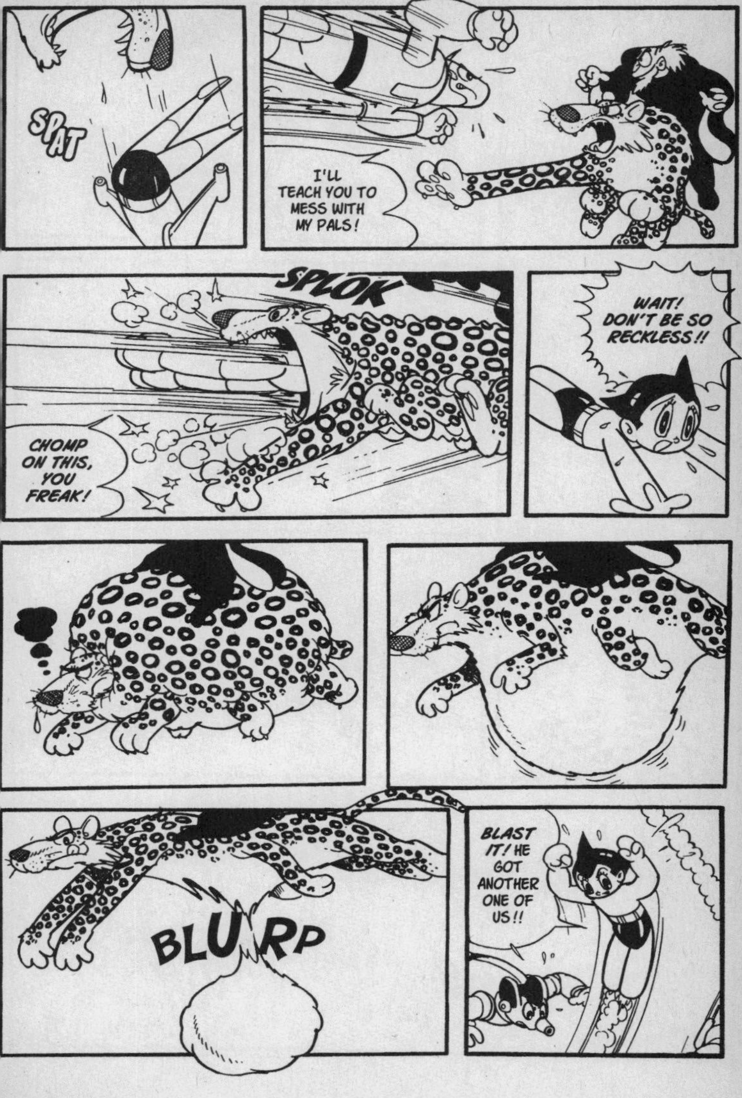
SPAT
I'LL TEACH YOU TO MESS WITH MY PALS!
SPLOK
CHOMP ON THIS, YOU FREAK!
WAIT! DON'T BE SO RECKLESS!!
BLURP
BLAST IT! HE GOT ANOTHER ONE OF US!!

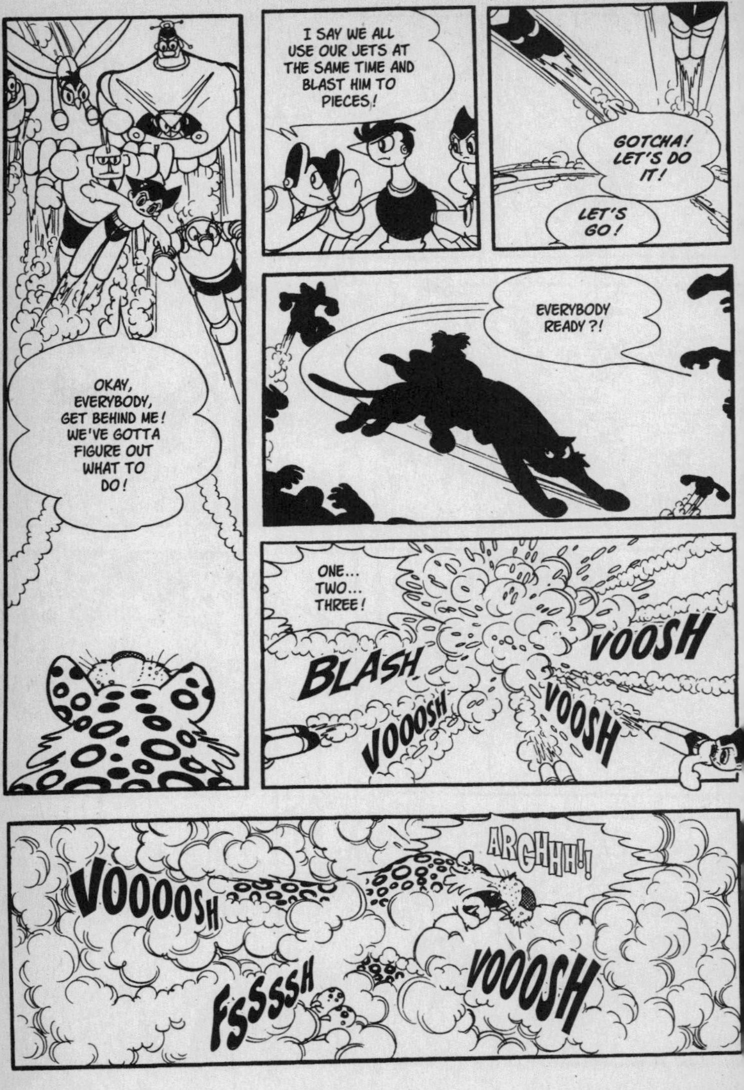
OKAY, EVERYBODY, GET BEHIND ME! WE'VE GOTTA FIGURE OUT WHAT TO DO!
I SAY WE ALL USE OUR JETS AT THE SAME TIME AND BLAST HIM TO PIECES!
GOTCHA! LET'S DO IT!
LET'S GO!
EVERYBODY READY?!
ONE... TWO... THREE!
BLASH
VOOSH
VOOOSH
VOOSH
VOOOOSH
ARGHHH!!
FSSSSH
VOOOSH

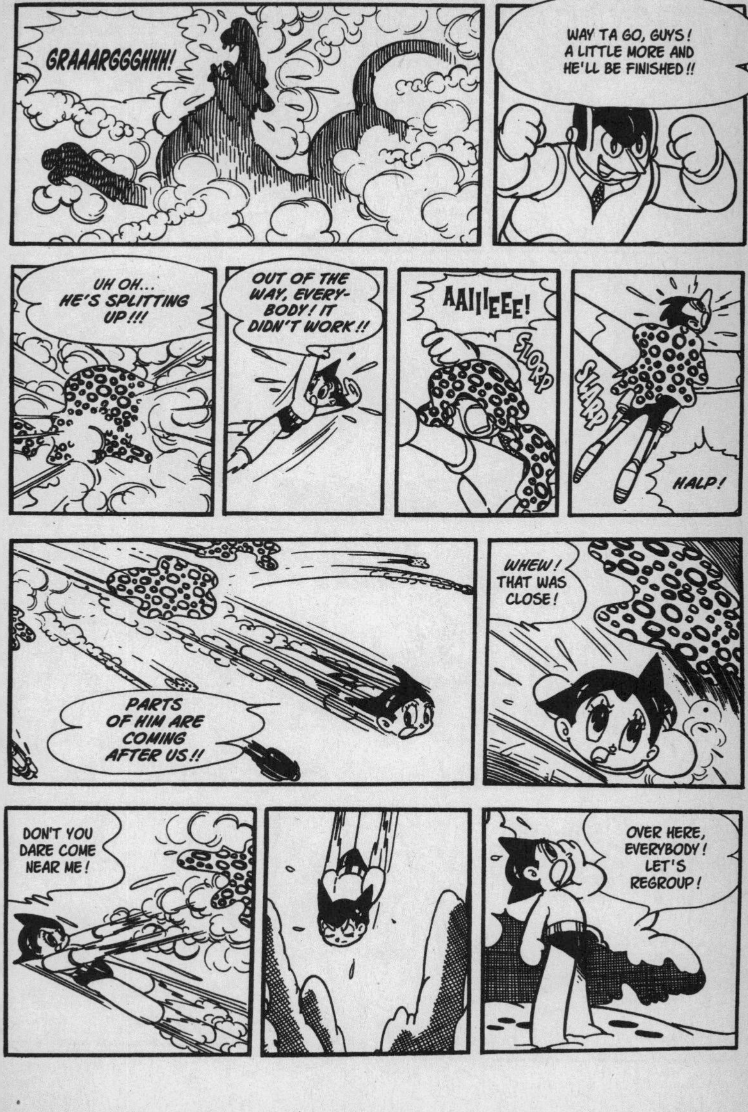
GRAAARGGGHHH!
WAY TA GO, GUYS! A LITTLE MORE AND HE'LL BE FINISHED!!
UH OH... HE'S SPLITTING UP!!!
OUT OF THE WAY, EVERY-BODY! IT DIDN'T WORK!!
AAIIIEEE!
SLORP
SLARP
HALP!
PARTS OF HIM ARE COMING AFTER US!!
WHEW! THAT WAS CLOSE!
DON'T YOU DARE COME NEAR ME!
OVER HERE, EVERYBODY! LET'S REGROUP!

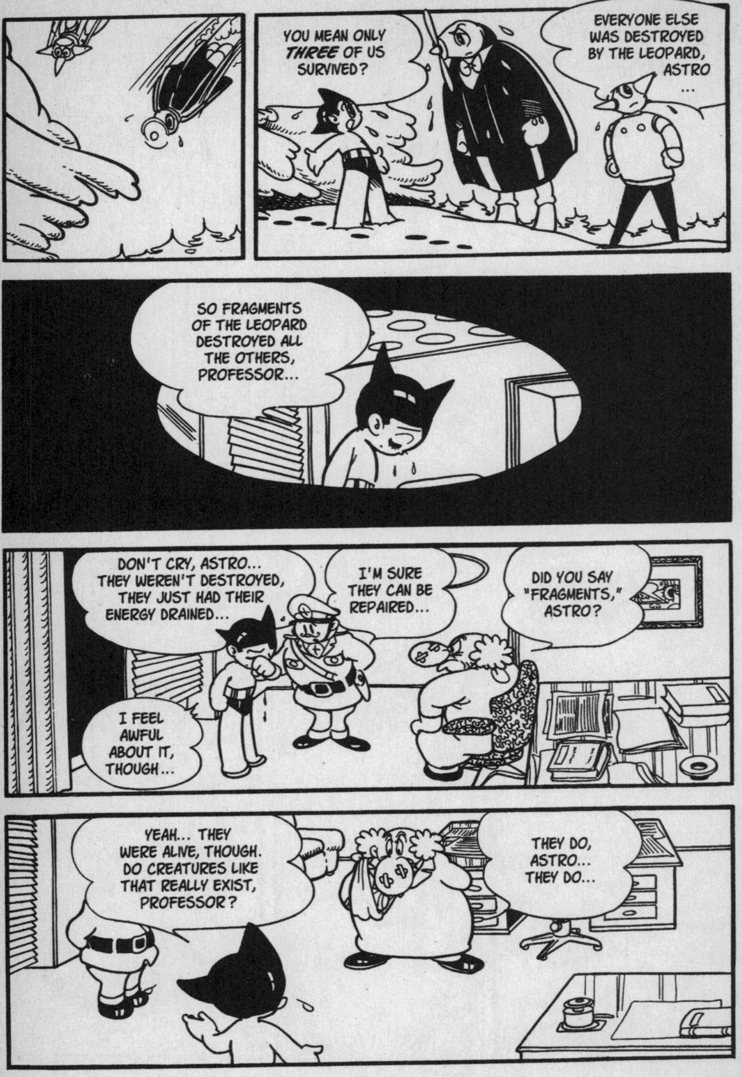
YOU MEAN ONLY *THREE* OF US SURVIVED?
EVERYONE ELSE WAS DESTROYED BY THE LEOPARD, ASTRO ...
SO FRAGMENTS OF THE LEOPARD DESTROYED ALL THE OTHERS, PROFESSOR...
DON'T CRY, ASTRO... THEY WEREN'T DESTROYED, THEY JUST HAD THEIR ENERGY DRAINED...
I FEEL AWFUL ABOUT IT, THOUGH...
I'M SURE THEY CAN BE REPAIRED...
DID YOU SAY "FRAGMENTS," ASTRO?
YEAH... THEY WERE ALIVE, THOUGH. DO CREATURES LIKE THAT REALLY EXIST, PROFESSOR?
THEY DO, ASTRO... THEY DO...

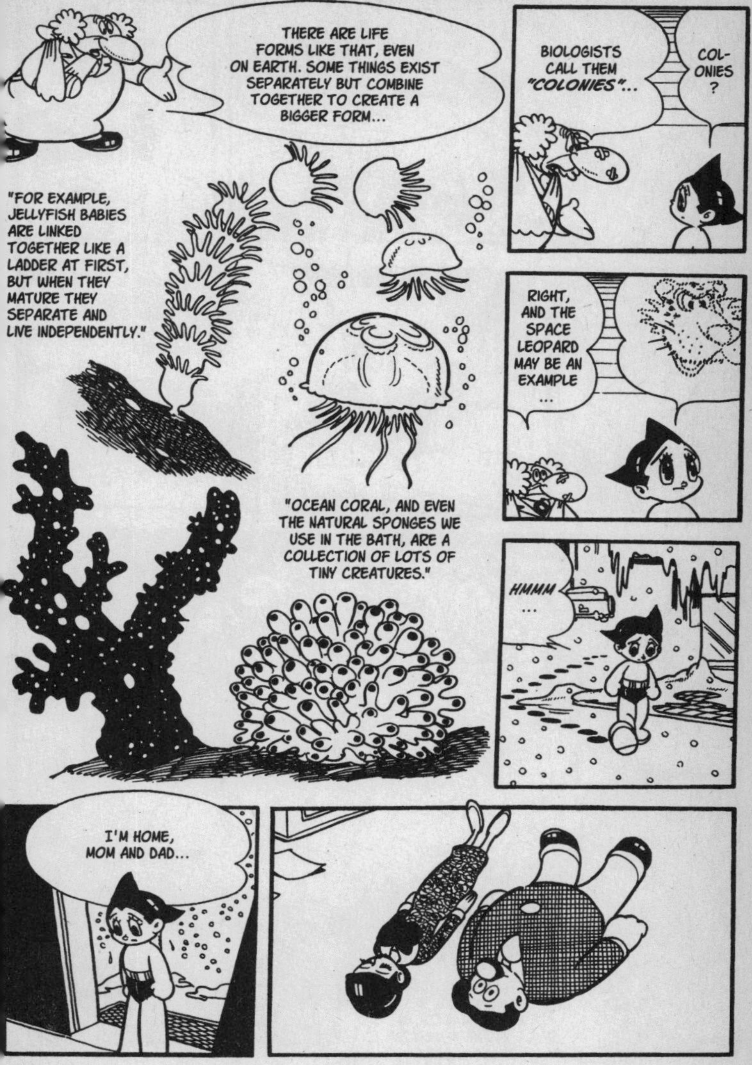
THERE ARE LIFE FORMS LIKE THAT, EVEN ON EARTH. SOME THINGS EXIST SEPARATELY BUT COMBINE TOGETHER TO CREATE A BIGGER FORM...
"FOR EXAMPLE, JELLYFISH BABIES ARE LINKED TOGETHER LIKE A LADDER AT FIRST, BUT WHEN THEY MATURE THEY SEPARATE AND LIVE INDEPENDENTLY."
"OCEAN CORAL, AND EVEN THE NATURAL SPONGES WE USE IN THE BATH, ARE A COLLECTION OF LOTS OF TINY CREATURES."
BIOLOGISTS CALL THEM "COLONIES"...
COL-ONIES ?
RIGHT, AND THE SPACE LEOPARD MAY BE AN EXAMPLE ...
HMMM ...
I'M HOME, MOM AND DAD...

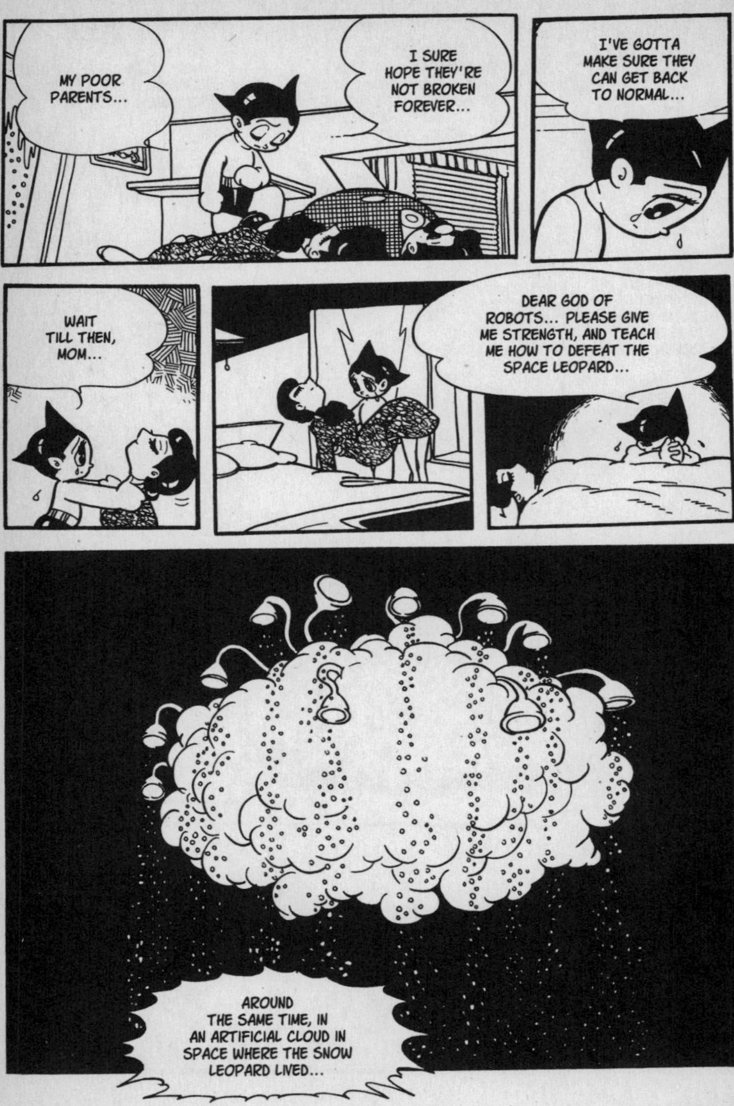
MY POOR PARENTS...
I SURE HOPE THEY'RE NOT BROKEN FOREVER...
I'VE GOTTA MAKE SURE THEY CAN GET BACK TO NORMAL...
WAIT TILL THEN, MOM...
DEAR GOD OF ROBOTS... PLEASE GIVE ME STRENGTH, AND TEACH ME HOW TO DEFEAT THE SPACE LEOPARD...
AROUND THE SAME TIME, IN AN ARTIFICIAL CLOUD IN SPACE WHERE THE SNOW LEOPARD LIVED...

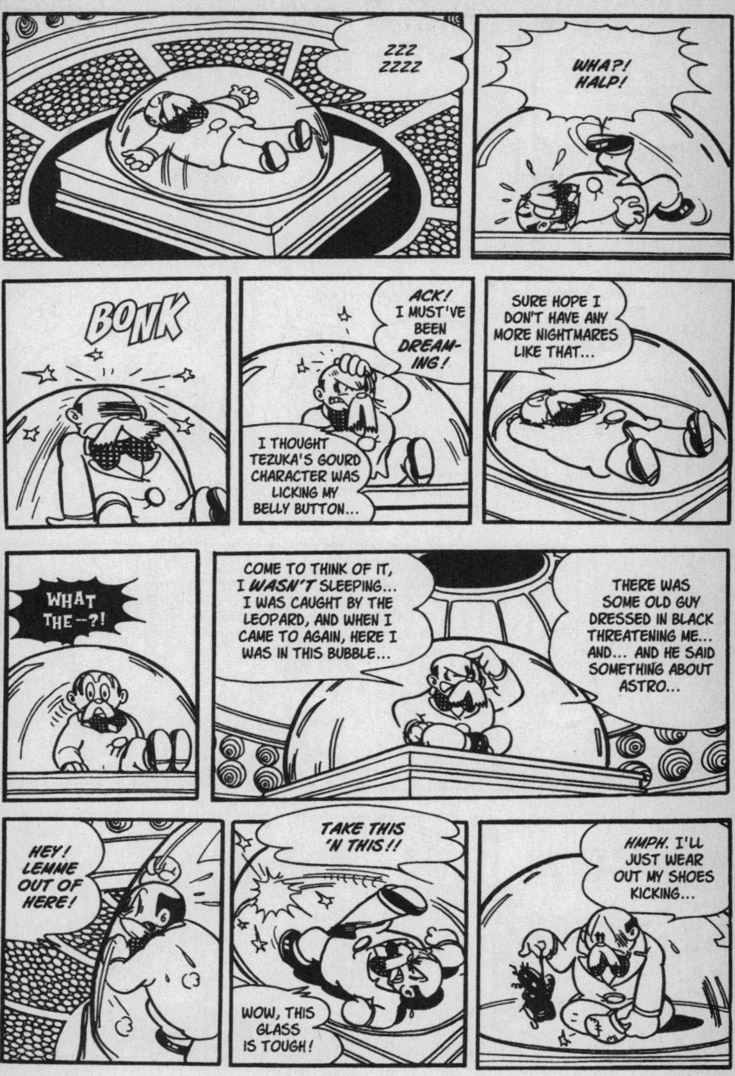
ZZZ
ZZZZ
WHA?! HALP!
BONK
ACK! I MUST'VE BEEN DREAMING!
I THOUGHT TEZUKA'S GOURD CHARACTER WAS LICKING MY BELLY BUTTON...
SURE HOPE I DON'T HAVE ANY MORE NIGHTMARES LIKE THAT...
WHAT THE--?!
COME TO THINK OF IT, I WASN'T SLEEPING... I WAS CAUGHT BY THE LEOPARD, AND WHEN I CAME TO AGAIN, HERE I WAS IN THIS BUBBLE...
THERE WAS SOME OLD GUY DRESSED IN BLACK THREATENING ME... AND... AND HE SAID SOMETHING ABOUT ASTRO...
HEY! LEMME OUT OF HERE!
TAKE THIS 'N THIS!!
WOW, THIS GLASS IS TOUGH!
HMPH. I'LL JUST WEAR OUT MY SHOES KICKING...

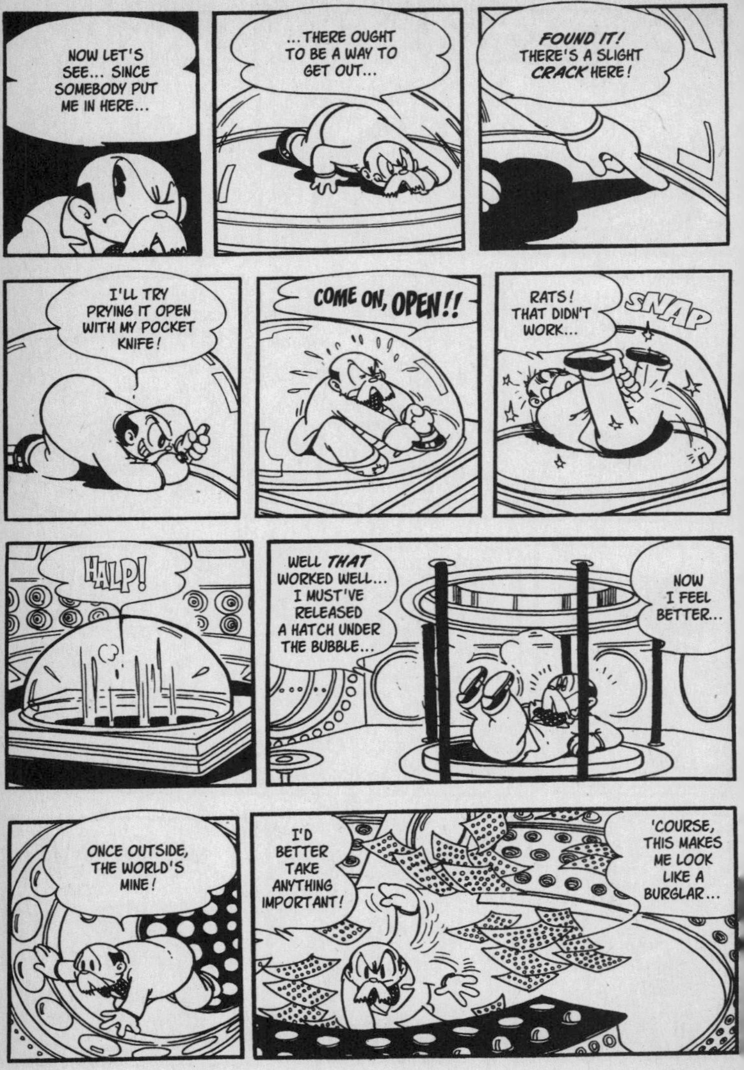
NOW LET'S SEE... SINCE SOMEBODY PUT ME IN HERE...
...THERE OUGHT TO BE A WAY TO GET OUT...
FOUND IT! THERE'S A SLIGHT CRACK HERE!
I'LL TRY PRYING IT OPEN WITH MY POCKET KNIFE!
COME ON, OPEN!!
RATS! THAT DIDN'T WORK...
SNAP
HALP!
WELL THAT WORKED WELL... I MUST'VE RELEASED A HATCH UNDER THE BUBBLE...
NOW I FEEL BETTER...
ONCE OUTSIDE, THE WORLD'S MINE!
I'D BETTER TAKE ANYTHING IMPORTANT!
'COURSE, THIS MAKES ME LOOK LIKE A BURGLAR...

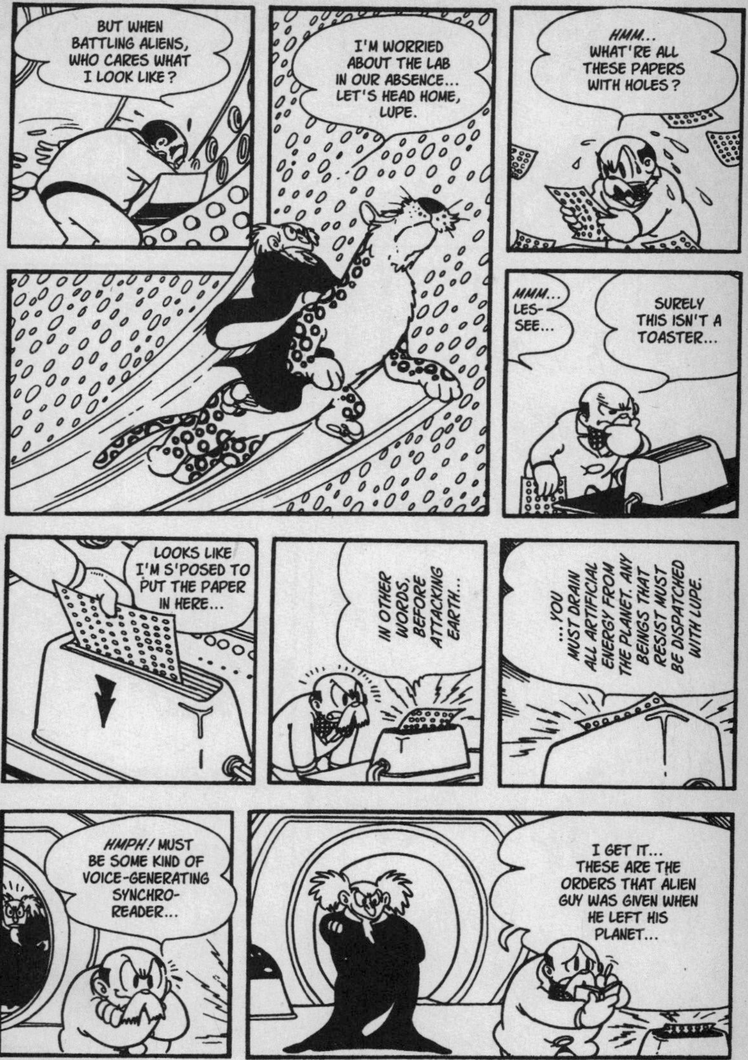

BUT WHEN BATTLING ALIENS, WHO CARES WHAT I LOOK LIKE?
I'M WORRIED ABOUT THE LAB IN OUR ABSENCE... LET'S HEAD HOME, LUPE.
HMM... WHAT'RE ALL THESE PAPERS WITH HOLES?
MMM... LES-SEE...
SURELY THIS ISN'T A TOASTER...
LOOKS LIKE I'M S'POSED TO PUT THE PAPER IN HERE...
IN OTHER WORDS, BEFORE ATTACKING EARTH...
...YOU MUST DRAIN ALL ARTIFICIAL ENERGY FROM THE PLANET. ANY BEINGS THAT RESIST MUST BE DISPATCHED WITH LUPE.
HMPH! MUST BE SOME KIND OF VOICE-GENERATING SYNCHRO-READER...
I GET IT... THESE ARE THE ORDERS THAT ALIEN GUY WAS GIVEN WHEN HE LEFT HIS PLANET...

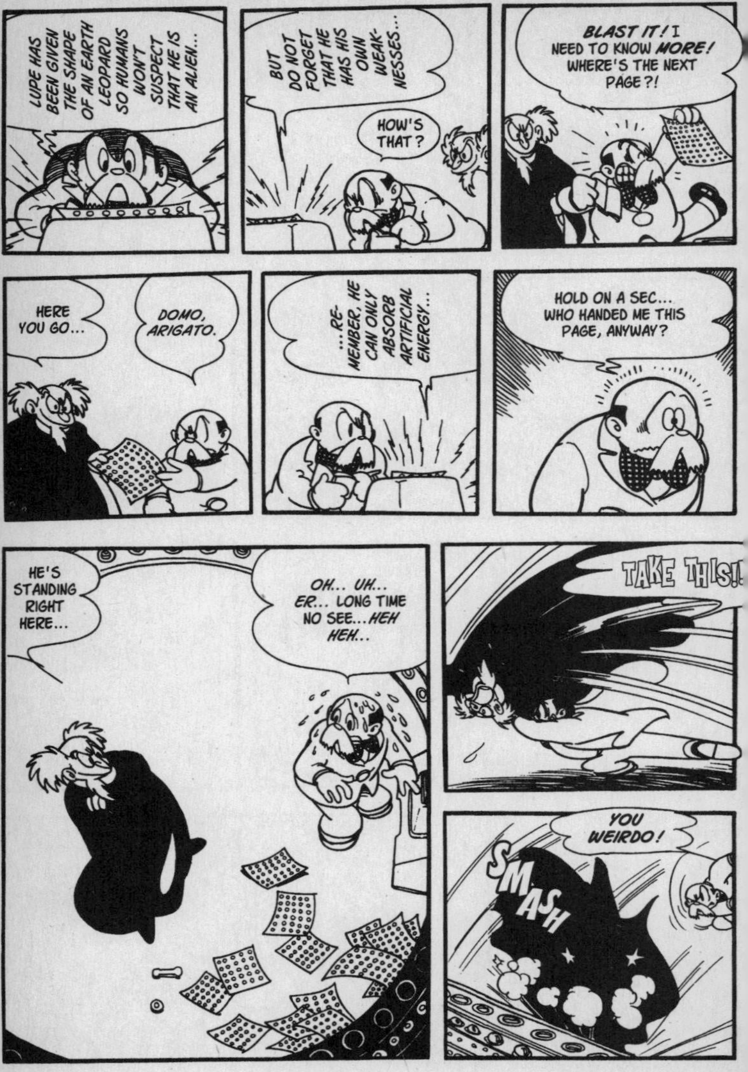
LUPE HAS BEEN GIVEN THE SHAPE OF AN EARTH LEOPARD SO HUMANS WON'T SUSPECT THAT HE IS AN ALIEN...
BUT DO NOT FORGET THAT HE HAS HIS OWN WEAK-NESSES...
HOW'S THAT?
BLAST IT! I NEED TO KNOW MORE! WHERE'S THE NEXT PAGE?!
HERE YOU GO...
DOMO, ARIGATO.
...RE-MEMBER, HE CAN ONLY ABSORB ARTIFICIAL ENERGY...
HOLD ON A SEC... WHO HANDED ME THIS PAGE, ANYWAY?
HE'S STANDING RIGHT HERE...
OH... UH... ER... LONG TIME NO SEE... HEH HEH...
TAKE THIS!
YOU WEIRDO!
SMASH

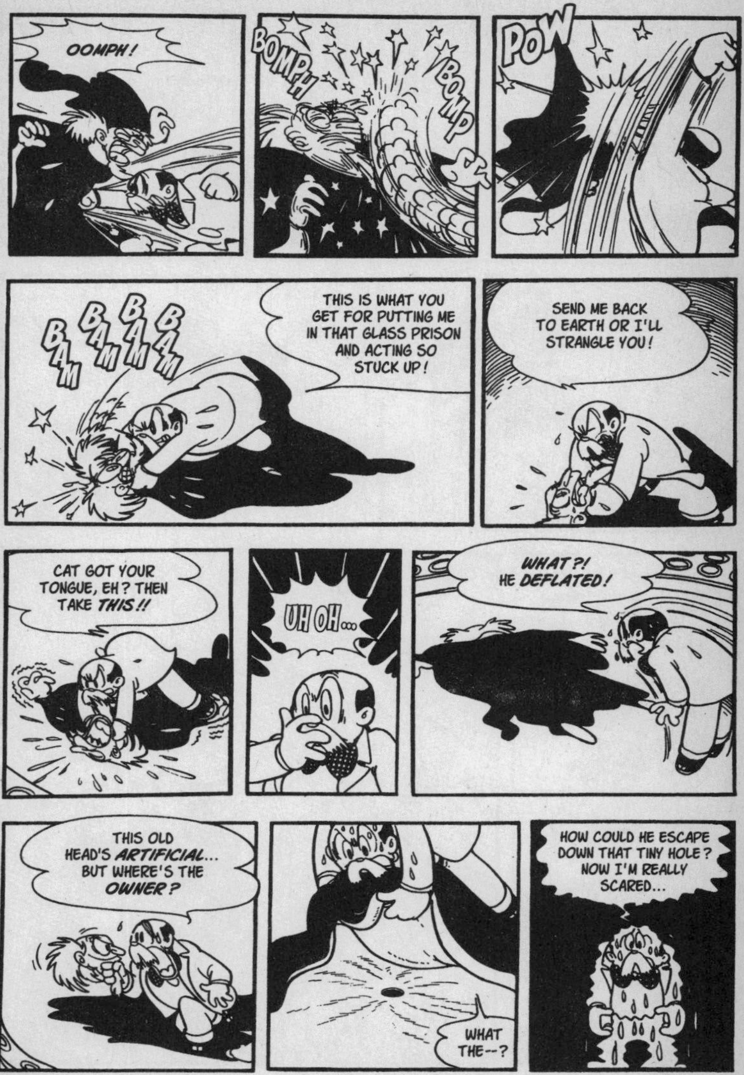
OOMPH!
BOMPH
BOMP
POW
BAM
BAM
BAM
BAM
THIS IS WHAT YOU GET FOR PUTTING ME IN THAT GLASS PRISON AND ACTING SO STUCK UP!
SEND ME BACK TO EARTH OR I'LL STRANGLE YOU!
CAT GOT YOUR TONGUE, EH? THEN TAKE *THIS!!*
UH OH...
WHAT?! HE *DEFLATED!*
THIS OLD HEAD'S *ARTIFICIAL*... BUT WHERE'S THE *OWNER?*
WHAT THE--?
HOW COULD HE ESCAPE DOWN THAT TINY HOLE? NOW I'M REALLY SCARED...

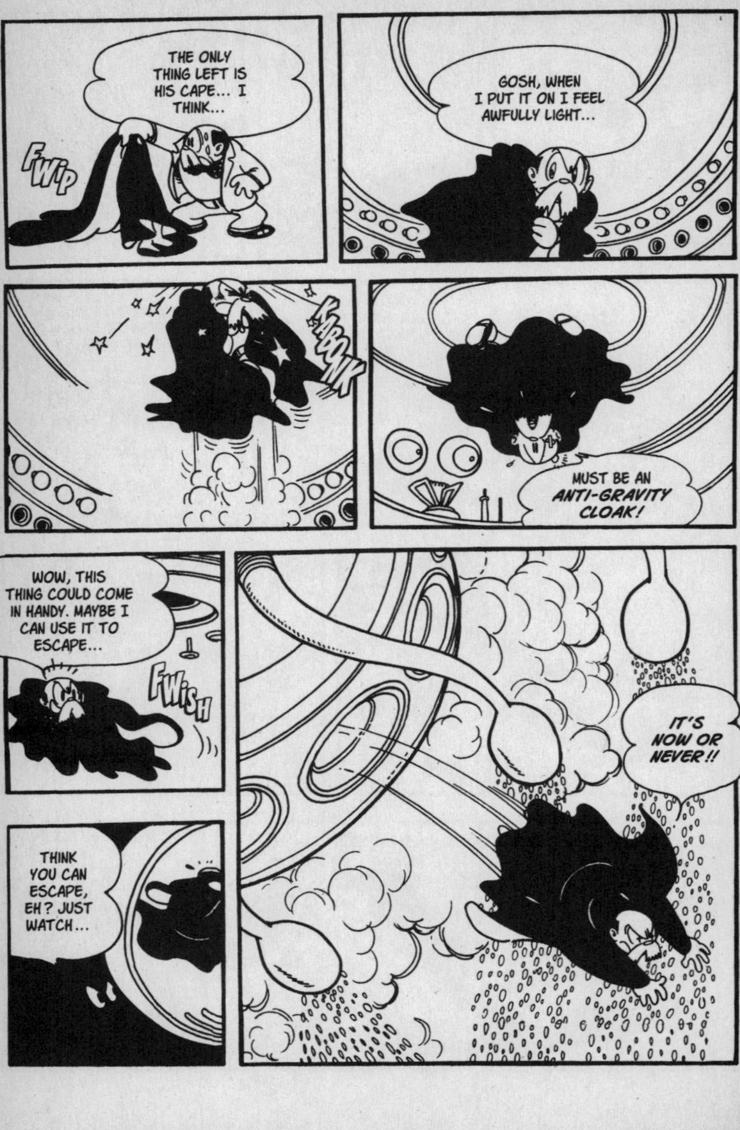
THE ONLY THING LEFT IS HIS CAPE... I THINK...
FWIP
GOSH, WHEN I PUT IT ON I FEEL AWFULLY LIGHT...
KABONK
MUST BE AN *ANTI-GRAVITY CLOAK!*
WOW, THIS THING COULD COME IN HANDY. MAYBE I CAN USE IT TO ESCAPE...
FWISH
THINK YOU CAN ESCAPE, EH? JUST WATCH...
IT'S NOW OR NEVER!!

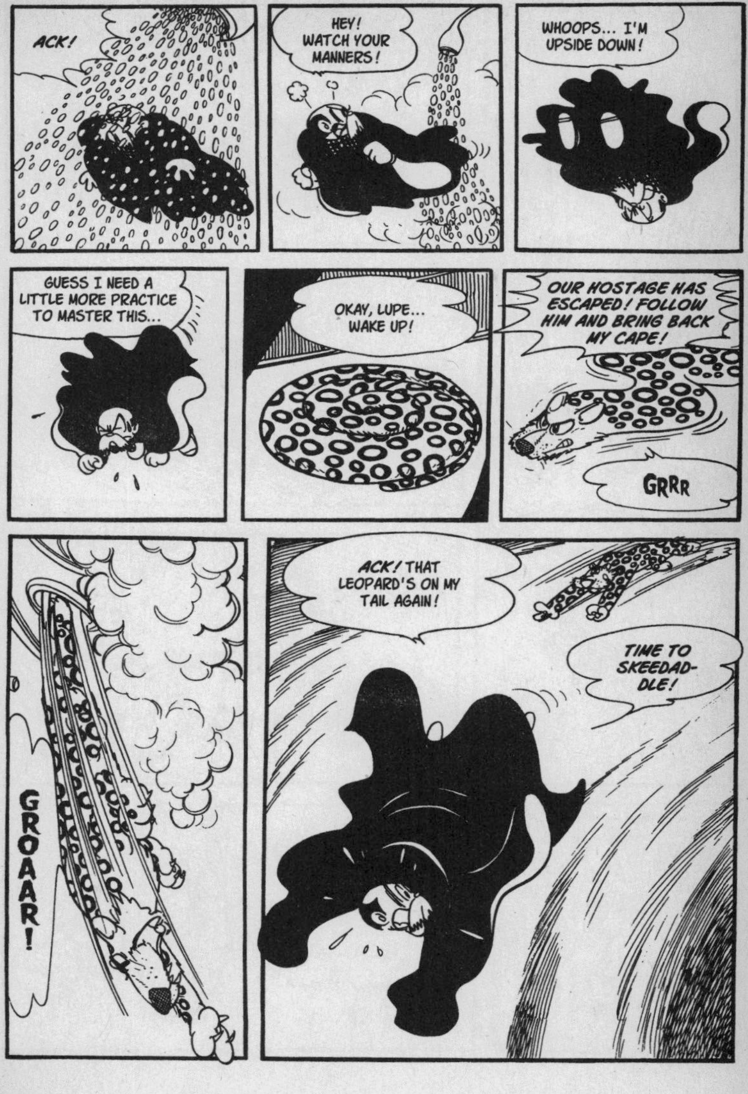
ACK!
HEY! WATCH YOUR MANNERS!
WHOOPS... I'M UPSIDE DOWN!
GUESS I NEED A LITTLE MORE PRACTICE TO MASTER THIS...
OKAY, LUPE... WAKE UP!
OUR HOSTAGE HAS ESCAPED! FOLLOW HIM AND BRING BACK MY CAPE!
GRRR
GROAAR!
ACK! THAT LEOPARD'S ON MY TAIL AGAIN!
TIME TO SKEEDAD-DLE!

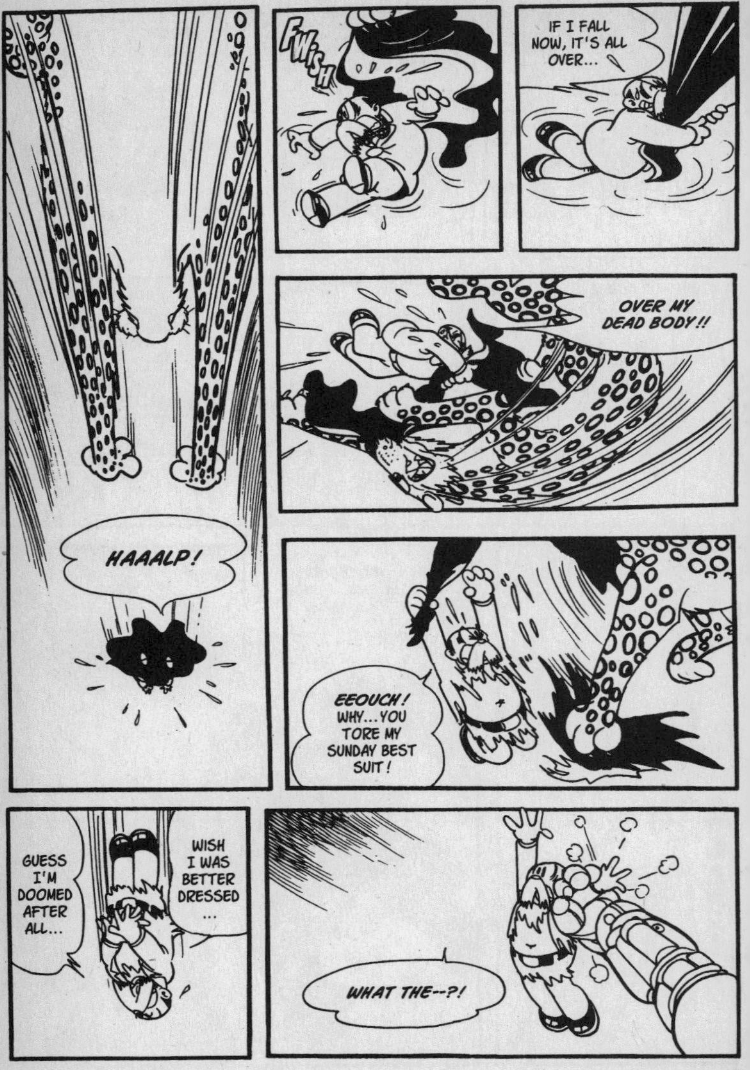
HAAALP!
FWISH
IF I FALL NOW, IT'S ALL OVER...
OVER MY DEAD BODY!!
EEOUCH! WHY...YOU TORE MY SUNDAY BEST SUIT!
GUESS I'M DOOMED AFTER ALL...
WISH I WAS BETTER DRESSED ...
WHAT THE--?!

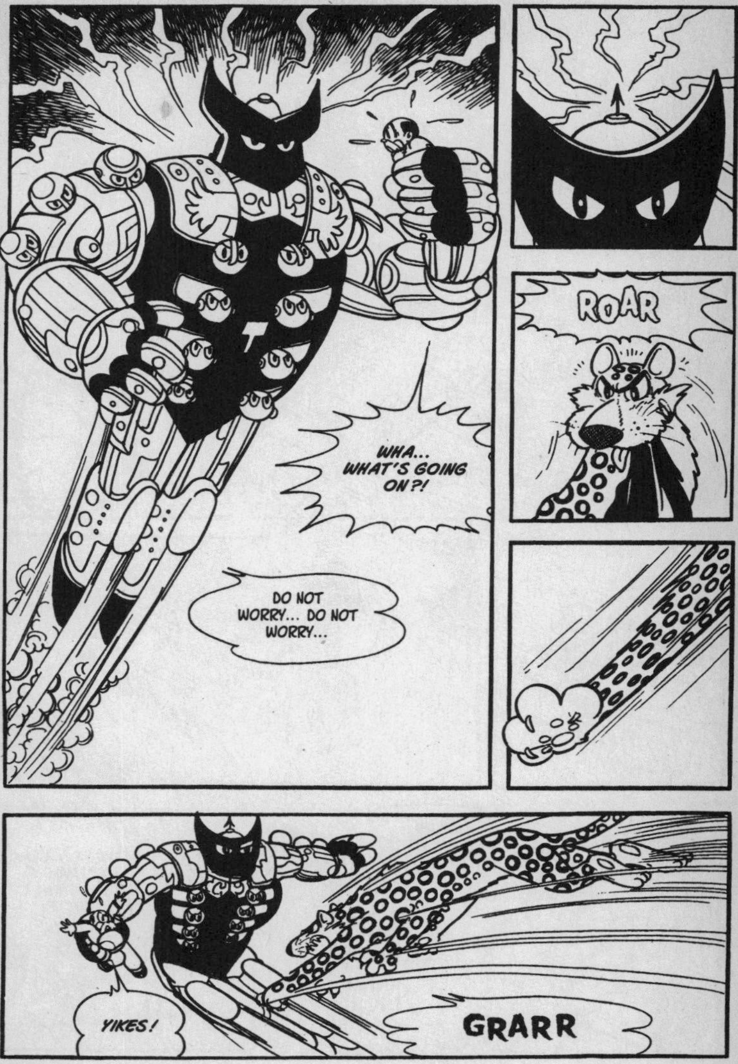
WHA... WHAT'S GOING ON?!
DO NOT WORRY... DO NOT WORRY...
ROAR
YIKES!
GRARR

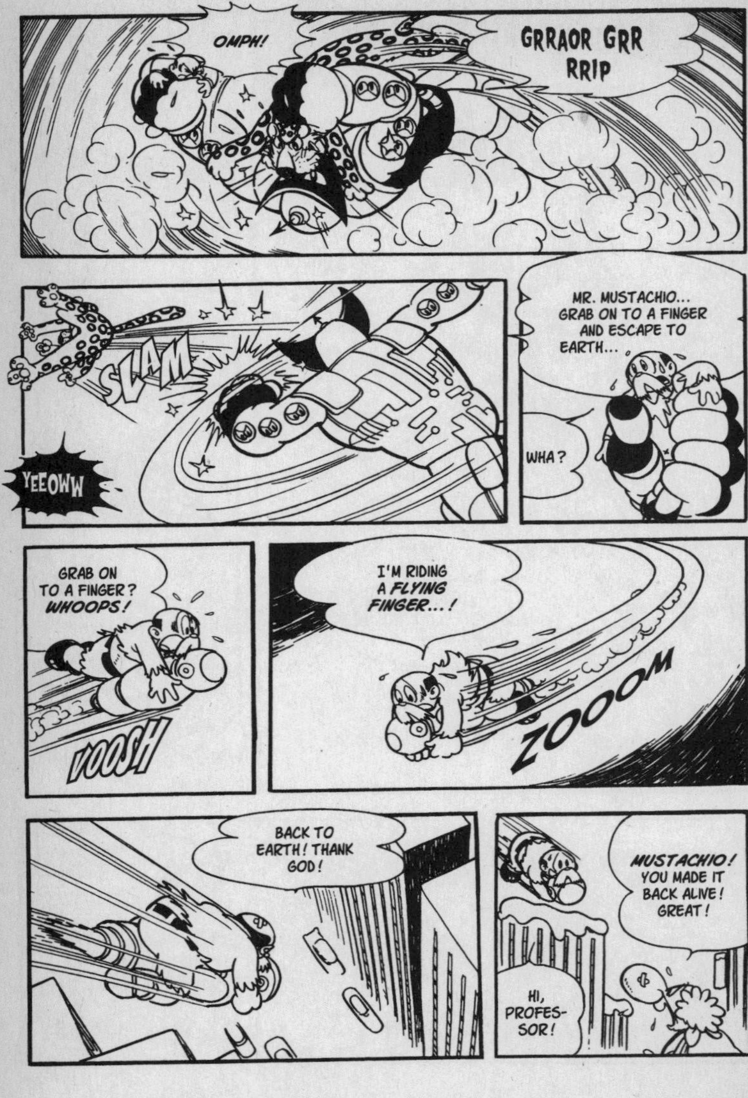
OMPH!
GRRAOR GRR RRIP
SLAM
YEEOWW
MR. MUSTACHIO... GRAB ON TO A FINGER AND ESCAPE TO EARTH...
WHA?
GRAB ON TO A FINGER? WHOOPS!
VOOSH
I'M RIDING A FLYING FINGER...!
ZOOOOM
BACK TO EARTH! THANK GOD!
MUSTACHIO! YOU MADE IT BACK ALIVE! GREAT!
HI, PROFES-SOR!

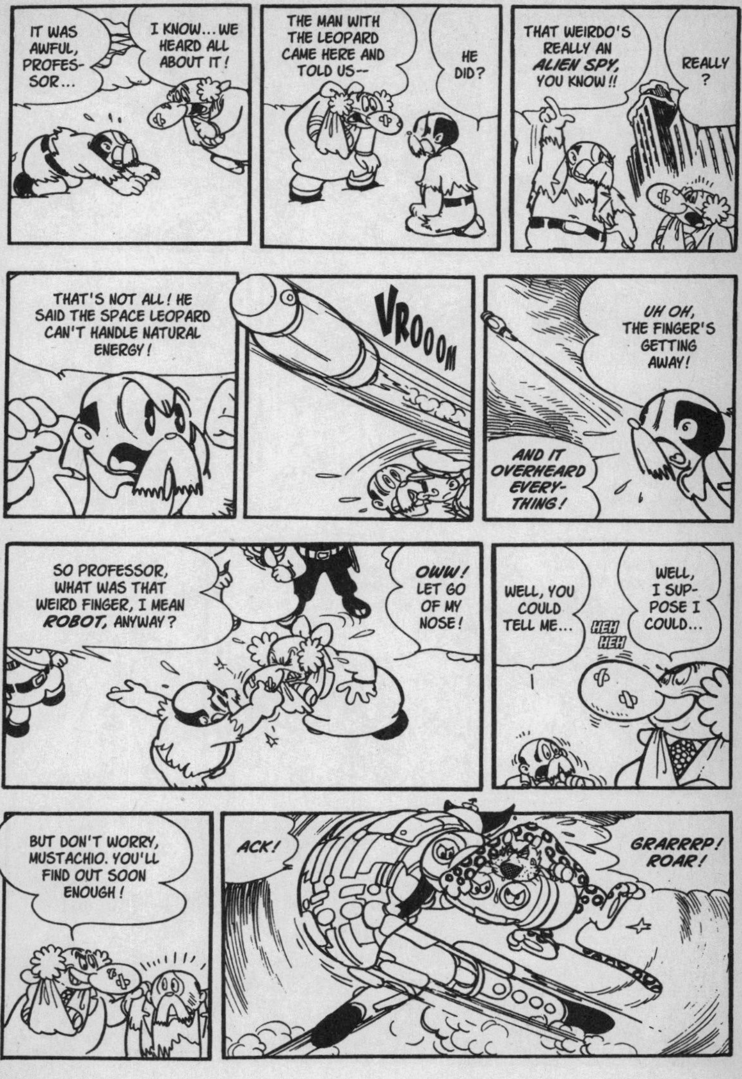
IT WAS AWFUL, PROFES-SOR...
I KNOW... WE HEARD ALL ABOUT IT!
THE MAN WITH THE LEOPARD CAME HERE AND TOLD US--
HE DID?
THAT WEIRDO'S REALLY AN ALIEN SPY, YOU KNOW!!
REALLY?
THAT'S NOT ALL! HE SAID THE SPACE LEOPARD CAN'T HANDLE NATURAL ENERGY!
VROOOM
UH OH, THE FINGER'S GETTING AWAY!
AND IT OVERHEARD EVERY-THING!
SO PROFESSOR, WHAT WAS THAT WEIRD FINGER, I MEAN ROBOT, ANYWAY?
OWW! LET GO OF MY NOSE!
WELL, YOU COULD TELL ME...
HEH HEH
WELL, I SUP-POSE I COULD...
BUT DON'T WORRY, MUSTACHIO. YOU'LL FIND OUT SOON ENOUGH!
ACK!
GRARRRP! ROAR!

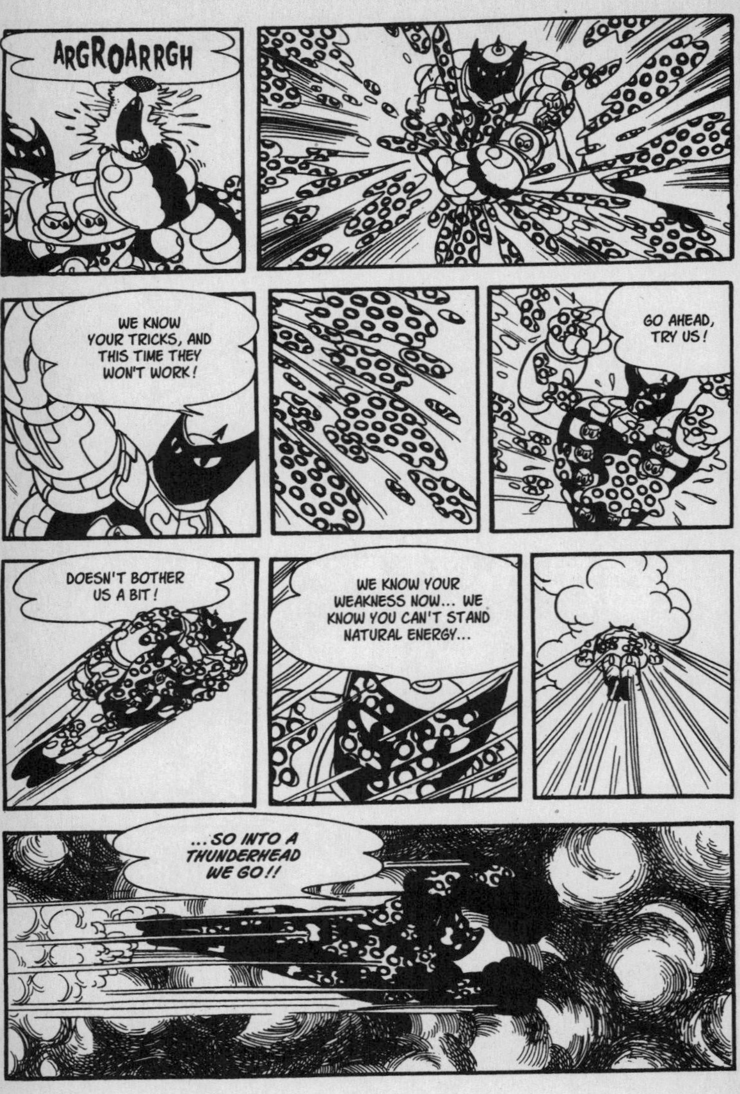
ARGROARRGH
WE KNOW YOUR TRICKS, AND THIS TIME THEY WON'T WORK!
GO AHEAD, TRY US!
DOESN'T BOTHER US A BIT!
WE KNOW YOUR WEAKNESS NOW... WE KNOW YOU CAN'T STAND NATURAL ENERGY...
...SO INTO A THUNDERHEAD WE GO!!

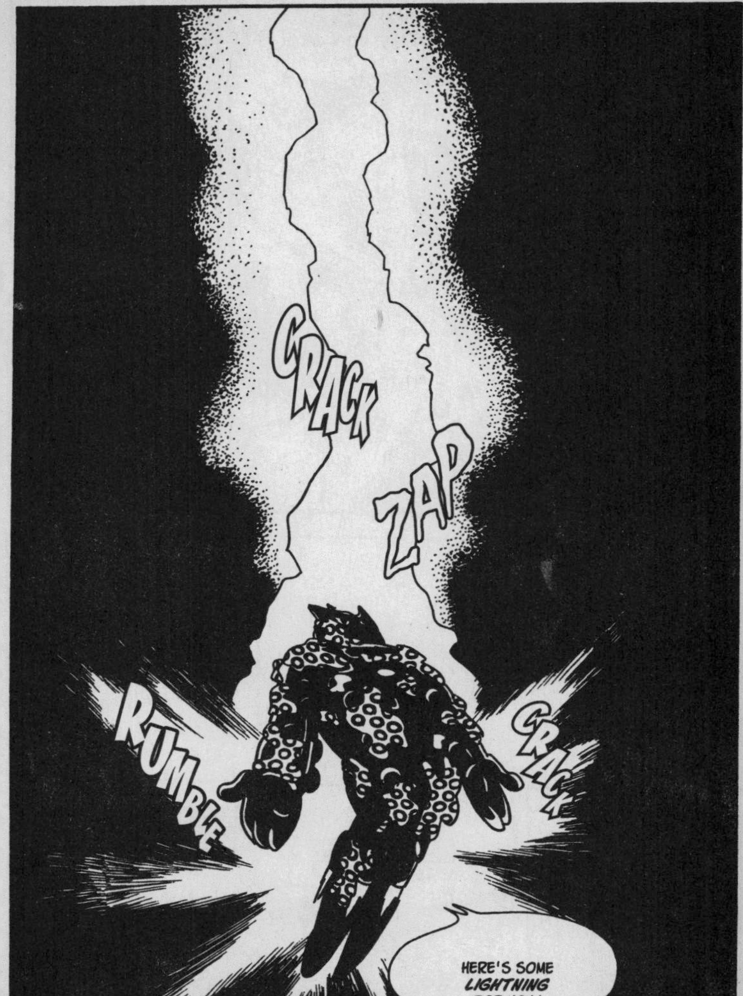
CRACK
ZAP
RUMBLE
CRACK
HERE'S SOME *LIGHTNING* FOR YOU!

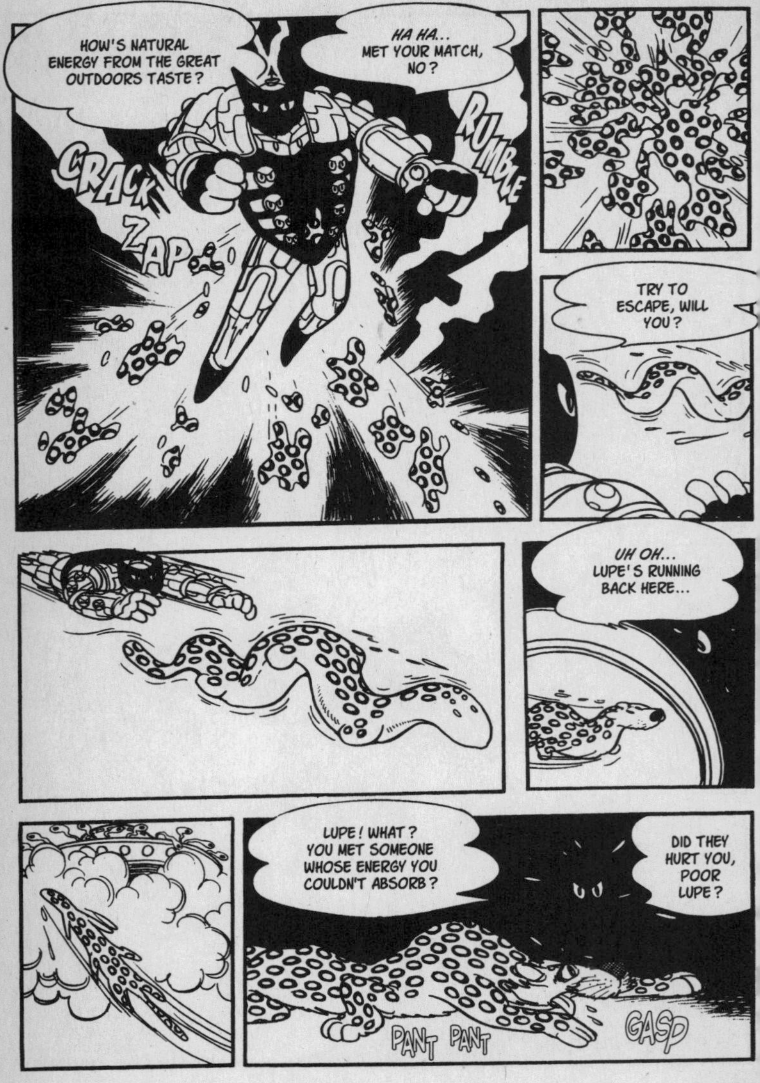
HOW'S NATURAL ENERGY FROM THE GREAT OUTDOORS TASTE?
HA HA... MET YOUR MATCH, NO?
RUMBLE
CRACK
ZAP
TRY TO ESCAPE, WILL YOU?
UH OH... LUPE'S RUNNING BACK HERE...
LUPE! WHAT? YOU MET SOMEONE WHOSE ENERGY YOU COULDN'T ABSORB?
DID THEY HURT YOU, POOR LUPE?
PANT PANT
GASP

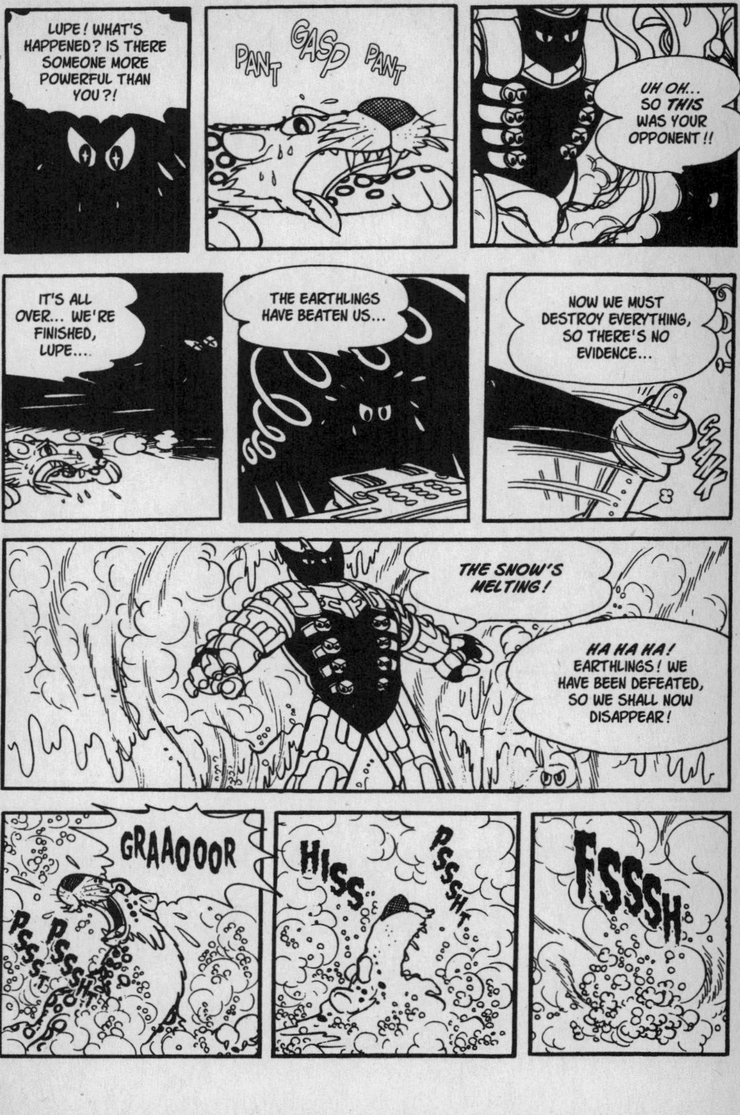
LUPE! WHAT'S HAPPENED? IS THERE SOMEONE MORE POWERFUL THAN YOU?!
PANT GASP PANT
UH OH... SO THIS WAS YOUR OPPONENT!!
IT'S ALL OVER... WE'RE FINISHED, LUPE....
THE EARTHLINGS HAVE BEATEN US...
NOW WE MUST DESTROY EVERYTHING, SO THERE'S NO EVIDENCE...
CLANK
THE SNOW'S MELTING!
HA HA HA! EARTHLINGS! WE HAVE BEEN DEFEATED, SO WE SHALL NOW DISAPPEAR!
GRAAOOOR
PSSST PSSSHT
HISS
PSSSHT
FSSSH

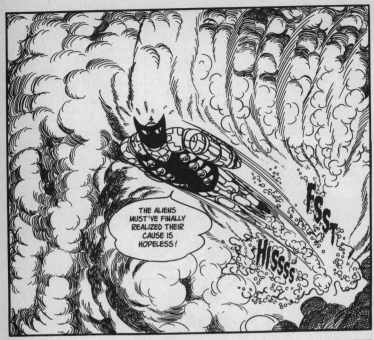

THE ALIENS MUST'VE FINALLY REALIZED THEIR CAUSE IS HOPELESS!

FSST

HISSSS

WELL DONE!! WELL DONE!

THE SPACE LEOPARD DISSOLVED ON HIS OWN...

HE COMMITTED SUICIDE?

146

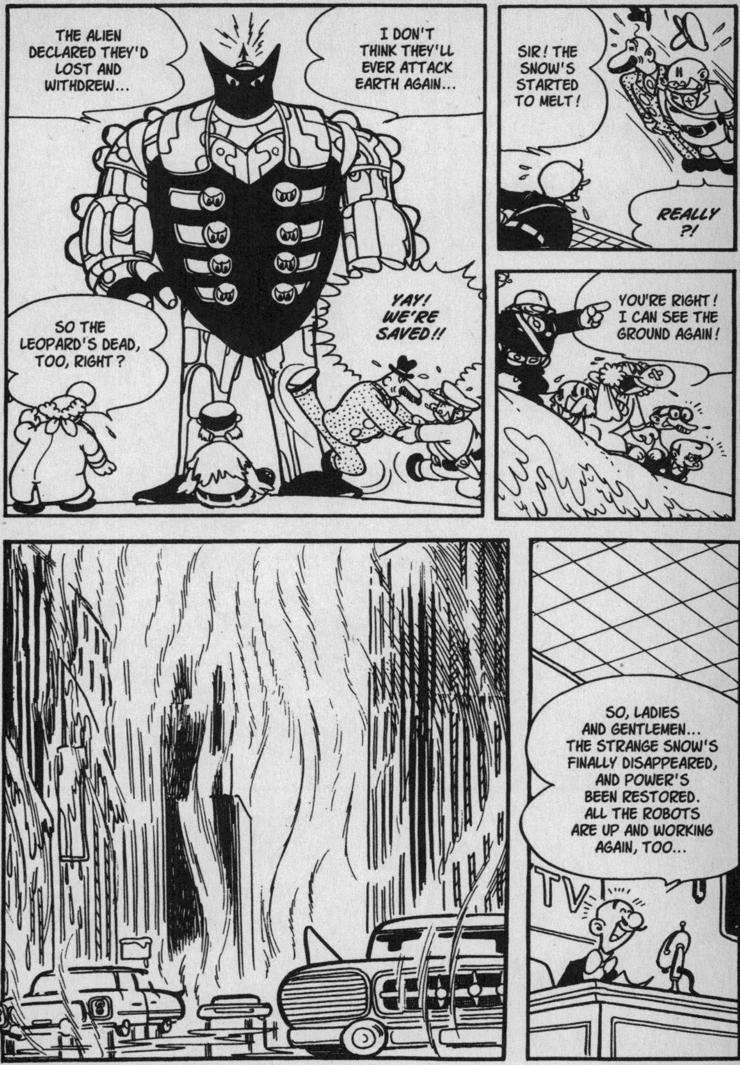
THE ALIEN DECLARED THEY'D LOST AND WITHDREW...
I DON'T THINK THEY'LL EVER ATTACK EARTH AGAIN...
SO THE LEOPARD'S DEAD, TOO, RIGHT?
YAY! WE'RE SAVED!!
SIR! THE SNOW'S STARTED TO MELT!
REALLY ?!
YOU'RE RIGHT! I CAN SEE THE GROUND AGAIN!
SO, LADIES AND GENTLEMEN... THE STRANGE SNOW'S FINALLY DISAPPEARED, AND POWER'S BEEN RESTORED. ALL THE ROBOTS ARE UP AND WORKING AGAIN, TOO...
TV

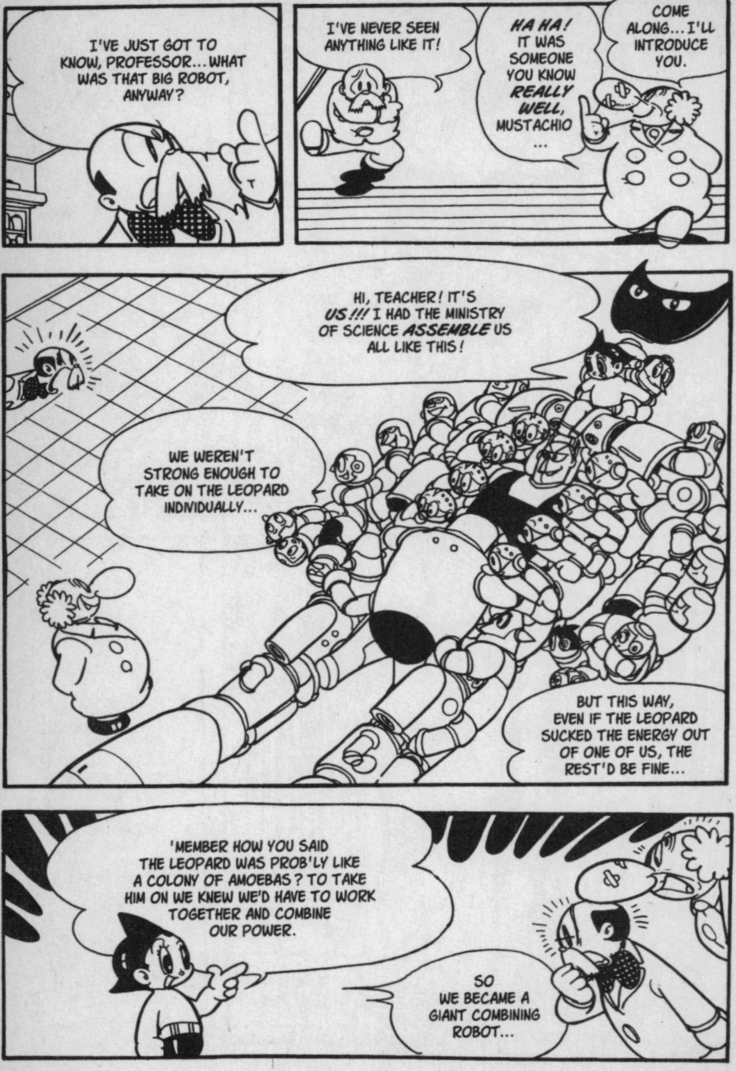

I'VE JUST GOT TO KNOW, PROFESSOR... WHAT WAS THAT BIG ROBOT, ANYWAY?
I'VE NEVER SEEN ANYTHING LIKE IT!
HA HA! IT WAS SOMEONE YOU KNOW REALLY WELL, MUSTACHIO ...
COME ALONG... I'LL INTRODUCE YOU.
HI, TEACHER! IT'S US!!! I HAD THE MINISTRY OF SCIENCE ASSEMBLE US ALL LIKE THIS!
WE WEREN'T STRONG ENOUGH TO TAKE ON THE LEOPARD INDIVIDUALLY...
BUT THIS WAY, EVEN IF THE LEOPARD SUCKED THE ENERGY OUT OF ONE OF US, THE REST'D BE FINE...
'MEMBER HOW YOU SAID THE LEOPARD WAS PROB'LY LIKE A COLONY OF AMOEBAS? TO TAKE HIM ON WE KNEW WE'D HAVE TO WORK TOGETHER AND COMBINE OUR POWER.
SO WE BECAME A GIANT COMBINING ROBOT...

THE ARTIFICIAL SUN

First serialized between December 1959 and
February 1960 in *Shonen* magazine.

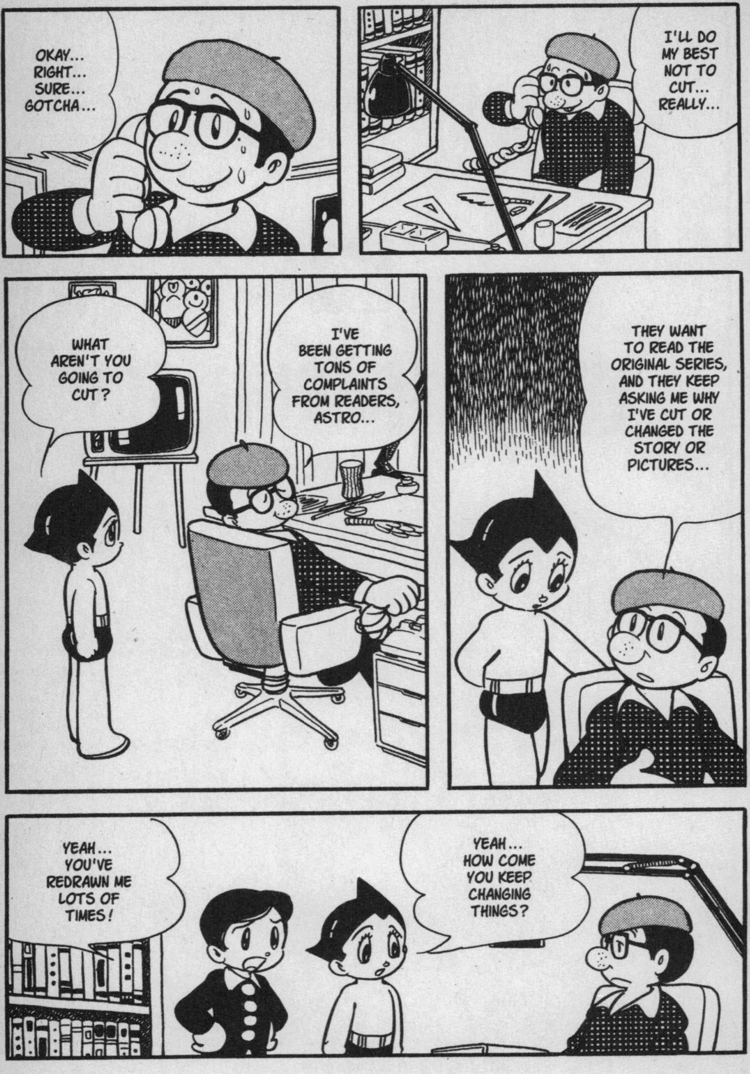
OKAY... RIGHT... SURE... GOTCHA...
I'LL DO MY BEST NOT TO CUT... REALLY...
WHAT AREN'T YOU GOING TO CUT?
I'VE BEEN GETTING TONS OF COMPLAINTS FROM READERS, ASTRO...
THEY WANT TO READ THE ORIGINAL SERIES, AND THEY KEEP ASKING ME WHY I'VE CUT OR CHANGED THE STORY OR PICTURES...
YEAH... YOU'VE REDRAWN ME LOTS OF TIMES!
YEAH... HOW COME YOU KEEP CHANGING THINGS?

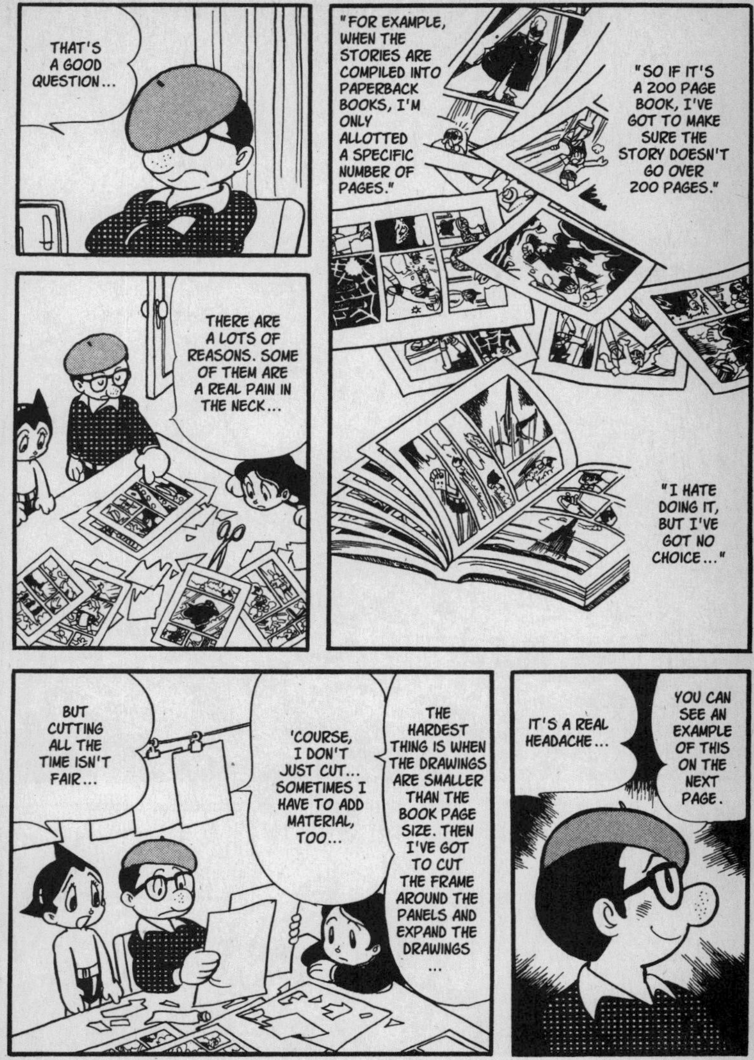
THAT'S A GOOD QUESTION...
"FOR EXAMPLE, WHEN THE STORIES ARE COMPILED INTO PAPERBACK BOOKS, I'M ONLY ALLOTTED A SPECIFIC NUMBER OF PAGES."
"SO IF IT'S A 200 PAGE BOOK, I'VE GOT TO MAKE SURE THE STORY DOESN'T GO OVER 200 PAGES."
THERE ARE A LOTS OF REASONS. SOME OF THEM ARE A REAL PAIN IN THE NECK...
"I HATE DOING IT, BUT I'VE GOT NO CHOICE..."
BUT CUTTING ALL THE TIME ISN'T FAIR...
'COURSE, I DON'T JUST CUT... SOMETIMES I HAVE TO ADD MATERIAL, TOO...
THE HARDEST THING IS WHEN THE DRAWINGS ARE SMALLER THAN THE BOOK PAGE SIZE. THEN I'VE GOT TO CUT THE FRAME AROUND THE PANELS AND EXPAND THE DRAWINGS ...
IT'S A REAL HEADACHE...
YOU CAN SEE AN EXAMPLE OF THIS ON THE NEXT PAGE.

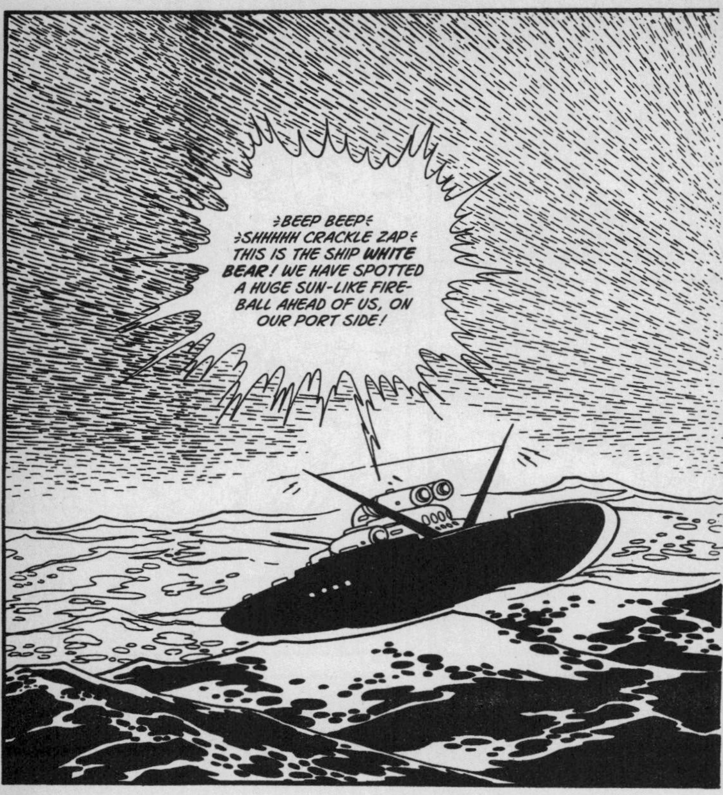
⋟BEEP BEEP⋞ ⋟SHHHHH CRACKLE ZAP⋞ THIS IS THE SHIP **WHITE BEAR**! WE HAVE SPOTTED A HUGE SUN-LIKE FIREBALL AHEAD OF US, ON OUR PORT SIDE!

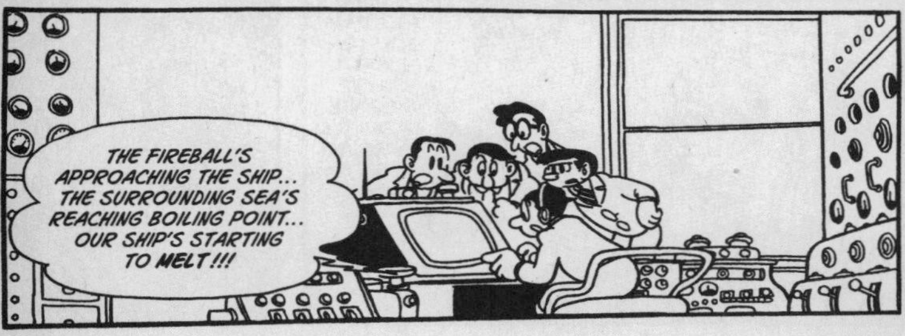
THE FIREBALL'S APPROACHING THE SHIP... THE SURROUNDING SEA'S REACHING BOILING POINT... OUR SHIP'S STARTING TO **MELT**!!!

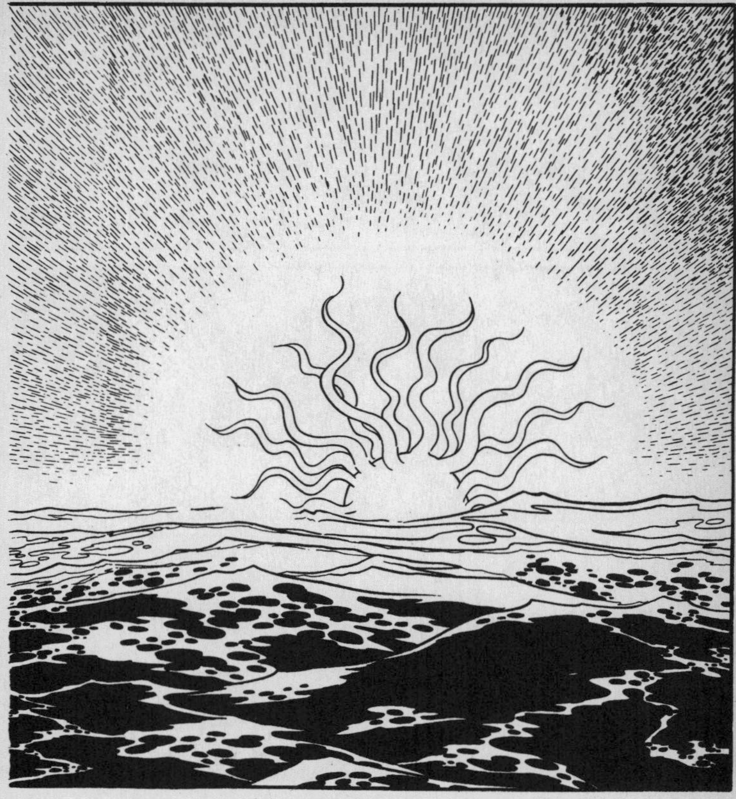

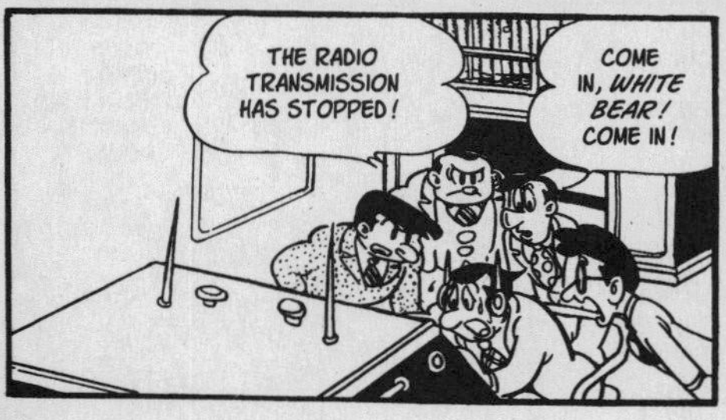

THE RADIO TRANSMISSION HAS STOPPED!
COME IN, *WHITE BEAR!* COME IN!

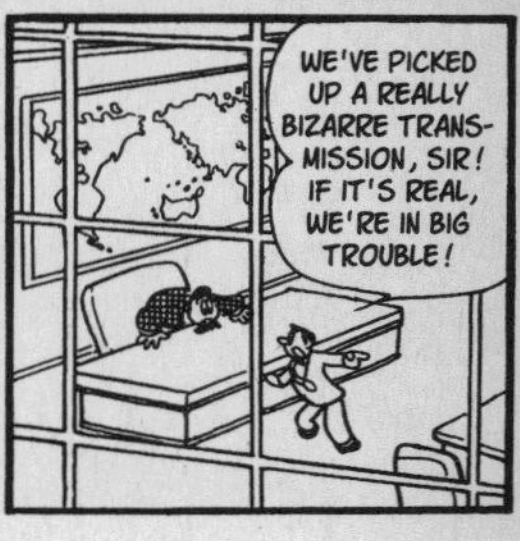

WE'VE PICKED UP A REALLY BIZARRE TRANS-MISSION, SIR! IF IT'S REAL, WE'RE IN BIG TROUBLE!

ALL RIGHT, MEN. I WANT YOU TO HEAD OUT AT TOP SPEED TO WHERE THAT SHIP IS, AND REPORT BACK TO ME!!

HOO-BOY!

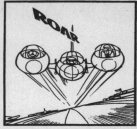

ROAR

WOW! THERE'S SO MUCH *MIST* I CAN HARDLY SEE...

SO WE FLY INTO IT?

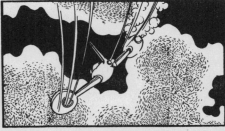

THE SEA'S SURFACE IS COVERED IN MIST...

QUICK! PULL UP!

WHEW... THAT WAS CLOSE!

WHERE'S THE *WHITE BEAR*?

IT'S MYST-IFYING!

HEY, THERE'S PIECES OF A SHIP FLOATING OVER THERE!

AN OIL SLICK! 'MUST BE WHERE THE POOR *WHITE BEAR* SANK!!

THE SEA SURFACE IS WEIRD! LOOKS LIKE IT'S BOILING!

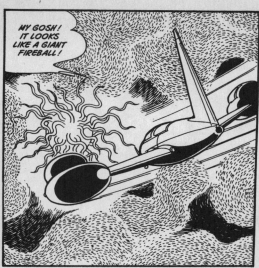

MY GOSH! IT LOOKS LIKE A GIANT FIREBALL!

FWIP

WE APPEAR TO HAVE UNEXPLAINABLE INCIDENTS OF THIS TYPE OCCURRING THROUGHOUT THE NORTH PACIFIC...

I·C·P·O

INTERNATIONAL COUNCIL OF POLICE ORGANIZATIONS

EVENTUALLY, AN EMERGENCY MEETING OF THE *I.C.P.O.* WAS HELD.

WELL, SUPERINTENDENT GENERAL, WHAT DO YOU THINK, SIR?

IN ADDITION TO PATROLLING THE AREA, WE SHOULD SEND IN A *SPECIAL AGENT*...

AGENT? ARE YOU SAYING THERE MIGHT BE A *CRIMINAL INTENT* BEHIND THIS, SIR?

MINOR GUYS

GENTLEMEN...THIS INCIDENT WAS NOT CAUSED BY AN UNDERSEA VOLCANO...

THE BIG GUY

155

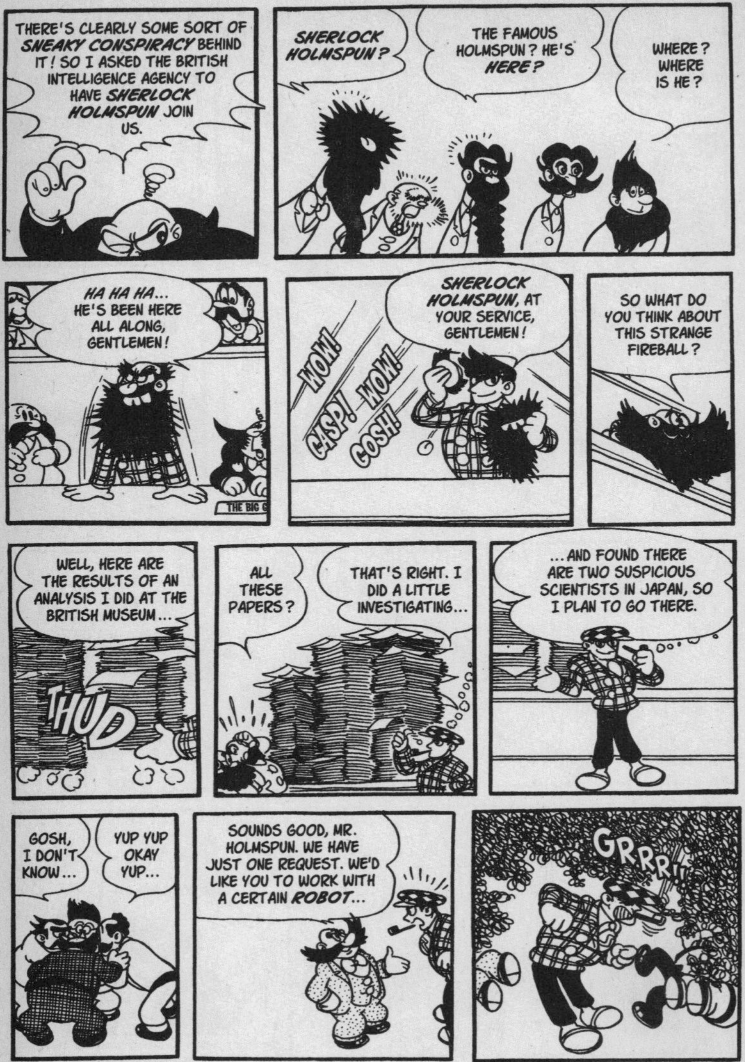
THERE'S CLEARLY SOME SORT OF SNEAKY CONSPIRACY BEHIND IT! SO I ASKED THE BRITISH INTELLIGENCE AGENCY TO HAVE SHERLOCK HOLMSPUN JOIN US.
SHERLOCK HOLMSPUN?
THE FAMOUS HOLMSPUN? HE'S HERE?
WHERE? WHERE IS HE?
HA HA HA... HE'S BEEN HERE ALL ALONG, GENTLEMEN!
THE BIG G
SHERLOCK HOLMSPUN, AT YOUR SERVICE, GENTLEMEN!
WOW!
GASP!
WOW!
GOSH!
SO WHAT DO YOU THINK ABOUT THIS STRANGE FIREBALL?
WELL, HERE ARE THE RESULTS OF AN ANALYSIS I DID AT THE BRITISH MUSEUM...
THUD
ALL THESE PAPERS?
THAT'S RIGHT. I DID A LITTLE INVESTIGATING...
...AND FOUND THERE ARE TWO SUSPICIOUS SCIENTISTS IN JAPAN, SO I PLAN TO GO THERE.
GOSH, I DON'T KNOW...
YUP YUP OKAY YUP...
SOUNDS GOOD, MR. HOLMSPUN. WE HAVE JUST ONE REQUEST. WE'D LIKE YOU TO WORK WITH A CERTAIN ROBOT...
GRRRR!

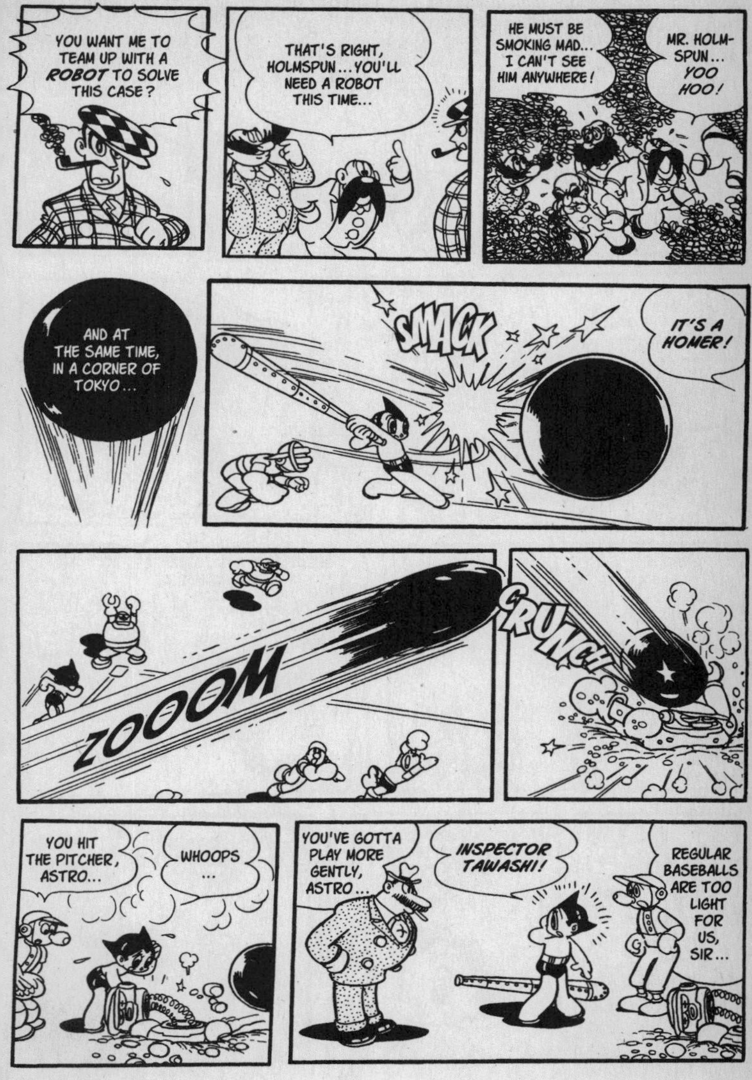
YOU WANT ME TO TEAM UP WITH A *ROBOT* TO SOLVE THIS CASE?
THAT'S RIGHT, HOLMSPUN... YOU'LL NEED A ROBOT THIS TIME...
HE MUST BE SMOKING MAD... I CAN'T SEE HIM ANYWHERE!
MR. HOLMSPUN... *YOO HOO!*
AND AT THE SAME TIME, IN A CORNER OF TOKYO...
SMACK
IT'S A HOMER!
ZOOOM
CRUNCH
YOU HIT THE PITCHER, ASTRO...
WHOOPS ...
YOU'VE GOTTA PLAY MORE GENTLY, ASTRO...
INSPECTOR TAWASHI!
REGULAR BASEBALLS ARE TOO LIGHT FOR US, SIR...

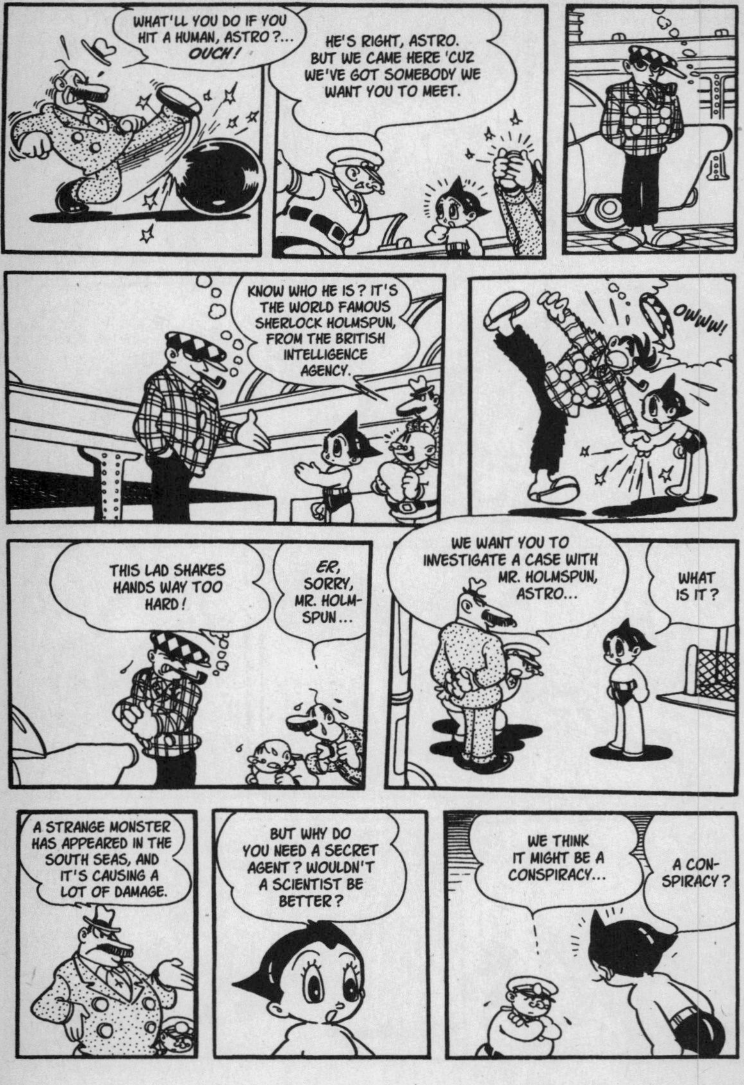
WHAT'LL YOU DO IF YOU HIT A HUMAN, ASTRO?... OUCH!
HE'S RIGHT, ASTRO. BUT WE CAME HERE 'CUZ WE'VE GOT SOMEBODY WE WANT YOU TO MEET.
KNOW WHO HE IS? IT'S THE WORLD FAMOUS SHERLOCK HOLMSPUN, FROM THE BRITISH INTELLIGENCE AGENCY.
OWWW!
THIS LAD SHAKES HANDS WAY TOO HARD!
ER, SORRY, MR. HOLM-SPUN...
WE WANT YOU TO INVESTIGATE A CASE WITH MR. HOLMSPUN, ASTRO...
WHAT IS IT?
A STRANGE MONSTER HAS APPEARED IN THE SOUTH SEAS, AND IT'S CAUSING A LOT OF DAMAGE.
BUT WHY DO YOU NEED A SECRET AGENT? WOULDN'T A SCIENTIST BE BETTER?
WE THINK IT MIGHT BE A CONSPIRACY...
A CON-SPIRACY?

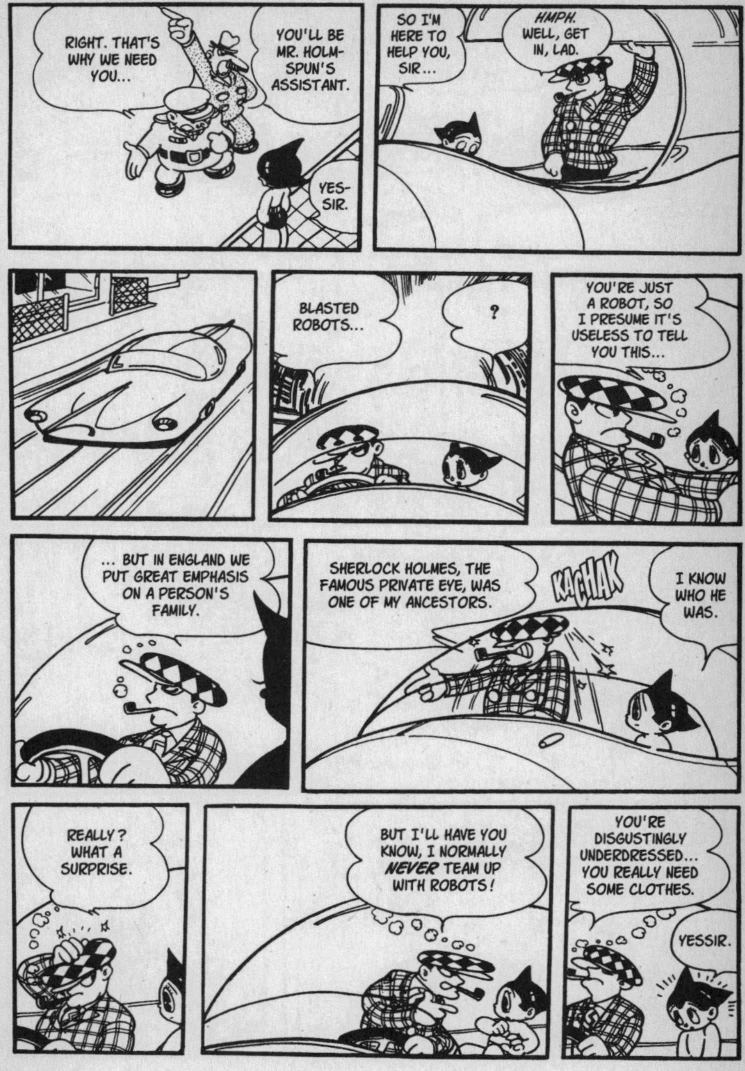
RIGHT. THAT'S WHY WE NEED YOU...
YOU'LL BE MR. HOLM-SPUN'S ASSISTANT.
YES-SIR.
SO I'M HERE TO HELP YOU, SIR...
HMPH. WELL, GET IN, LAD.
BLASTED ROBOTS...
?
YOU'RE JUST A ROBOT, SO I PRESUME IT'S USELESS TO TELL YOU THIS...
... BUT IN ENGLAND WE PUT GREAT EMPHASIS ON A PERSON'S FAMILY.
SHERLOCK HOLMES, THE FAMOUS PRIVATE EYE, WAS ONE OF MY ANCESTORS.
KACHAK
I KNOW WHO HE WAS.
REALLY? WHAT A SURPRISE.
BUT I'LL HAVE YOU KNOW, I NORMALLY NEVER TEAM UP WITH ROBOTS!
YOU'RE DISGUSTINGLY UNDERDRESSED... YOU REALLY NEED SOME CLOTHES.
YESSIR.

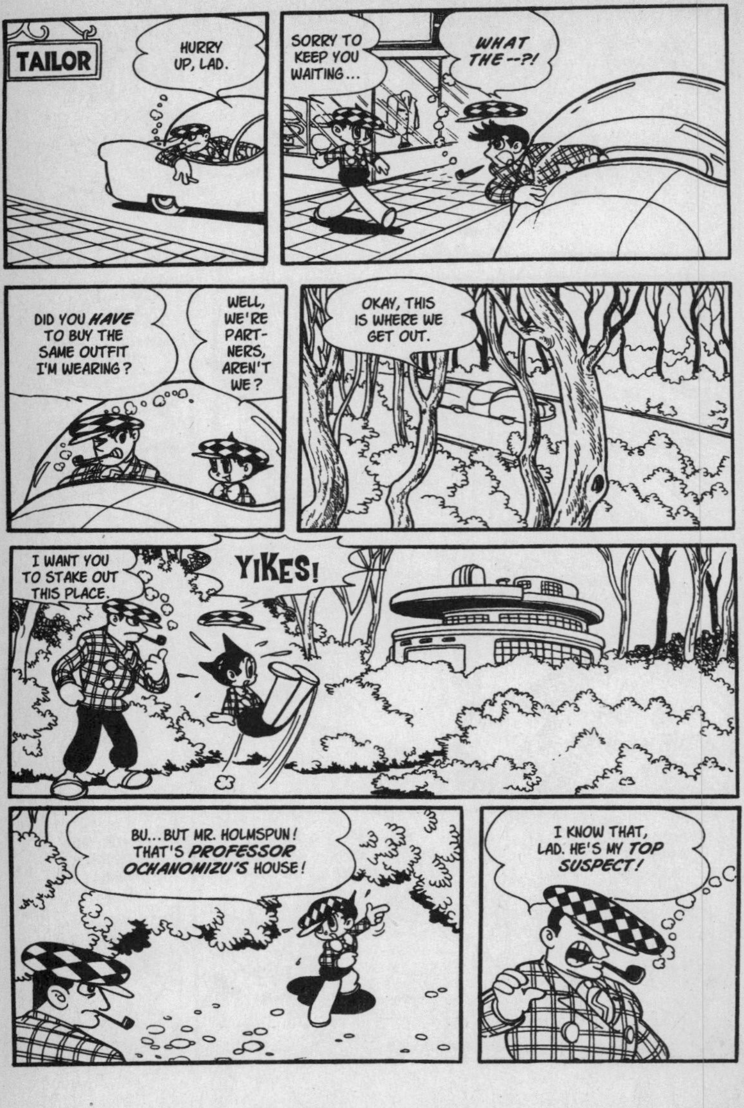
TAILOR
HURRY UP, LAD.
SORRY TO KEEP YOU WAITING...
WHAT THE--?!
DID YOU HAVE TO BUY THE SAME OUTFIT I'M WEARING?
WELL, WE'RE PART-NERS, AREN'T WE?
OKAY, THIS IS WHERE WE GET OUT.
I WANT YOU TO STAKE OUT THIS PLACE.
YIKES!
BU...BUT MR. HOLMSPUN! THAT'S PROFESSOR OCHANOMIZU'S HOUSE!
I KNOW THAT, LAD. HE'S MY TOP SUSPECT!

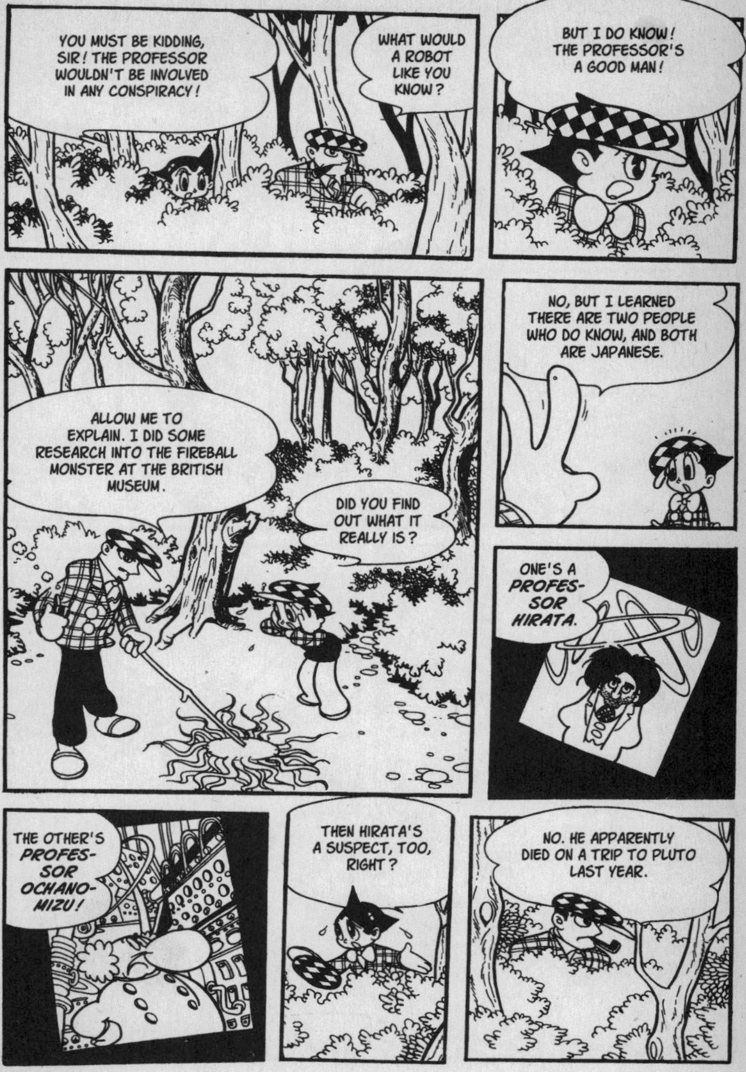
YOU MUST BE KIDDING, SIR! THE PROFESSOR WOULDN'T BE INVOLVED IN ANY CONSPIRACY!
WHAT WOULD A ROBOT LIKE YOU KNOW?
BUT I DO KNOW! THE PROFESSOR'S A GOOD MAN!
ALLOW ME TO EXPLAIN. I DID SOME RESEARCH INTO THE FIREBALL MONSTER AT THE BRITISH MUSEUM.
DID YOU FIND OUT WHAT IT REALLY IS?
NO, BUT I LEARNED THERE ARE TWO PEOPLE WHO DO KNOW, AND BOTH ARE JAPANESE.
ONE'S A PROFESSOR HIRATA.
THE OTHER'S PROFESSOR OCHANOMIZU!
THEN HIRATA'S A SUSPECT, TOO, RIGHT?
NO. HE APPARENTLY DIED ON A TRIP TO PLUTO LAST YEAR.

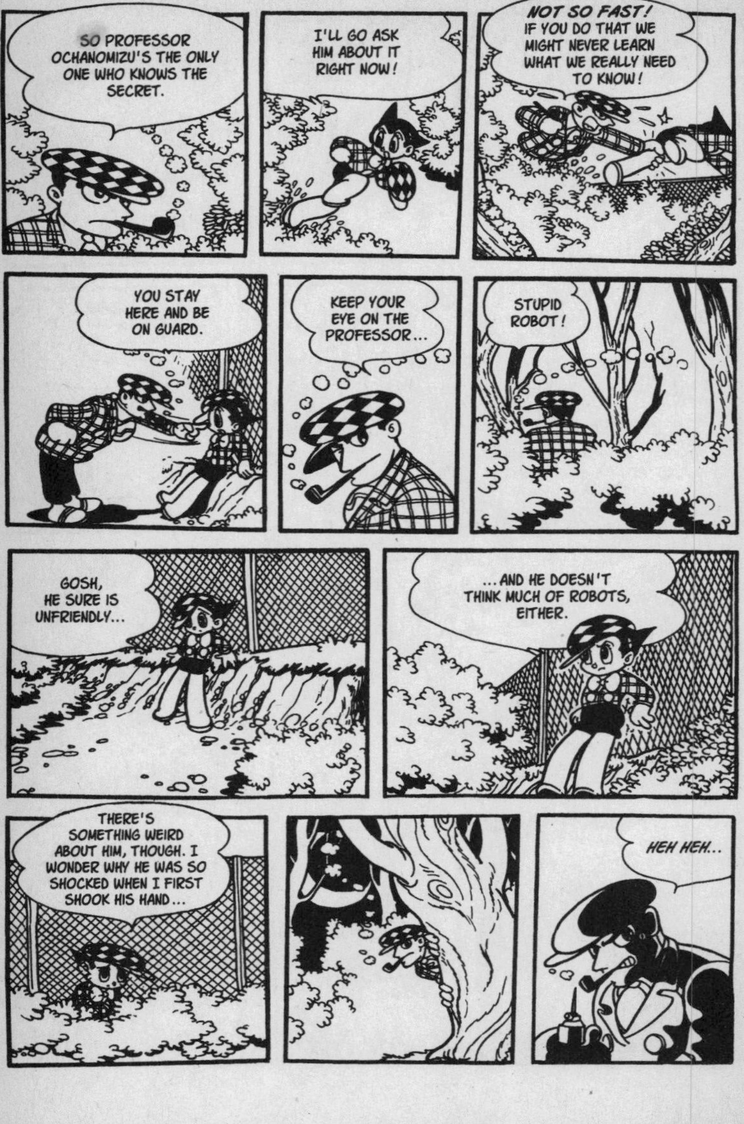
SO PROFESSOR OCHANOMIZU'S THE ONLY ONE WHO KNOWS THE SECRET.
I'LL GO ASK HIM ABOUT IT RIGHT NOW!
NOT SO FAST! IF YOU DO THAT WE MIGHT NEVER LEARN WHAT WE REALLY NEED TO KNOW!
YOU STAY HERE AND BE ON GUARD.
KEEP YOUR EYE ON THE PROFESSOR...
STUPID ROBOT!
GOSH, HE SURE IS UNFRIENDLY...
...AND HE DOESN'T THINK MUCH OF ROBOTS, EITHER.
THERE'S SOMETHING WEIRD ABOUT HIM, THOUGH. I WONDER WHY HE WAS SO SHOCKED WHEN I FIRST SHOOK HIS HAND...
HEH HEH...

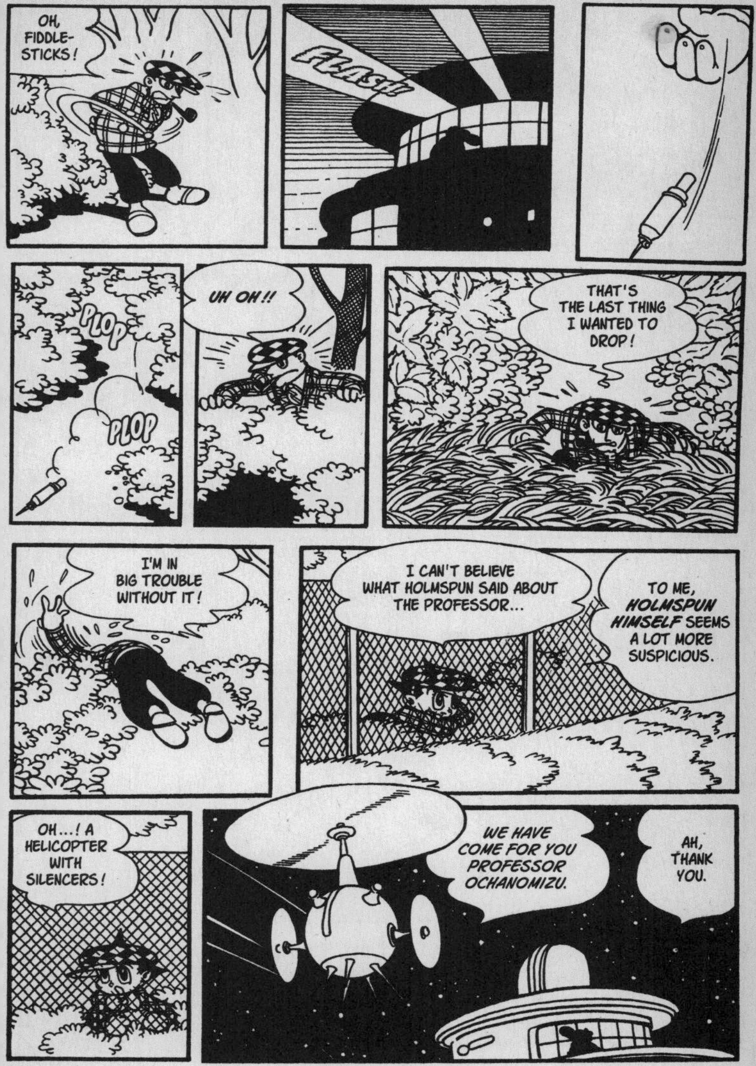
OH, FIDDLE-STICKS!
FLASH!
UH OH!!
PLOP
PLOP
THAT'S THE LAST THING I WANTED TO DROP!
I'M IN BIG TROUBLE WITHOUT IT!
I CAN'T BELIEVE WHAT HOLMSPUN SAID ABOUT THE PROFESSOR...
TO ME, HOLMSPUN HIMSELF SEEMS A LOT MORE SUSPICIOUS.
OH...! A HELICOPTER WITH SILENCERS!
WE HAVE COME FOR YOU PROFESSOR OCHANOMIZU.
AH, THANK YOU.

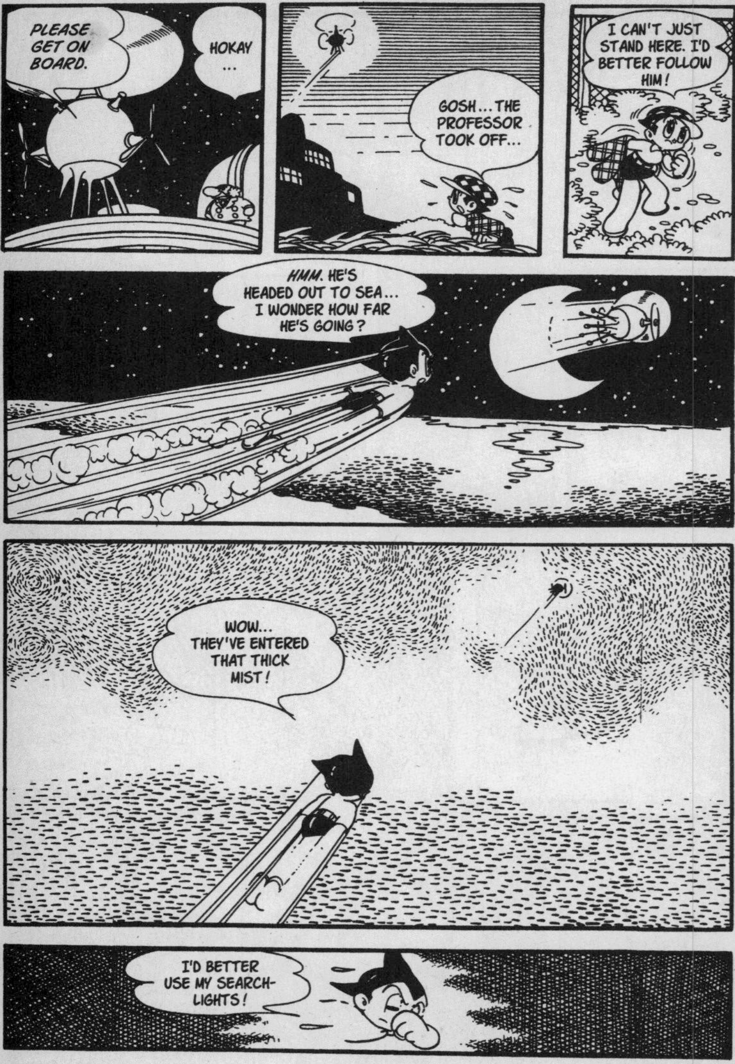
PLEASE GET ON BOARD.
HOKAY ...
GOSH ... THE PROFESSOR TOOK OFF...
I CAN'T JUST STAND HERE. I'D BETTER FOLLOW HIM!
HMM. HE'S HEADED OUT TO SEA... I WONDER HOW FAR HE'S GOING?
WOW... THEY'VE ENTERED THAT THICK MIST!
I'D BETTER USE MY SEARCH-LIGHTS!

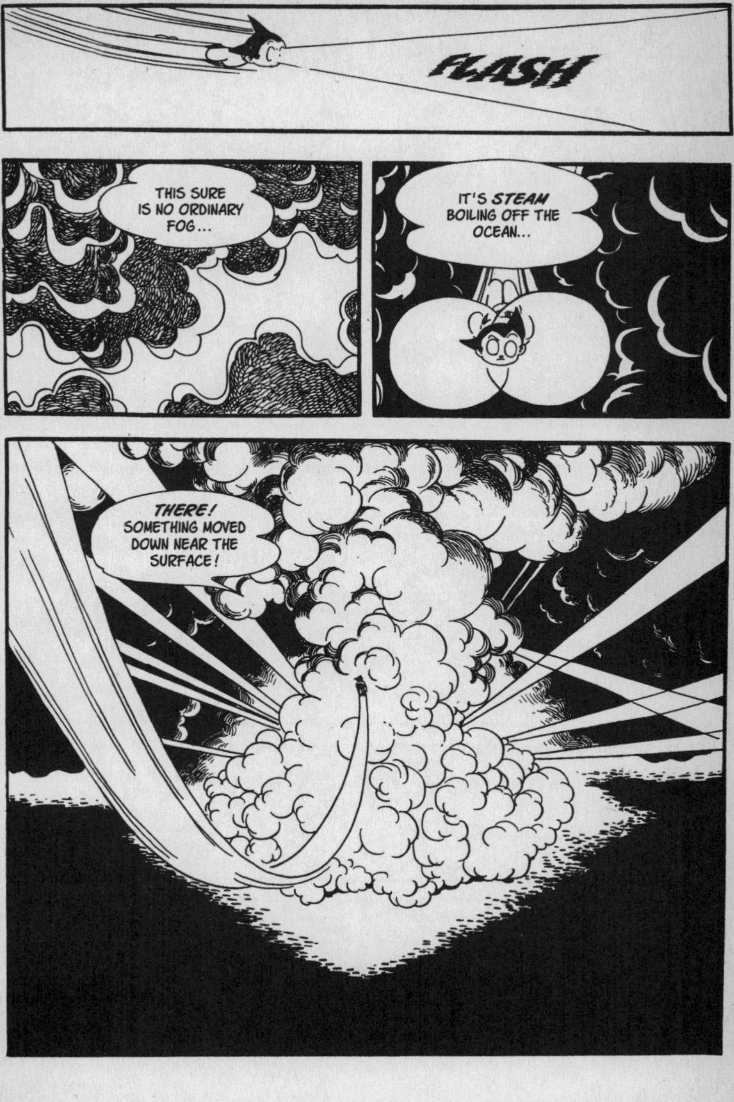
FLASH
THIS SURE IS NO ORDINARY FOG...
IT'S STEAM BOILING OFF THE OCEAN...
THERE! SOMETHING MOVED DOWN NEAR THE SURFACE!

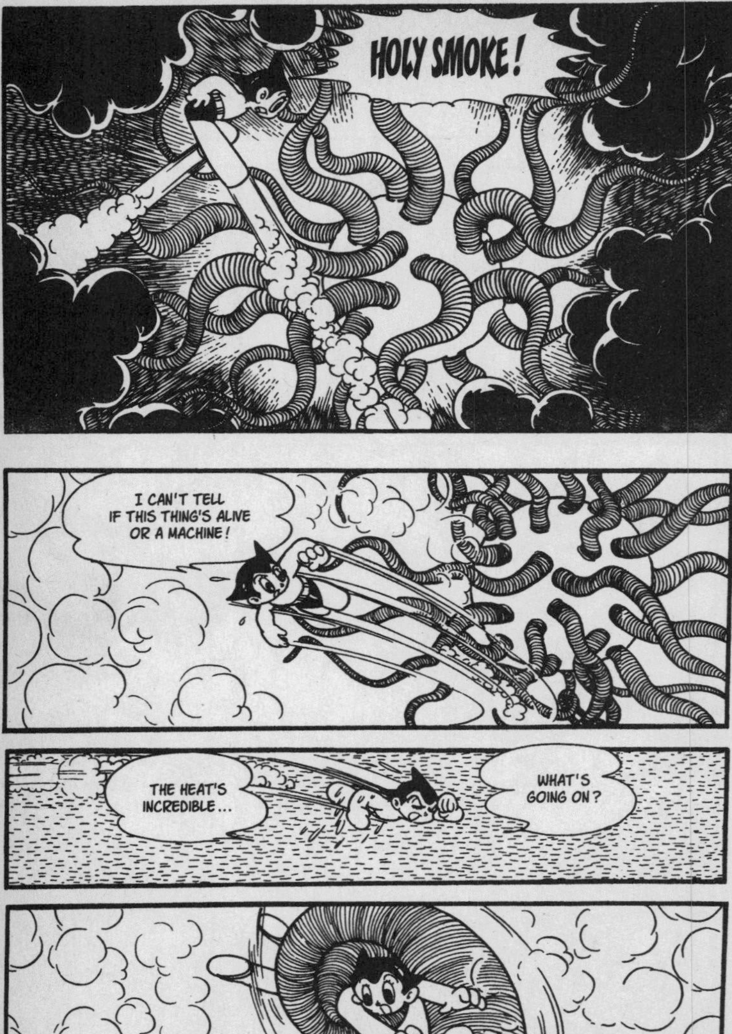
HOLY SMOKE!
I CAN'T TELL IF THIS THING'S ALIVE OR A MACHINE!
THE HEAT'S INCREDIBLE...
WHAT'S GOING ON?

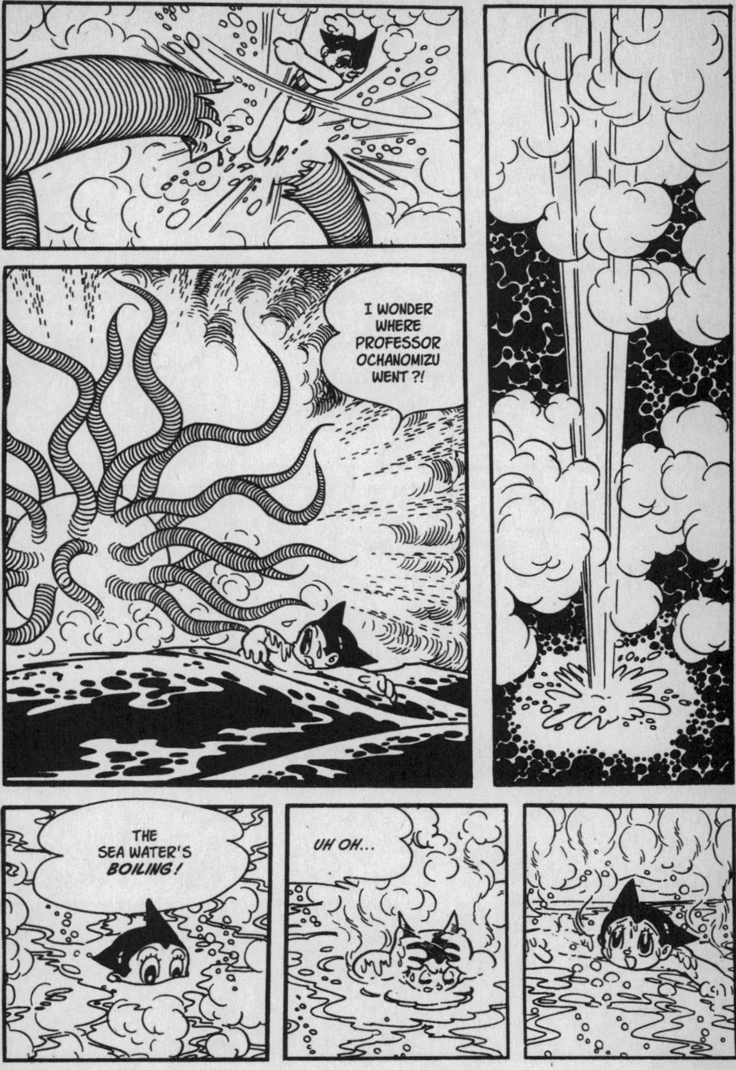
I WONDER WHERE PROFESSOR OCHANOMIZU WENT ?!
THE SEA WATER'S *BOILING !*
UH OH...

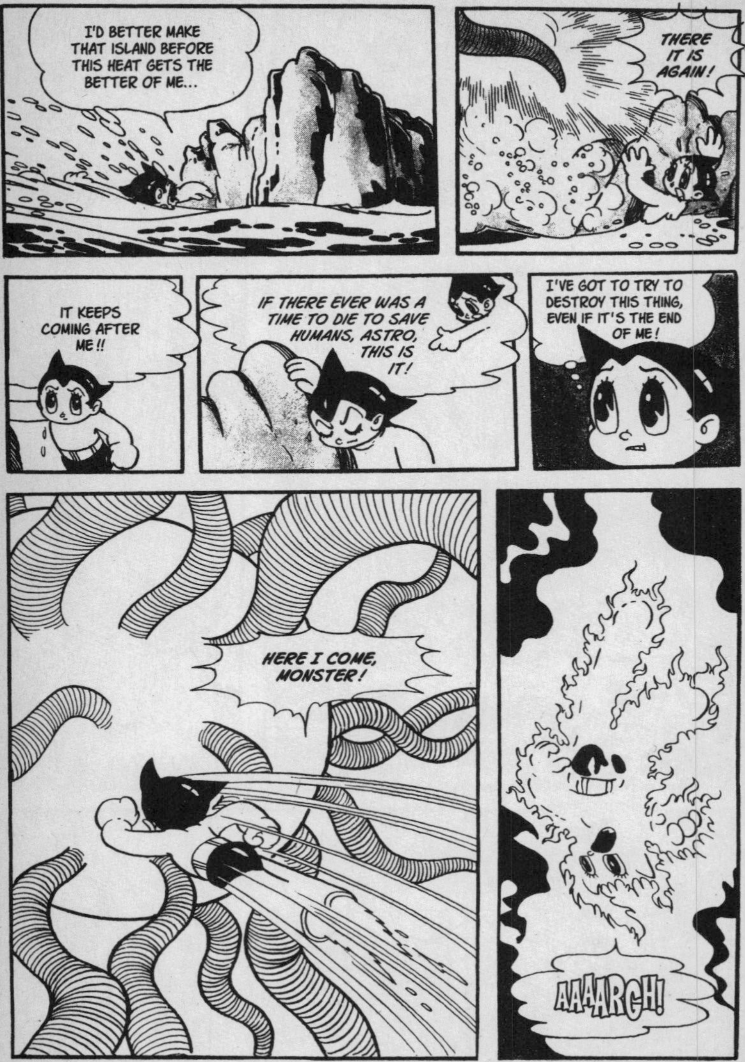
I'D BETTER MAKE THAT ISLAND BEFORE THIS HEAT GETS THE BETTER OF ME...
THERE IT IS AGAIN!
IT KEEPS COMING AFTER ME!!
IF THERE EVER WAS A TIME TO DIE TO SAVE HUMANS, ASTRO, THIS IS IT!
I'VE GOT TO TRY TO DESTROY THIS THING, EVEN IF IT'S THE END OF ME!
HERE I COME, MONSTER!
AAAARGH!

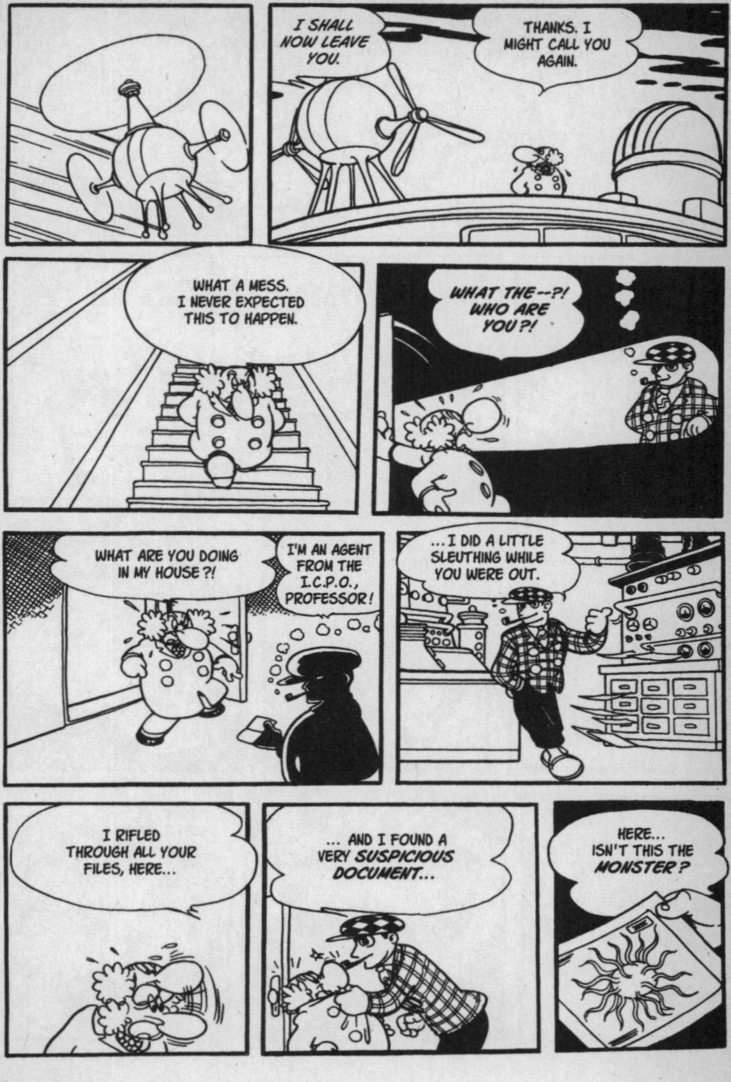
I SHALL NOW LEAVE YOU.
THANKS. I MIGHT CALL YOU AGAIN.
WHAT A MESS. I NEVER EXPECTED THIS TO HAPPEN.
WHAT THE--?! WHO ARE YOU?!
WHAT ARE YOU DOING IN MY HOUSE?!
I'M AN AGENT FROM THE I.C.P.O., PROFESSOR!
...I DID A LITTLE SLEUTHING WHILE YOU WERE OUT.
I RIFLED THROUGH ALL YOUR FILES, HERE...
... AND I FOUND A VERY SUSPICIOUS DOCUMENT...
HERE... ISN'T THIS THE MONSTER?

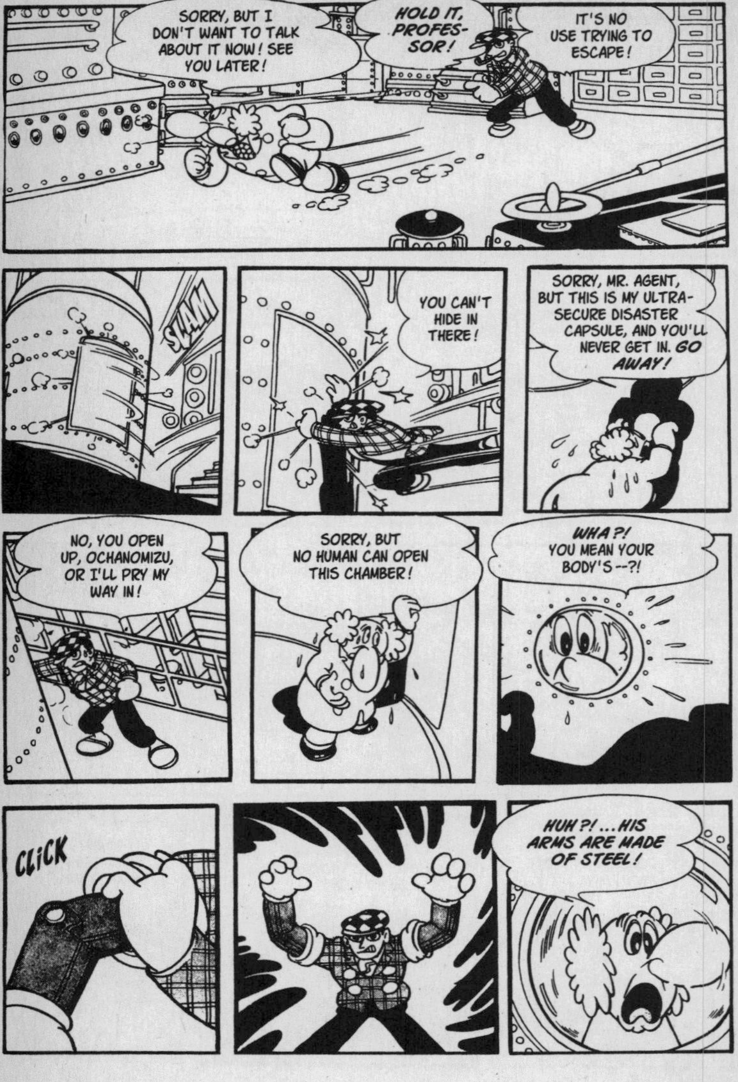
SORRY, BUT I DON'T WANT TO TALK ABOUT IT NOW! SEE YOU LATER!
HOLD IT, PROFES-SOR!
IT'S NO USE TRYING TO ESCAPE!
SLAM
YOU CAN'T HIDE IN THERE!
SORRY, MR. AGENT, BUT THIS IS MY ULTRA-SECURE DISASTER CAPSULE, AND YOU'LL NEVER GET IN. GO AWAY!
NO, YOU OPEN UP, OCHANOMIZU, OR I'LL PRY MY WAY IN!
SORRY, BUT NO HUMAN CAN OPEN THIS CHAMBER!
WHA?! YOU MEAN YOUR BODY'S --?!
CLICK
HUH?! ...HIS ARMS ARE MADE OF STEEL!

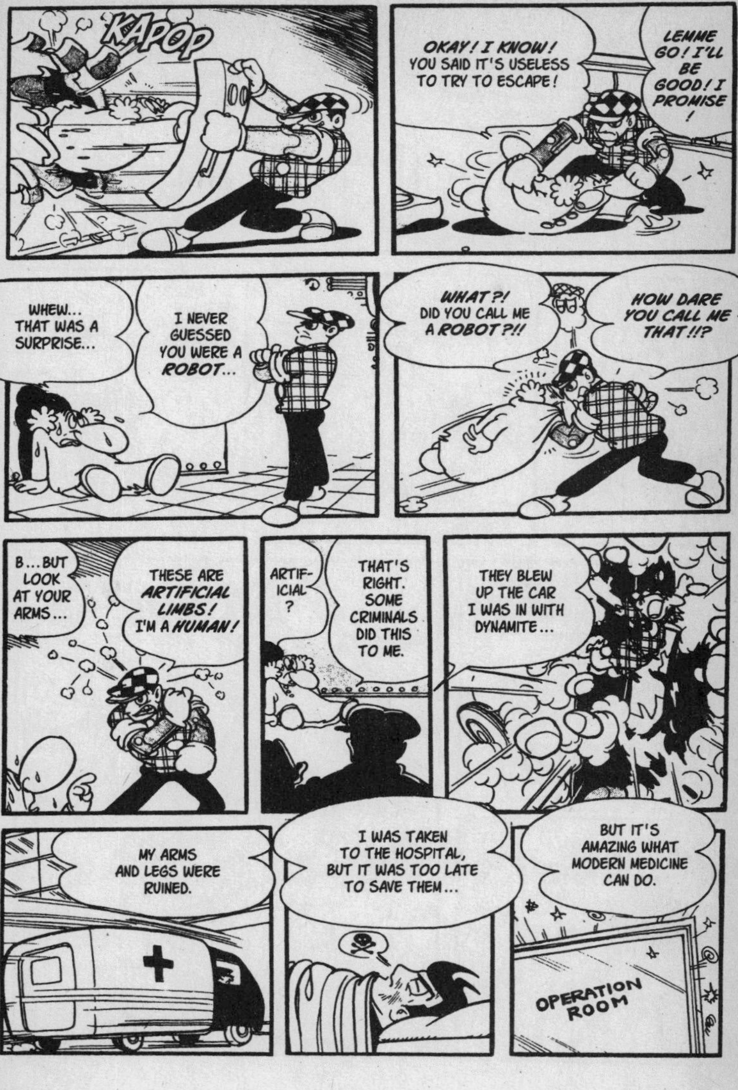
KAPOP
OKAY! I KNOW! YOU SAID IT'S USELESS TO TRY TO ESCAPE!
LEMME GO! I'LL BE GOOD! I PROMISE!
WHEW... THAT WAS A SURPRISE...
I NEVER GUESSED YOU WERE A ROBOT...
WHAT?! DID YOU CALL ME A ROBOT?!!
HOW DARE YOU CALL ME THAT!!?
B... BUT LOOK AT YOUR ARMS...
THESE ARE ARTIFICIAL LIMBS! I'M A HUMAN!
ARTIFICIAL?
THAT'S RIGHT. SOME CRIMINALS DID THIS TO ME.
THEY BLEW UP THE CAR I WAS IN WITH DYNAMITE...
MY ARMS AND LEGS WERE RUINED.
I WAS TAKEN TO THE HOSPITAL, BUT IT WAS TOO LATE TO SAVE THEM...
BUT IT'S AMAZING WHAT MODERN MEDICINE CAN DO.
OPERATION ROOM

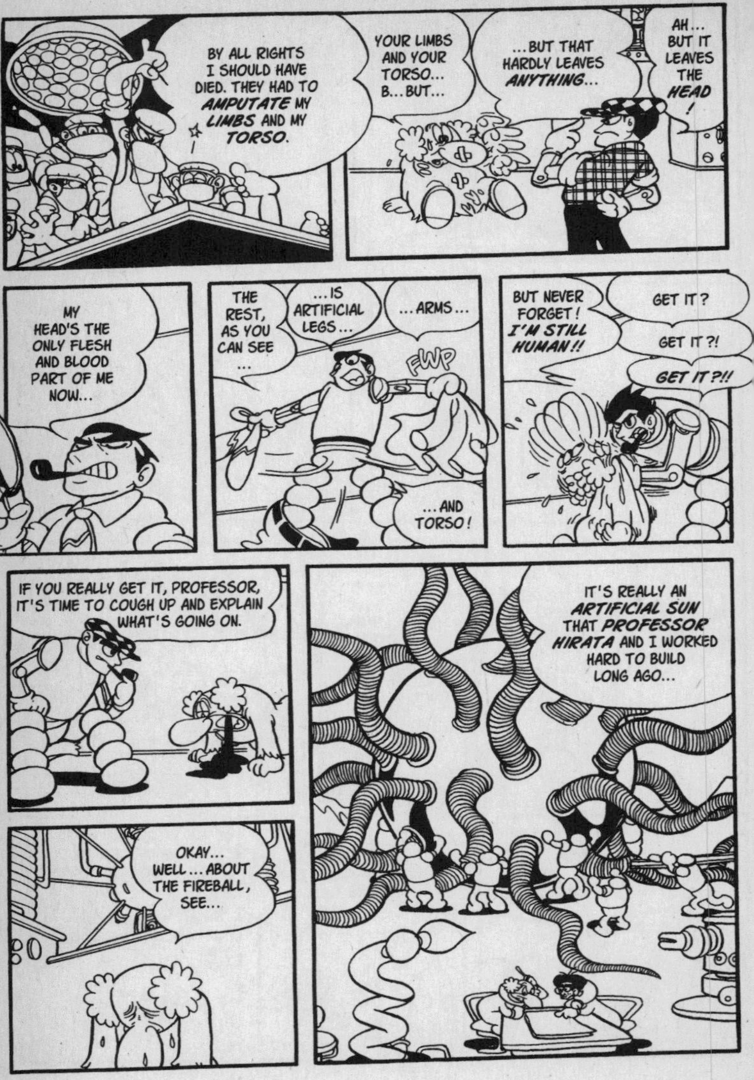
BY ALL RIGHTS I SHOULD HAVE DIED. THEY HAD TO AMPUTATE MY LIMBS AND MY TORSO.
YOUR LIMBS AND YOUR TORSO... B...BUT...
...BUT THAT HARDLY LEAVES ANYTHING...
AH... BUT IT LEAVES THE HEAD!
MY HEAD'S THE ONLY FLESH AND BLOOD PART OF ME NOW...
THE REST, AS YOU CAN SEE ...
...IS ARTIFICIAL LEGS...
...ARMS...
FWP
...AND TORSO!
BUT NEVER FORGET! I'M STILL HUMAN!!
GET IT?
GET IT?!
GET IT?!!
IF YOU REALLY GET IT, PROFESSOR, IT'S TIME TO COUGH UP AND EXPLAIN WHAT'S GOING ON.
OKAY... WELL... ABOUT THE FIREBALL, SEE...
IT'S REALLY AN ARTIFICIAL SUN THAT PROFESSOR HIRATA AND I WORKED HARD TO BUILD LONG AGO...

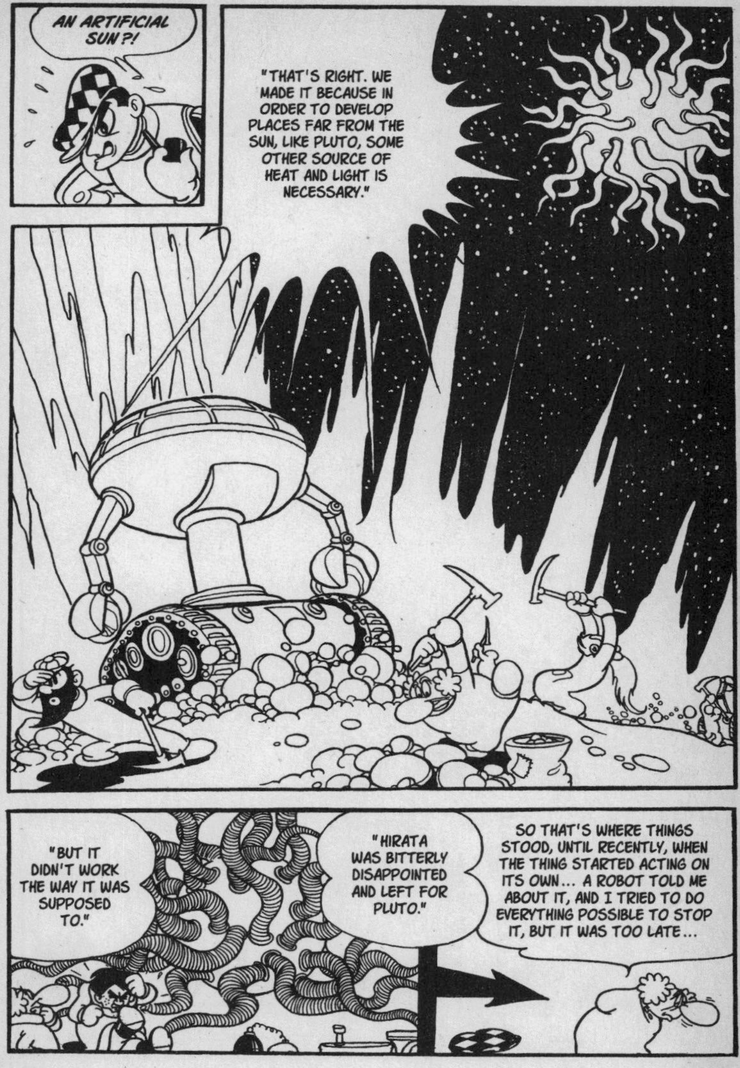
AN ARTIFICIAL SUN?!
"THAT'S RIGHT. WE MADE IT BECAUSE IN ORDER TO DEVELOP PLACES FAR FROM THE SUN, LIKE PLUTO, SOME OTHER SOURCE OF HEAT AND LIGHT IS NECESSARY."
"BUT IT DIDN'T WORK THE WAY IT WAS SUPPOSED TO."
"HIRATA WAS BITTERLY DISAPPOINTED AND LEFT FOR PLUTO."
SO THAT'S WHERE THINGS STOOD, UNTIL RECENTLY, WHEN THE THING STARTED ACTING ON ITS OWN... A ROBOT TOLD ME ABOUT IT, AND I TRIED TO DO EVERYTHING POSSIBLE TO STOP IT, BUT IT WAS TOO LATE...

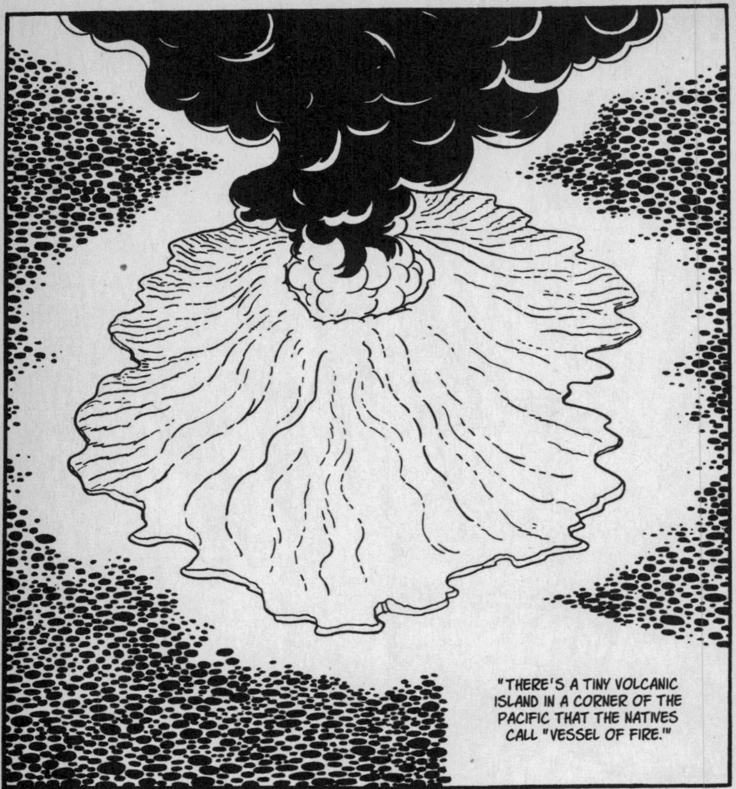
"THERE'S A TINY VOLCANIC ISLAND IN A CORNER OF THE PACIFIC THAT THE NATIVES CALL "VESSEL OF FIRE.'"

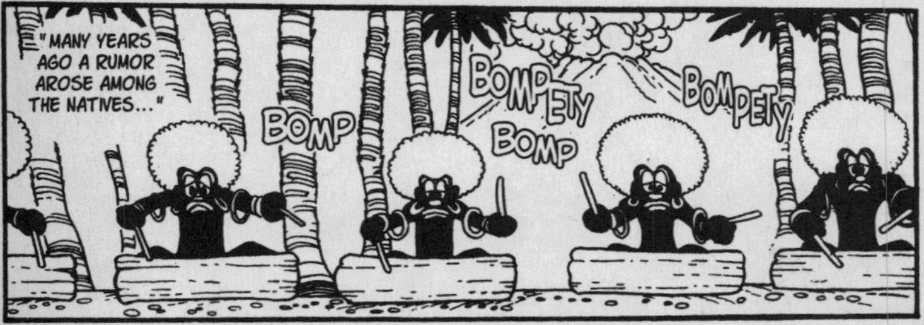
"MANY YEARS AGO A RUMOR AROSE AMONG THE NATIVES..."
BOMP
BOMPETY
BOMP
BOMPETY

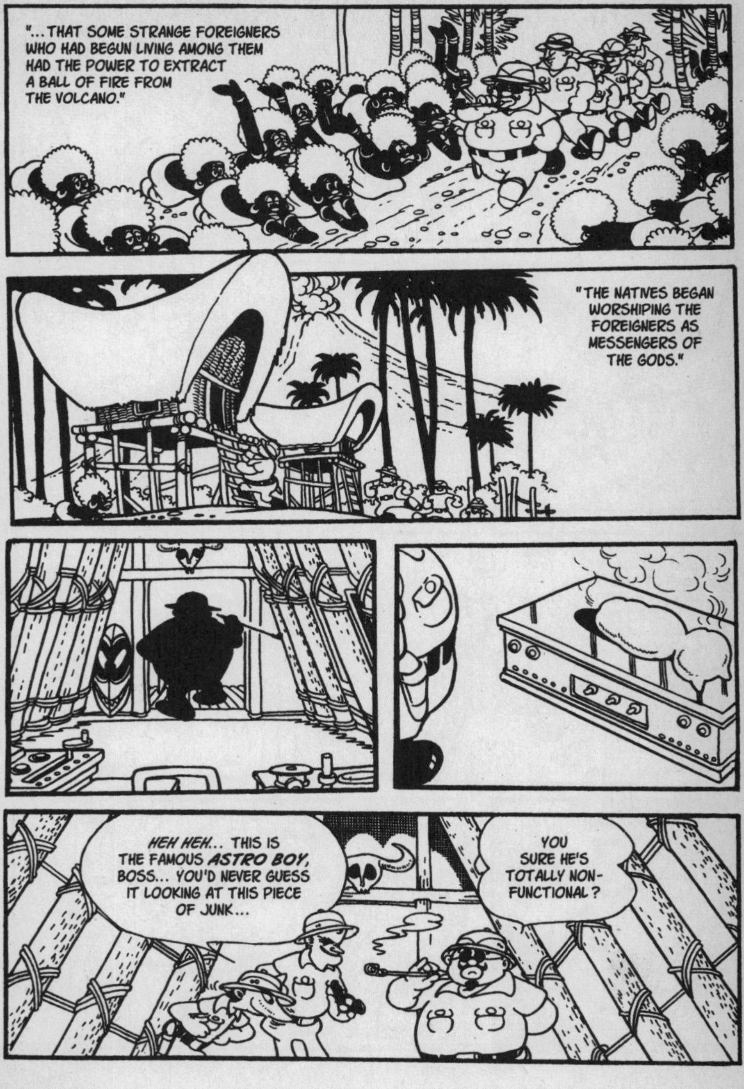
"...THAT SOME STRANGE FOREIGNERS WHO HAD BEGUN LIVING AMONG THEM HAD THE POWER TO EXTRACT A BALL OF FIRE FROM THE VOLCANO."
"THE NATIVES BEGAN WORSHIPING THE FOREIGNERS AS MESSENGERS OF THE GODS."
HEH HEH... THIS IS THE FAMOUS ***ASTRO BOY,*** BOSS... YOU'D NEVER GUESS IT LOOKING AT THIS PIECE OF JUNK...
YOU SURE HE'S TOTALLY NON-FUNCTIONAL?

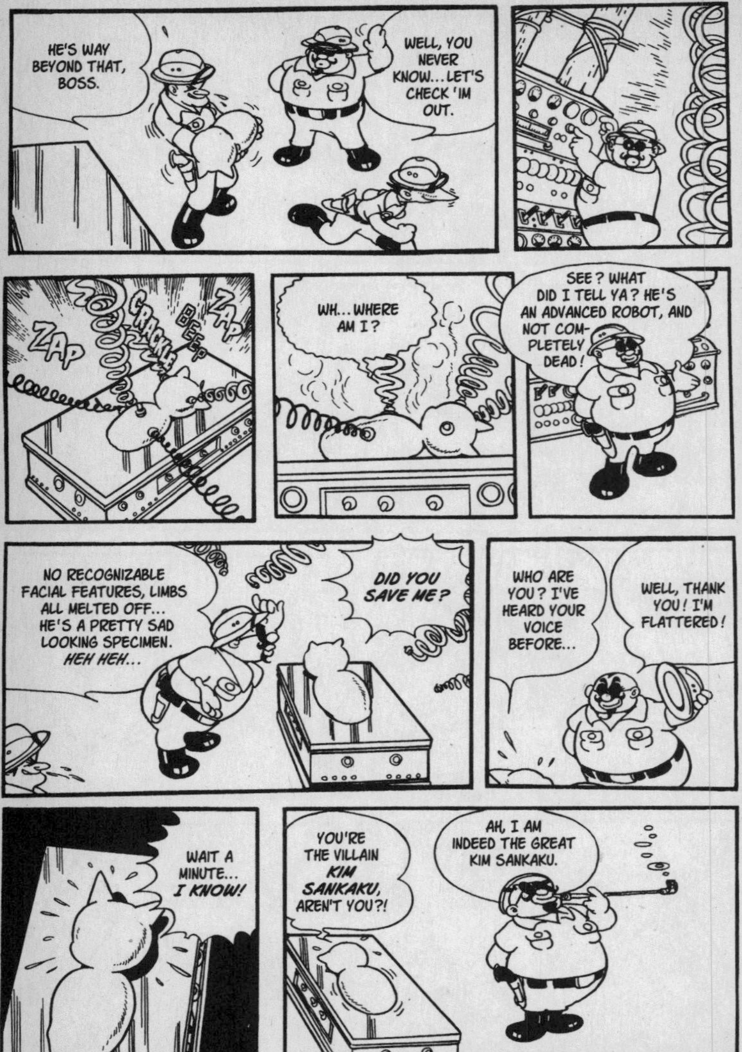
HE'S WAY BEYOND THAT, BOSS.
WELL, YOU NEVER KNOW...LET'S CHECK 'IM OUT.
ZAP
CRACKLE
BEEP
ZAP
WH...WHERE AM I?
SEE? WHAT DID I TELL YA? HE'S AN ADVANCED ROBOT, AND NOT COMPLETELY DEAD!
NO RECOGNIZABLE FACIAL FEATURES, LIMBS ALL MELTED OFF... HE'S A PRETTY SAD LOOKING SPECIMEN. *HEH HEH...*
DID YOU SAVE ME?
WHO ARE YOU? I'VE HEARD YOUR VOICE BEFORE...
WELL, THANK YOU! I'M FLATTERED!
WAIT A MINUTE... *I KNOW!*
YOU'RE THE VILLAIN *KIM SANKAKU*, AREN'T YOU?!
AH, I AM INDEED THE GREAT KIM SANKAKU.

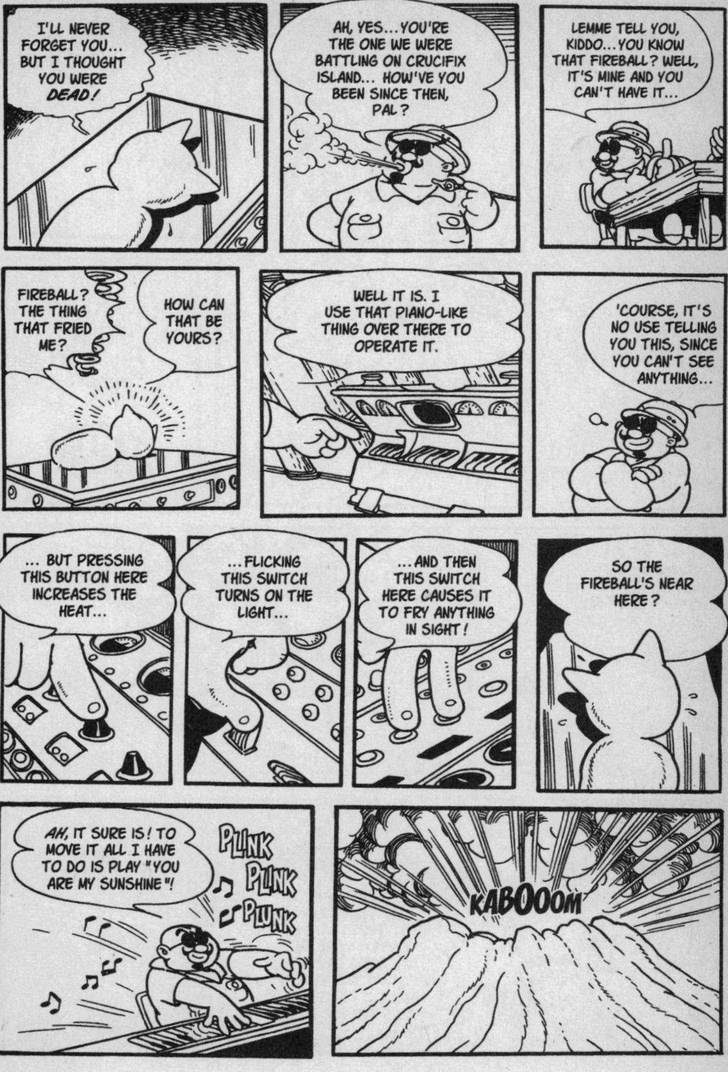
I'LL NEVER FORGET YOU... BUT I THOUGHT YOU WERE DEAD!
AH, YES...YOU'RE THE ONE WE WERE BATTLING ON CRUCIFIX ISLAND... HOW'VE YOU BEEN SINCE THEN, PAL?
LEMME TELL YOU, KIDDO...YOU KNOW THAT FIREBALL? WELL, IT'S MINE AND YOU CAN'T HAVE IT...
FIREBALL? THE THING THAT FRIED ME?
HOW CAN THAT BE YOURS?
WELL IT IS. I USE THAT PIANO-LIKE THING OVER THERE TO OPERATE IT.
'COURSE, IT'S NO USE TELLING YOU THIS, SINCE YOU CAN'T SEE ANYTHING...
... BUT PRESSING THIS BUTTON HERE INCREASES THE HEAT...
...FLICKING THIS SWITCH TURNS ON THE LIGHT...
...AND THEN THIS SWITCH HERE CAUSES IT TO FRY ANYTHING IN SIGHT!
SO THE FIREBALL'S NEAR HERE?
AH, IT SURE IS! TO MOVE IT ALL I HAVE TO DO IS PLAY "YOU ARE MY SUNSHINE"!
PLINK
PLINK
PLUNK
KABOOOM

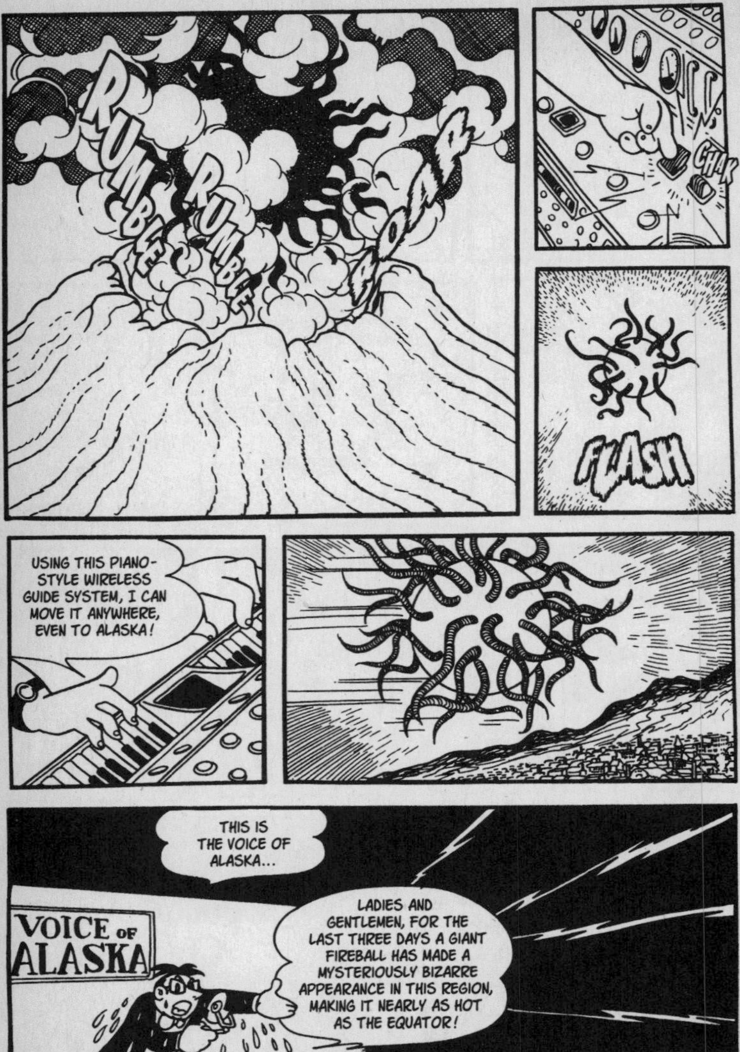
RUMBLE
RUMBLE
POP
CHAK
FLASH
USING THIS PIANO-STYLE WIRELESS GUIDE SYSTEM, I CAN MOVE IT ANYWHERE, EVEN TO ALASKA!
THIS IS THE VOICE OF ALASKA...
VOICE OF ALASKA
LADIES AND GENTLEMEN, FOR THE LAST THREE DAYS A GIANT FIREBALL HAS MADE A MYSTERIOUSLY BIZARRE APPEARANCE IN THIS REGION, MAKING IT NEARLY AS HOT AS THE EQUATOR!

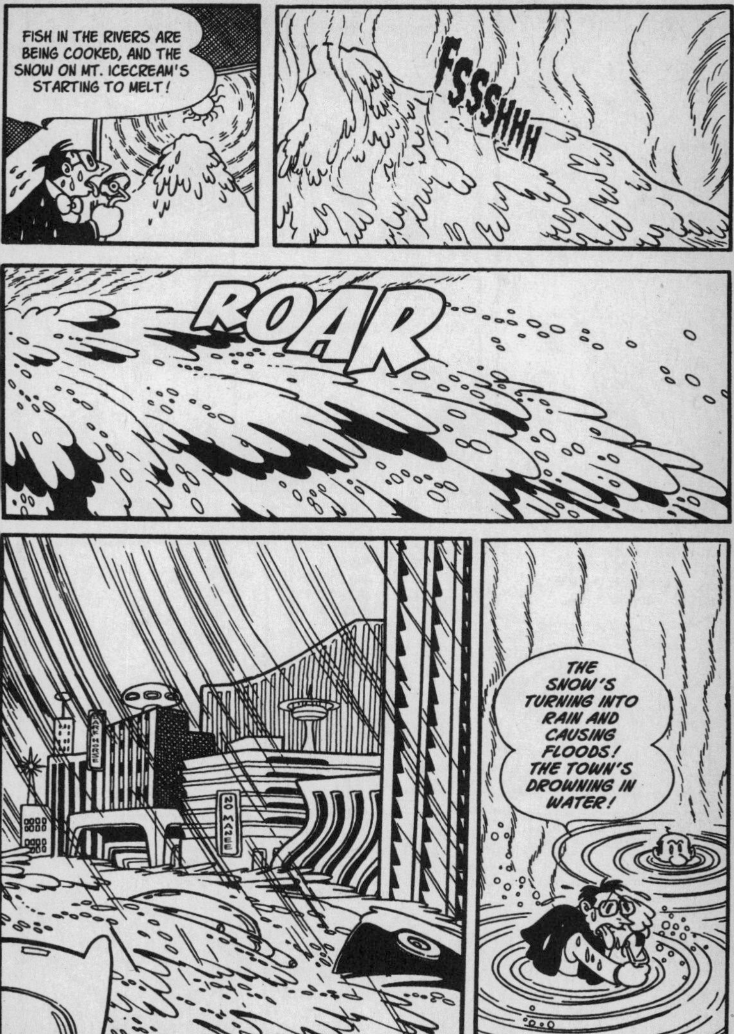
FISH IN THE RIVERS ARE BEING COOKED, AND THE SNOW ON MT. ICECREAM'S STARTING TO MELT!
FSSSHHH
ROAR
NO MANEE
THE SNOW'S TURNING INTO RAIN AND CAUSING FLOODS! THE TOWN'S DROWNING IN WATER!

RECONNAISSANCE PLANES TRYING TO APPROACH THE BURNING ORB SIMPLY MELT...

SCIENTISTS ARE PUTTING THEIR QUIRKY HEADS TOGETHER AND TRYING TO FIGURE THIS OUT...

...BUT EACH SCIENTIST THINKS EVERYONE ELSE IS UNQUALIFIED, SO NOBODY CAN AGREE ON ANYTHING.

WELL, HERE'S AN ODD-LOOKING FELLOW WHO'S JUST SHOWED UP AT THE CONFERENCE HALL.

DO ME A FAVOR AND GIVE THIS TO THE SCIENTISTS...

I'LL BE WAITING FOR THEIR ANSWER... *HEH HEH HEH...*

HE WAS AWFULLY STRANGE, AND DISAPPEARED IMMEDIATELY AFTER HANDING ME THE LETTER.

WHAT THE --?!

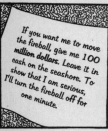

If you want me to move the fireball, give me 100 million dollars. Leave it in cash on the seashore. To show that I am serious, I'll turn the fireball off for one minute.

I'D SAY ANYONE WHO'D WRITE A LETTER LIKE THIS...

...HAS GOT TO BE SOME STUPID *PRANKSTER!*

WAIT!! LOOK AT THAT!!

180

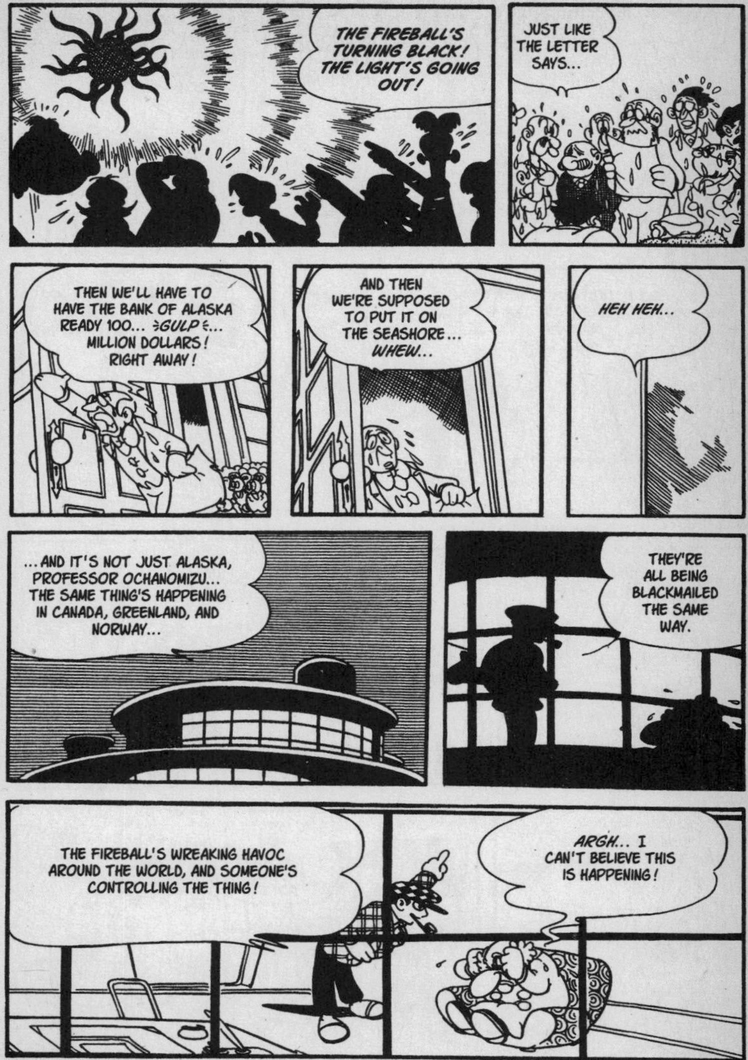
THE FIREBALL'S TURNING BLACK! THE LIGHT'S GOING OUT!
JUST LIKE THE LETTER SAYS...
THEN WE'LL HAVE TO HAVE THE BANK OF ALASKA READY 100... *GULP*... MILLION DOLLARS! RIGHT AWAY!
AND THEN WE'RE SUPPOSED TO PUT IT ON THE SEASHORE... *WHEW*...
HEH HEH...
...AND IT'S NOT JUST ALASKA, PROFESSOR OCHANOMIZU... THE SAME THING'S HAPPENING IN CANADA, GREENLAND, AND NORWAY...
THEY'RE ALL BEING BLACKMAILED THE SAME WAY.
THE FIREBALL'S WREAKING HAVOC AROUND THE WORLD, AND SOMEONE'S CONTROLLING THE THING!
ARGH... I CAN'T BELIEVE THIS IS HAPPENING!

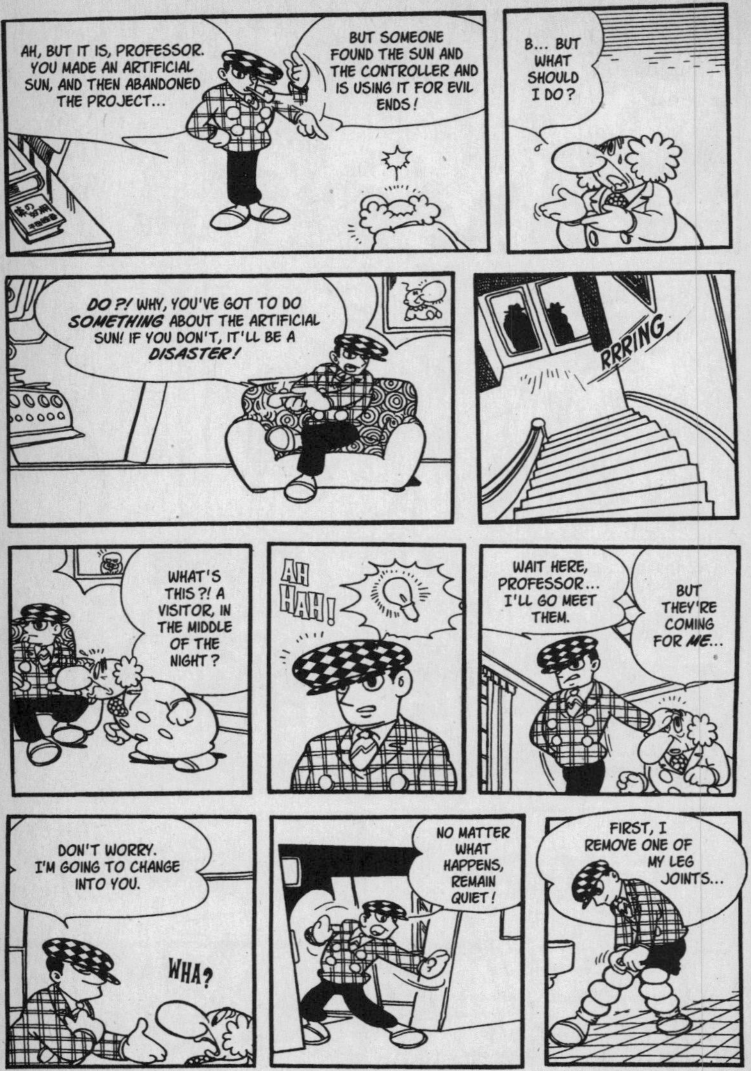
AH, BUT IT IS, PROFESSOR. YOU MADE AN ARTIFICIAL SUN, AND THEN ABANDONED THE PROJECT...
BUT SOMEONE FOUND THE SUN AND THE CONTROLLER AND IS USING IT FOR EVIL ENDS!
B... BUT WHAT SHOULD I DO?
DO?! WHY, YOU'VE GOT TO DO SOMETHING ABOUT THE ARTIFICIAL SUN! IF YOU DON'T, IT'LL BE A DISASTER!
RRRING
WHAT'S THIS?! A VISITOR, IN THE MIDDLE OF THE NIGHT?
AH HAH!
WAIT HERE, PROFESSOR... I'LL GO MEET THEM.
BUT THEY'RE COMING FOR ME...
DON'T WORRY. I'M GOING TO CHANGE INTO YOU.
WHA?
NO MATTER WHAT HAPPENS, REMAIN QUIET!
FIRST, I REMOVE ONE OF MY LEG JOINTS...

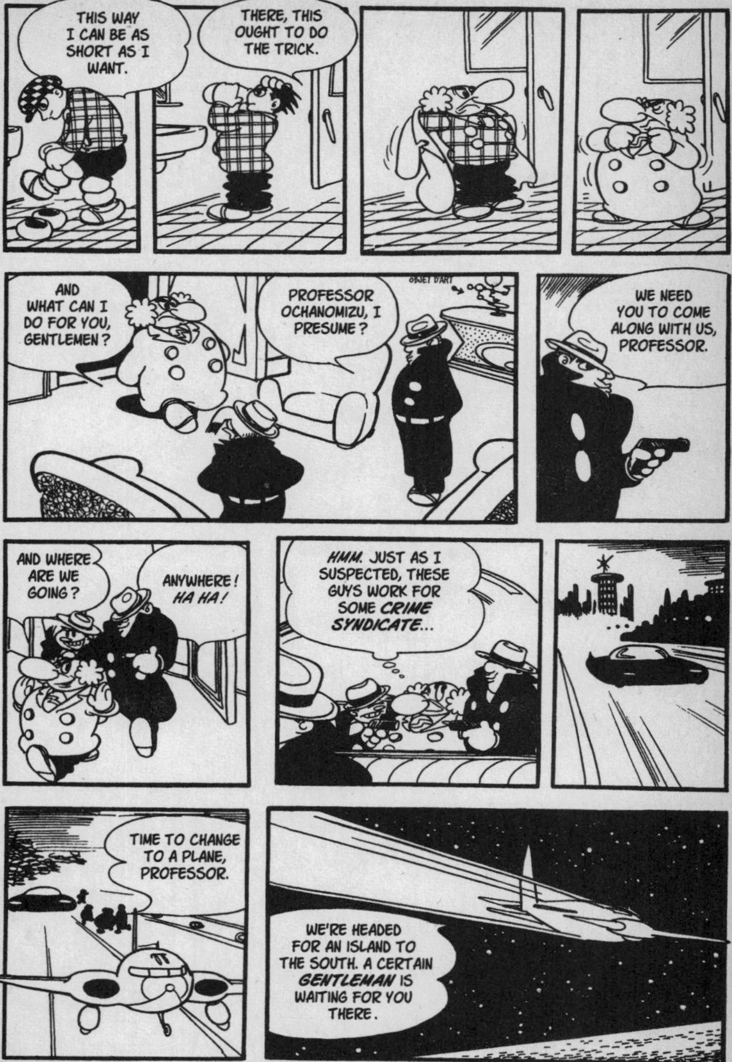
THIS WAY I CAN BE AS SHORT AS I WANT.
THERE, THIS OUGHT TO DO THE TRICK.
AND WHAT CAN I DO FOR YOU, GENTLEMEN?
PROFESSOR OCHANOMIZU, I PRESUME?
OBJET D'ART
WE NEED YOU TO COME ALONG WITH US, PROFESSOR.
AND WHERE ARE WE GOING?
ANYWHERE! *HA HA!*
HMM. JUST AS I SUSPECTED, THESE GUYS WORK FOR SOME *CRIME SYNDICATE*...
TIME TO CHANGE TO A PLANE, PROFESSOR.
WE'RE HEADED FOR AN ISLAND TO THE SOUTH. A CERTAIN *GENTLEMAN* IS WAITING FOR YOU THERE.

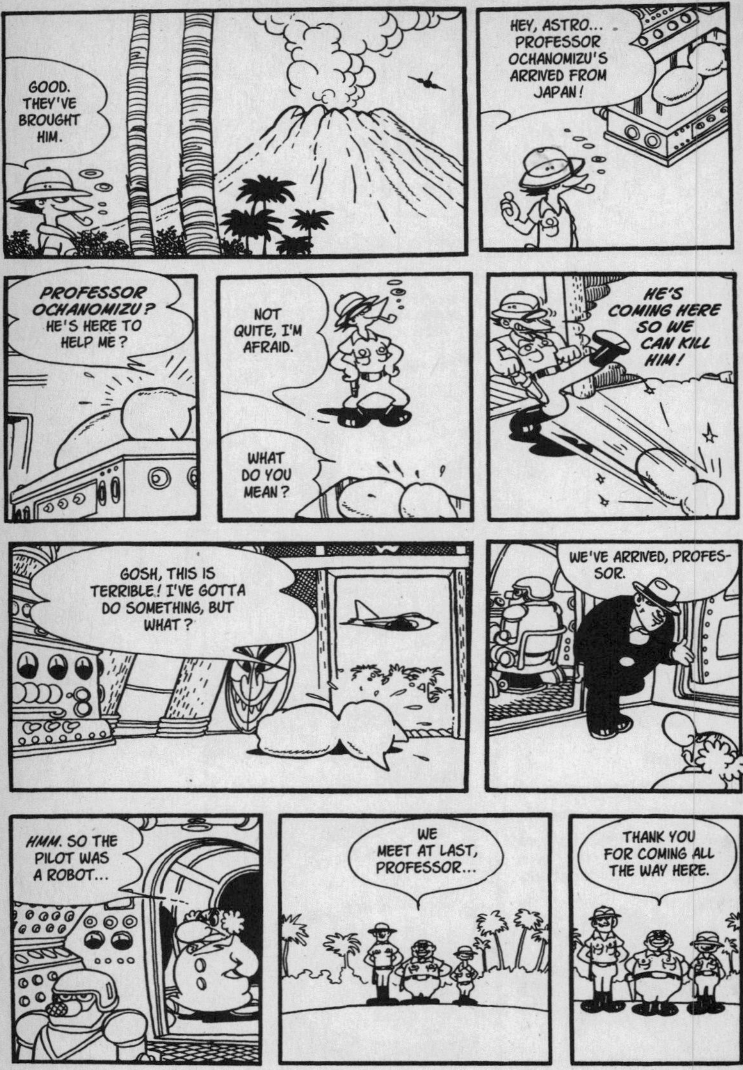
GOOD. THEY'VE BROUGHT HIM.
HEY, ASTRO... PROFESSOR OCHANOMIZU'S ARRIVED FROM JAPAN!
PROFESSOR OCHANOMIZU? HE'S HERE TO HELP ME?
NOT QUITE, I'M AFRAID.
WHAT DO YOU MEAN?
HE'S COMING HERE SO WE CAN KILL HIM!
GOSH, THIS IS TERRIBLE! I'VE GOTTA DO SOMETHING, BUT WHAT?
WE'VE ARRIVED, PROFES-SOR.
HMM. SO THE PILOT WAS A ROBOT...
WE MEET AT LAST, PROFESSOR...
THANK YOU FOR COMING ALL THE WAY HERE.

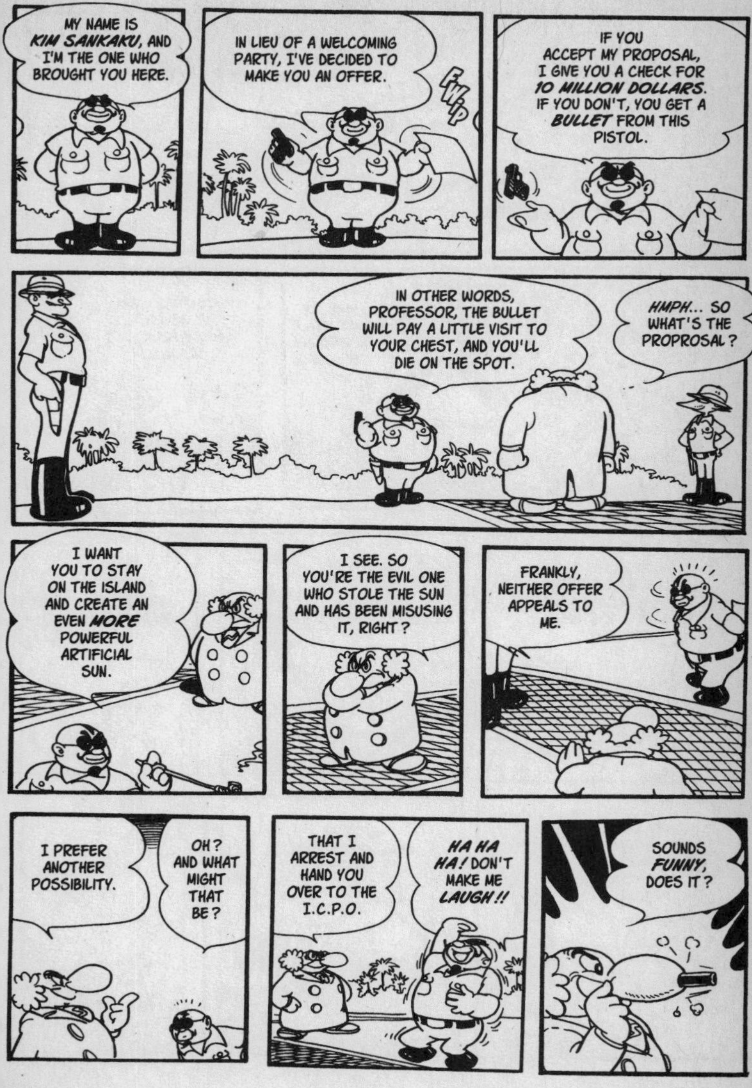

MY NAME IS KIM SANKAKU, AND I'M THE ONE WHO BROUGHT YOU HERE.
IN LIEU OF A WELCOMING PARTY, I'VE DECIDED TO MAKE YOU AN OFFER.
FWIP
IF YOU ACCEPT MY PROPOSAL, I GIVE YOU A CHECK FOR 10 MILLION DOLLARS. IF YOU DON'T, YOU GET A BULLET FROM THIS PISTOL.
IN OTHER WORDS, PROFESSOR, THE BULLET WILL PAY A LITTLE VISIT TO YOUR CHEST, AND YOU'LL DIE ON THE SPOT.
HMPH... SO WHAT'S THE PROPROSAL?
I WANT YOU TO STAY ON THE ISLAND AND CREATE AN EVEN MORE POWERFUL ARTIFICIAL SUN.
I SEE. SO YOU'RE THE EVIL ONE WHO STOLE THE SUN AND HAS BEEN MISUSING IT, RIGHT?
FRANKLY, NEITHER OFFER APPEALS TO ME.
I PREFER ANOTHER POSSIBILITY.
OH? AND WHAT MIGHT THAT BE?
THAT I ARREST AND HAND YOU OVER TO THE I.C.P.O.
HA HA HA! DON'T MAKE ME LAUGH!!
SOUNDS FUNNY, DOES IT?

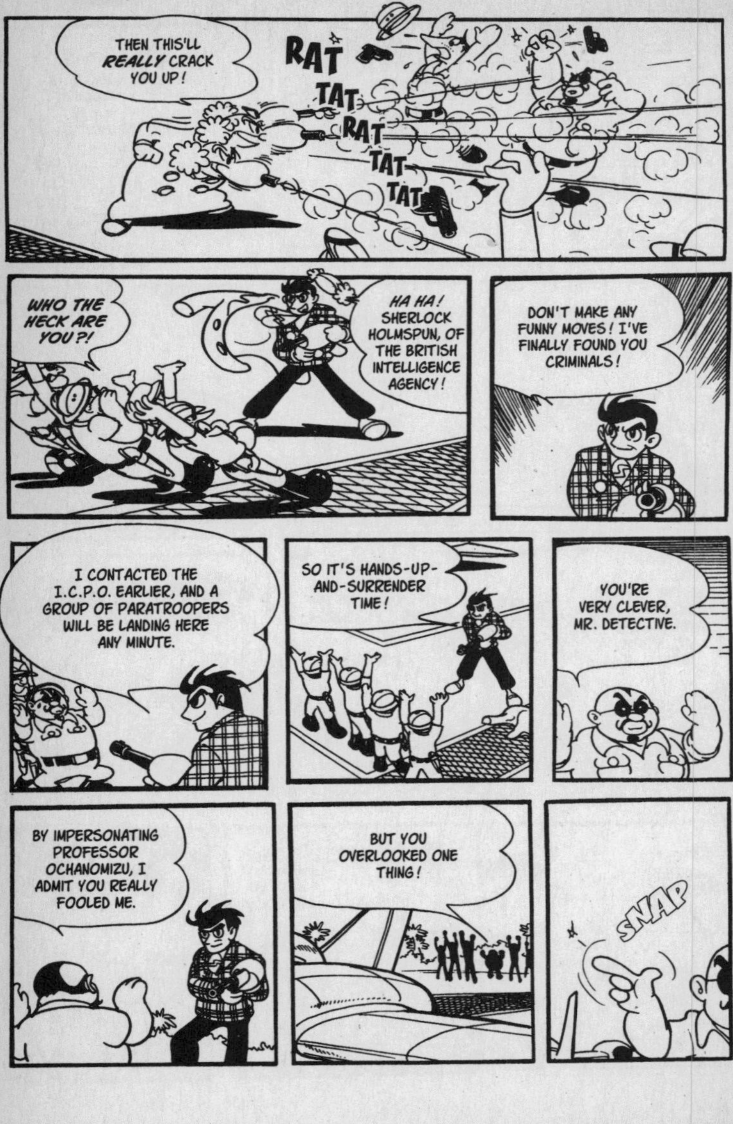

THEN THIS'LL *REALLY* CRACK YOU UP!
RAT TAT RAT TAT TAT
WHO THE HECK ARE YOU?!
HA HA! SHERLOCK HOLMSPUN, OF THE BRITISH INTELLIGENCE AGENCY!
DON'T MAKE ANY FUNNY MOVES! I'VE FINALLY FOUND YOU CRIMINALS!
I CONTACTED THE I.C.P.O. EARLIER, AND A GROUP OF PARATROOPERS WILL BE LANDING HERE ANY MINUTE.
SO IT'S HANDS-UP-AND-SURRENDER TIME!
YOU'RE VERY CLEVER, MR. DETECTIVE.
BY IMPERSONATING PROFESSOR OCHANOMIZU, I ADMIT YOU REALLY FOOLED ME.
BUT YOU OVERLOOKED ONE THING!
SNAP

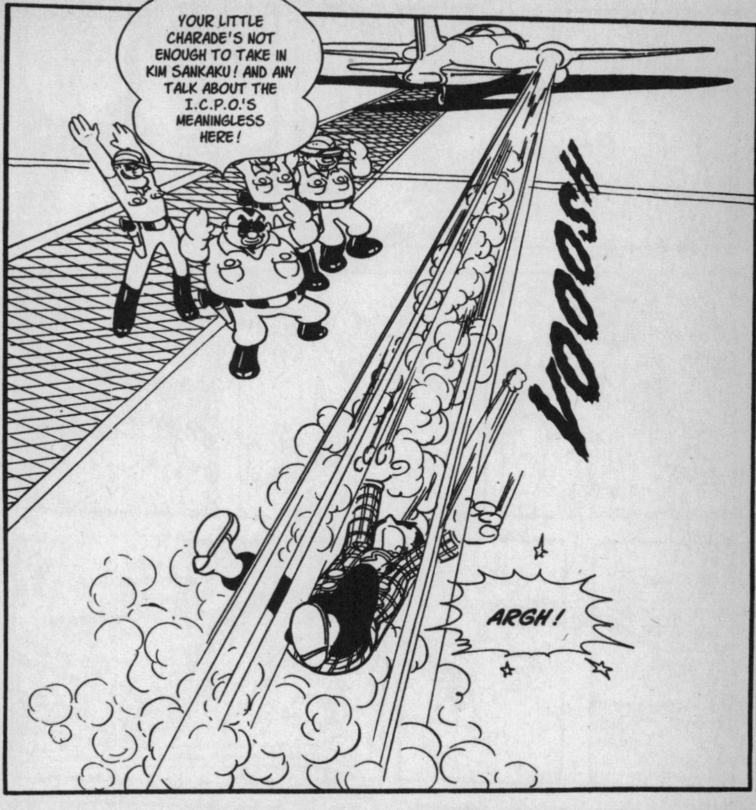
YOUR LITTLE CHARADE'S NOT ENOUGH TO TAKE IN KIM SANKAKU! AND ANY TALK ABOUT THE I.C.P.O.'S MEANINGLESS HERE!
VOOOSH
ARGH!

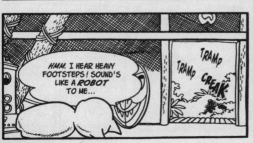

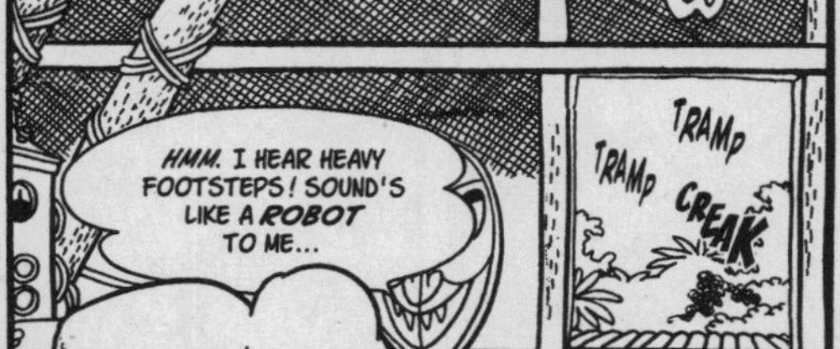
HMM. I HEAR HEAVY FOOTSTEPS! SOUND'S LIKE A *ROBOT* TO ME...
TRAMP
TRAMP
CREAK

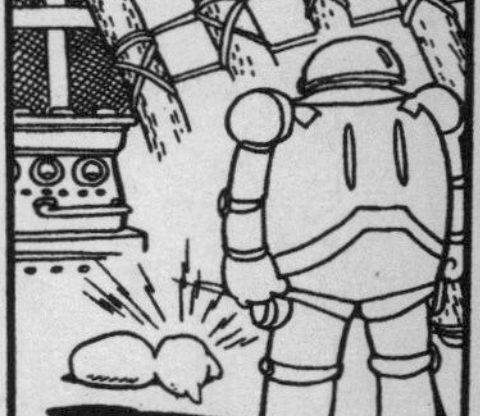

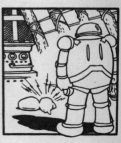

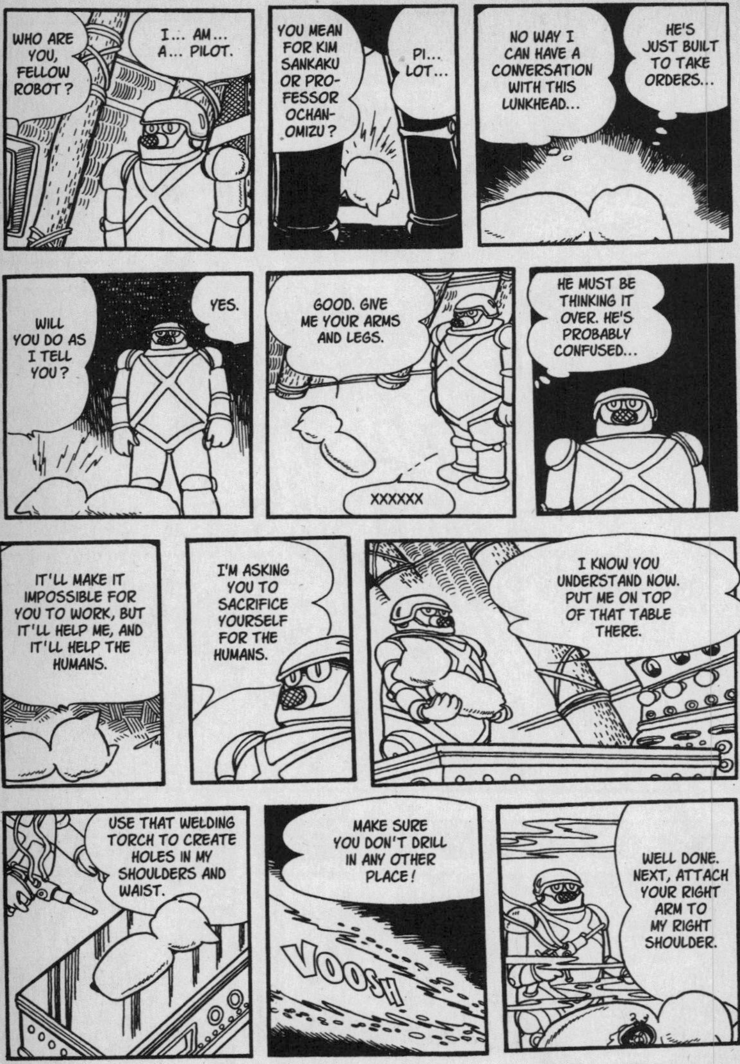

WHO ARE YOU, FELLOW ROBOT?
I... AM... A... PILOT.
YOU MEAN FOR KIM SANKAKU OR PRO-FESSOR OCHAN-OMIZU?
PI... LOT...
NO WAY I CAN HAVE A CONVERSATION WITH THIS LUNKHEAD...
HE'S JUST BUILT TO TAKE ORDERS...
WILL YOU DO AS I TELL YOU?
YES.
GOOD. GIVE ME YOUR ARMS AND LEGS.
XXXXXX
HE MUST BE THINKING IT OVER. HE'S PROBABLY CONFUSED...
IT'LL MAKE IT IMPOSSIBLE FOR YOU TO WORK, BUT IT'LL HELP ME, AND IT'LL HELP THE HUMANS.
I'M ASKING YOU TO SACRIFICE YOURSELF FOR THE HUMANS.
I KNOW YOU UNDERSTAND NOW. PUT ME ON TOP OF THAT TABLE THERE.
USE THAT WELDING TORCH TO CREATE HOLES IN MY SHOULDERS AND WAIST.
MAKE SURE YOU DON'T DRILL IN ANY OTHER PLACE!
VOOSH
WELL DONE. NEXT, ATTACH YOUR RIGHT ARM TO MY RIGHT SHOULDER.

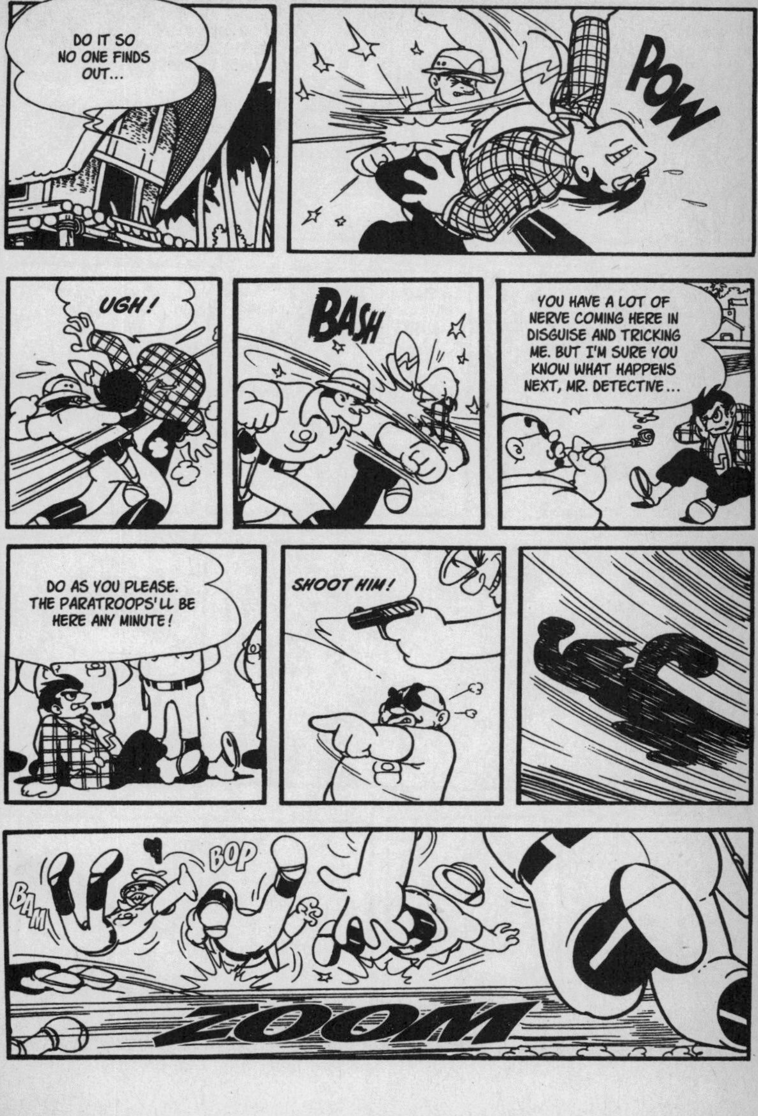
DO IT SO NO ONE FINDS OUT...
POW
UGH!
BASH
YOU HAVE A LOT OF NERVE COMING HERE IN DISGUISE AND TRICKING ME. BUT I'M SURE YOU KNOW WHAT HAPPENS NEXT, MR. DETECTIVE...
DO AS YOU PLEASE. THE PARATROOPS'LL BE HERE ANY MINUTE!
SHOOT HIM!
BAM
BOP
ZOOM

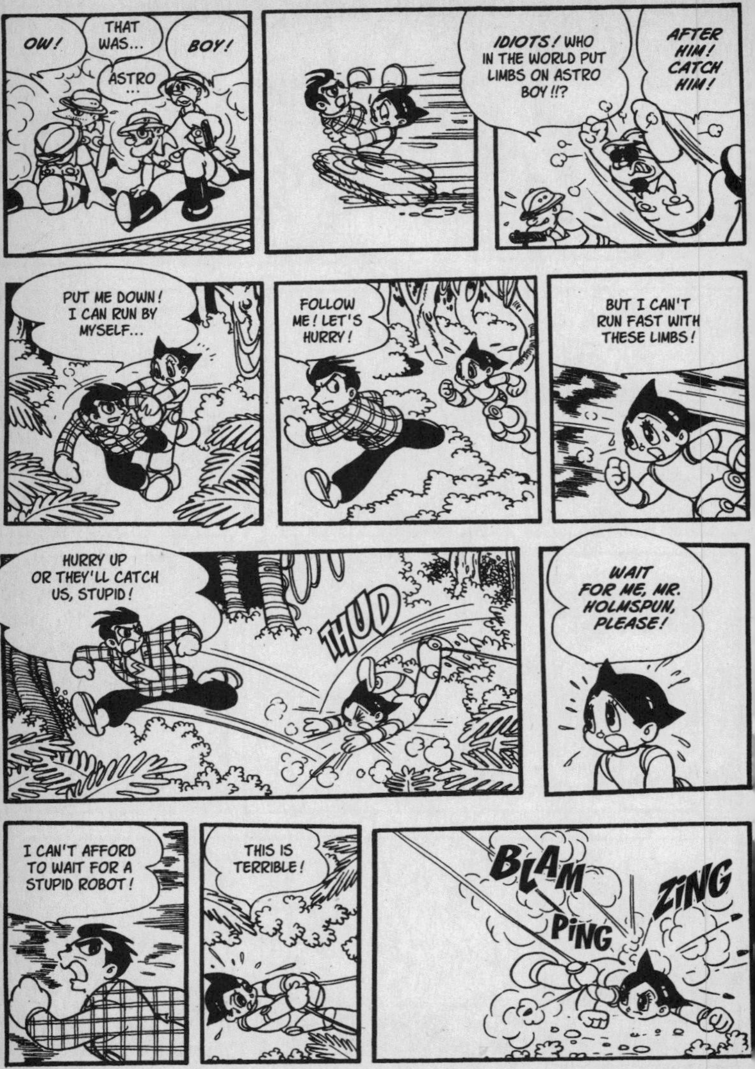
OW!
THAT WAS...
ASTRO ...
BOY!
IDIOTS! WHO IN THE WORLD PUT LIMBS ON ASTRO BOY!!?
AFTER HIM! CATCH HIM!
PUT ME DOWN! I CAN RUN BY MYSELF...
FOLLOW ME! LET'S HURRY!
BUT I CAN'T RUN FAST WITH THESE LIMBS!
HURRY UP OR THEY'LL CATCH US, STUPID!
THUD
WAIT FOR ME, MR. HOLMSPUN, PLEASE!
I CAN'T AFFORD TO WAIT FOR A STUPID ROBOT!
THIS IS TERRIBLE!
BLAM
PING
ZING

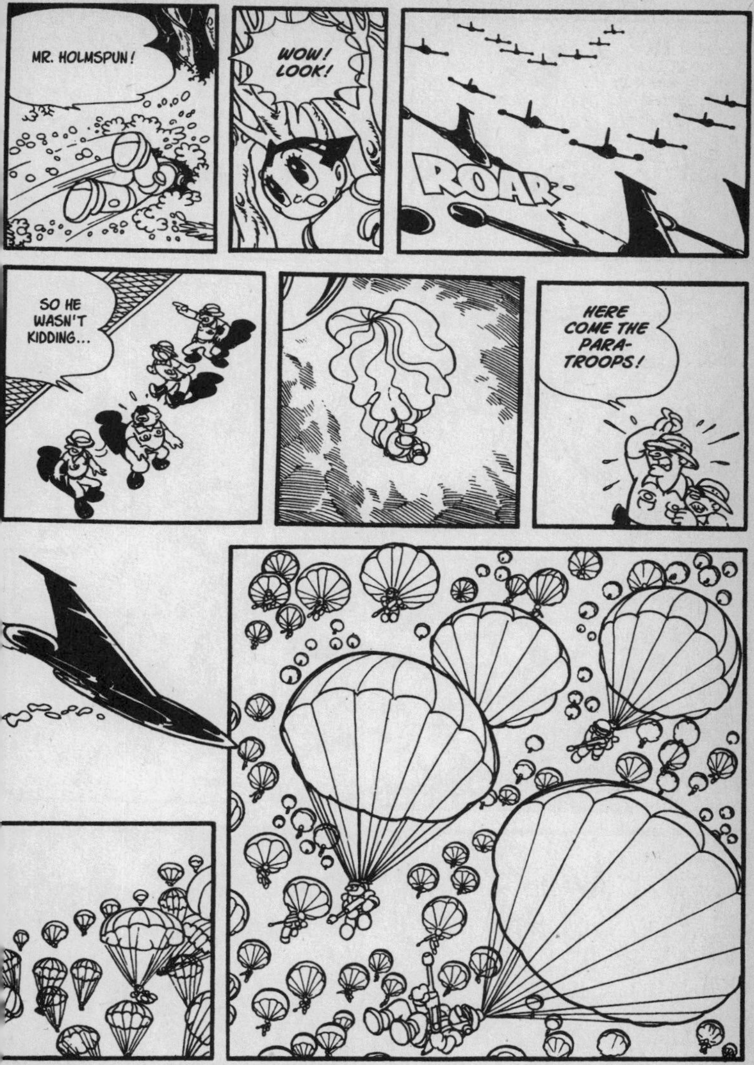
MR. HOLMSPUN!
WOW! LOOK!
ROAR
SO HE WASN'T KIDDING...
HERE COME THE PARA-TROOPS!

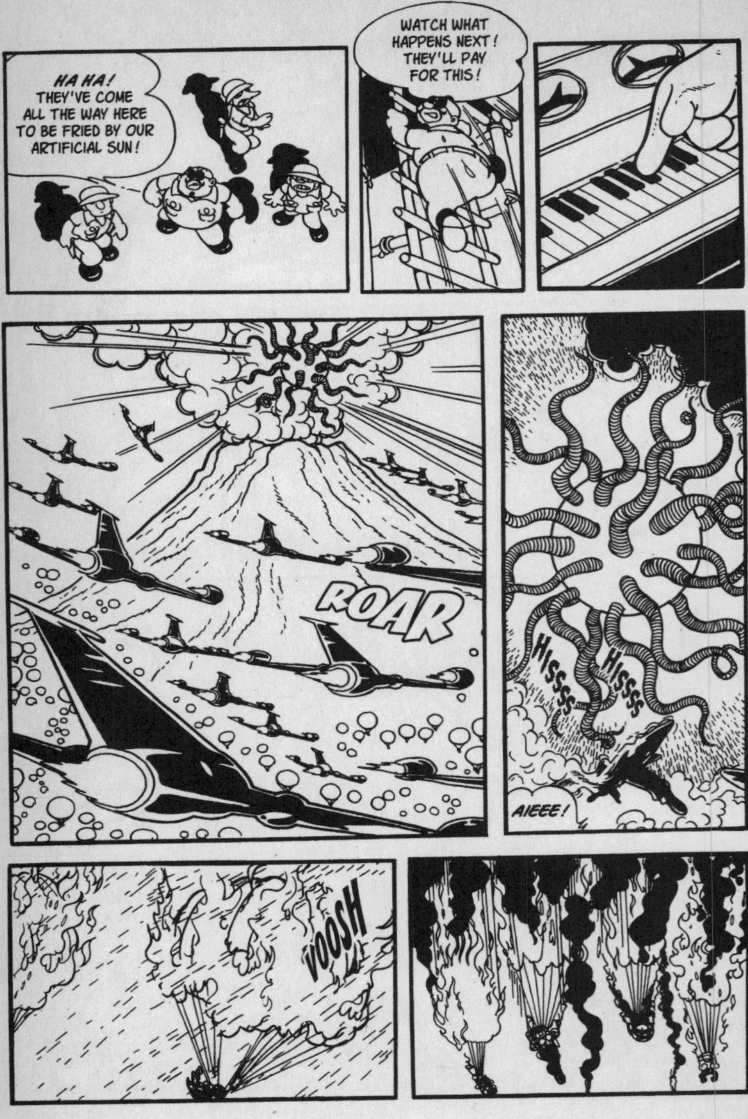
HA HA! THEY'VE COME ALL THE WAY HERE TO BE FRIED BY OUR ARTIFICIAL SUN!
WATCH WHAT HAPPENS NEXT! THEY'LL PAY FOR THIS!
ROAR
HISSSS
HISSSS
AIEEE!
VOOSH

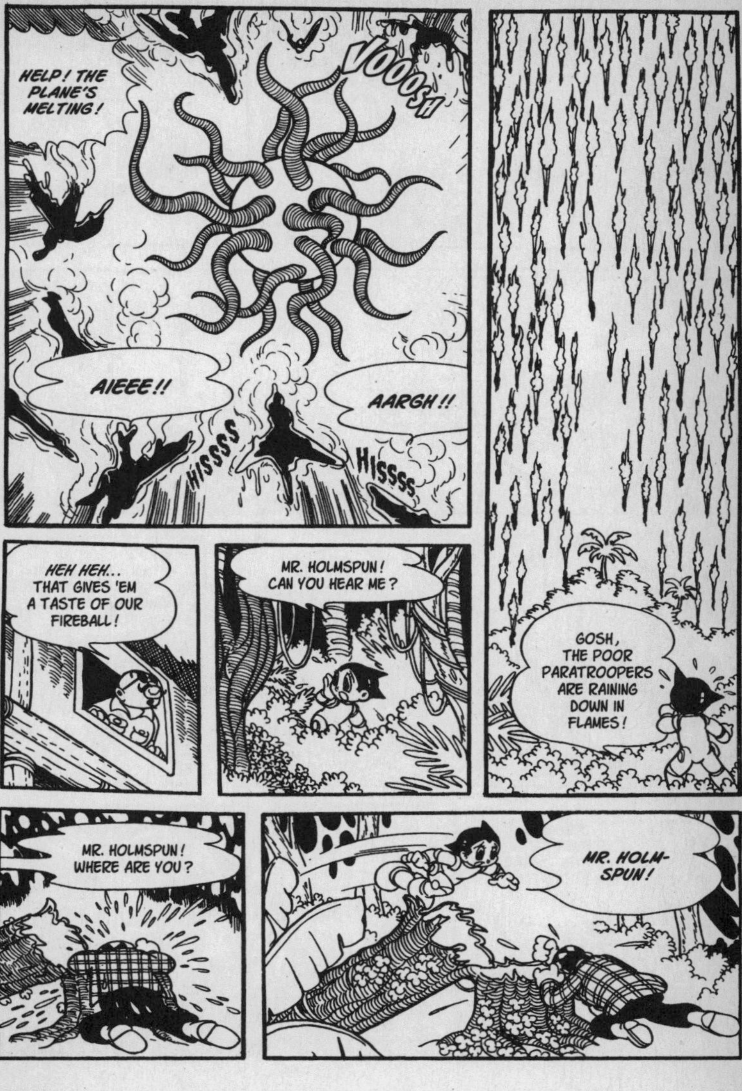
HELP! THE PLANE'S MELTING!
VOOOSH
AIEEE!!
AARGH!!
HISSSS
HISSSS
HEH HEH... THAT GIVES 'EM A TASTE OF OUR FIREBALL!
MR. HOLMSPUN! CAN YOU HEAR ME?
GOSH, THE POOR PARATROOPERS ARE RAINING DOWN IN FLAMES!
MR. HOLMSPUN! WHERE ARE YOU?
MR. HOLM-SPUN!

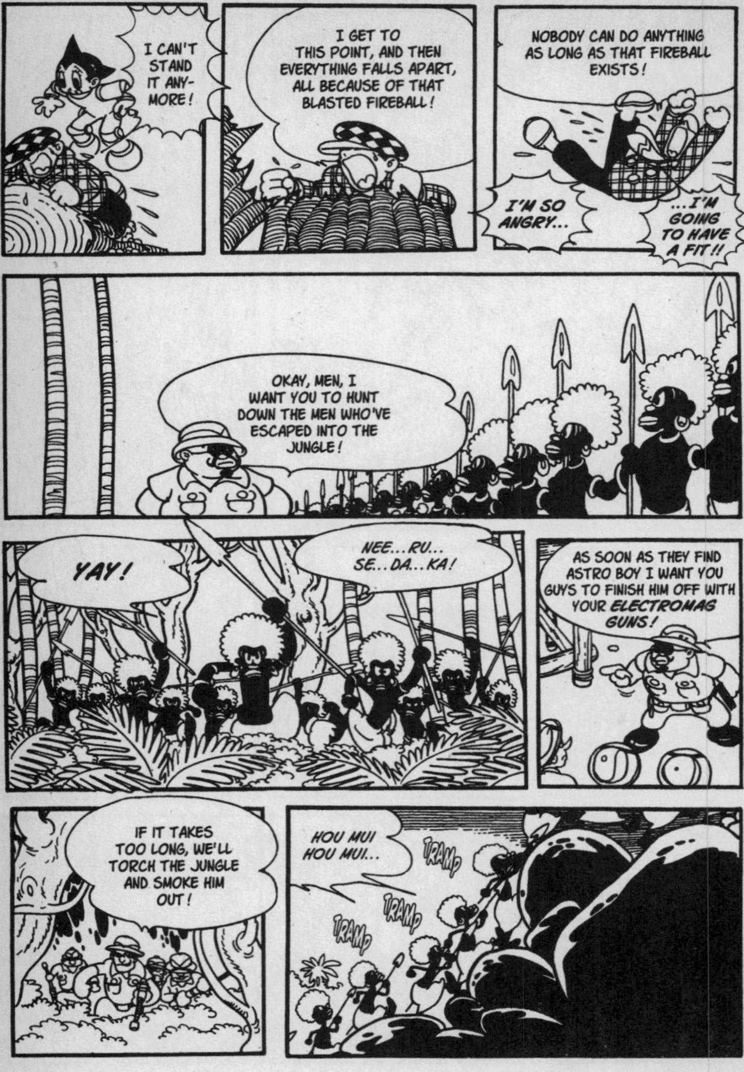
I CAN'T STAND IT ANY-MORE!
I GET TO THIS POINT, AND THEN EVERYTHING FALLS APART, ALL BECAUSE OF THAT BLASTED FIREBALL!
NOBODY CAN DO ANYTHING AS LONG AS THAT FIREBALL EXISTS!
I'M SO ANGRY...
...I'M GOING TO HAVE A FIT!!
OKAY, MEN, I WANT YOU TO HUNT DOWN THE MEN WHO'VE ESCAPED INTO THE JUNGLE!
YAY!
NEE...RU... SE...DA...KA!
AS SOON AS THEY FIND ASTRO BOY I WANT YOU GUYS TO FINISH HIM OFF WITH YOUR ELECTROMAG GUNS!
IF IT TAKES TOO LONG, WE'LL TORCH THE JUNGLE AND SMOKE HIM OUT!
HOU MUI HOU MUI...
TRAMP
TRAMP
TRAMP

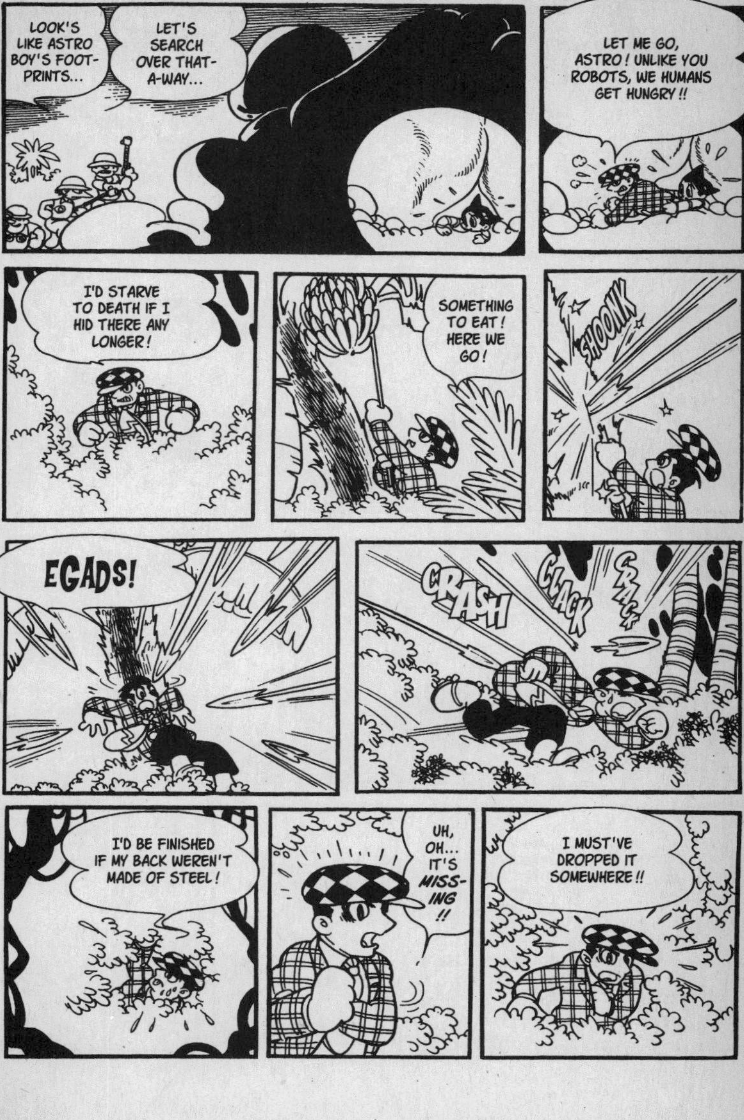

LOOK'S LIKE ASTRO BOY'S FOOT-PRINTS...
LET'S SEARCH OVER THAT-A-WAY...
LET ME GO, ASTRO! UNLIKE YOU ROBOTS, WE HUMANS GET HUNGRY!!
I'D STARVE TO DEATH IF I HID THERE ANY LONGER!
SOMETHING TO EAT! HERE WE GO!
SHOONK
EGADS!
CRASH
CLACK
CRACK
I'D BE FINISHED IF MY BACK WEREN'T MADE OF STEEL!
UH, OH... IT'S MISSING!!
I MUST'VE DROPPED IT SOMEWHERE!!

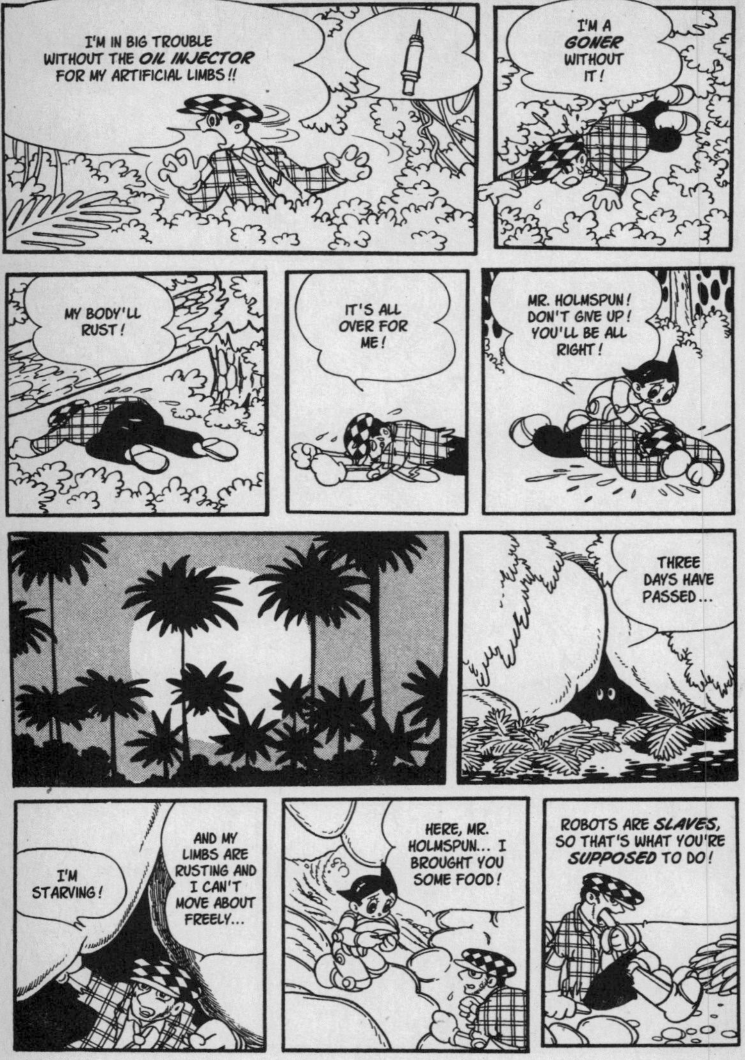
I'M IN BIG TROUBLE WITHOUT THE OIL INJECTOR FOR MY ARTIFICIAL LIMBS!!
I'M A GONER WITHOUT IT!
MY BODY'LL RUST!
IT'S ALL OVER FOR ME!
MR. HOLMSPUN! DON'T GIVE UP! YOU'LL BE ALL RIGHT!
THREE DAYS HAVE PASSED...
I'M STARVING!
AND MY LIMBS ARE RUSTING AND I CAN'T MOVE ABOUT FREELY...
HERE, MR. HOLMSPUN... I BROUGHT YOU SOME FOOD!
ROBOTS ARE SLAVES, SO THAT'S WHAT YOU'RE SUPPOSED TO DO!

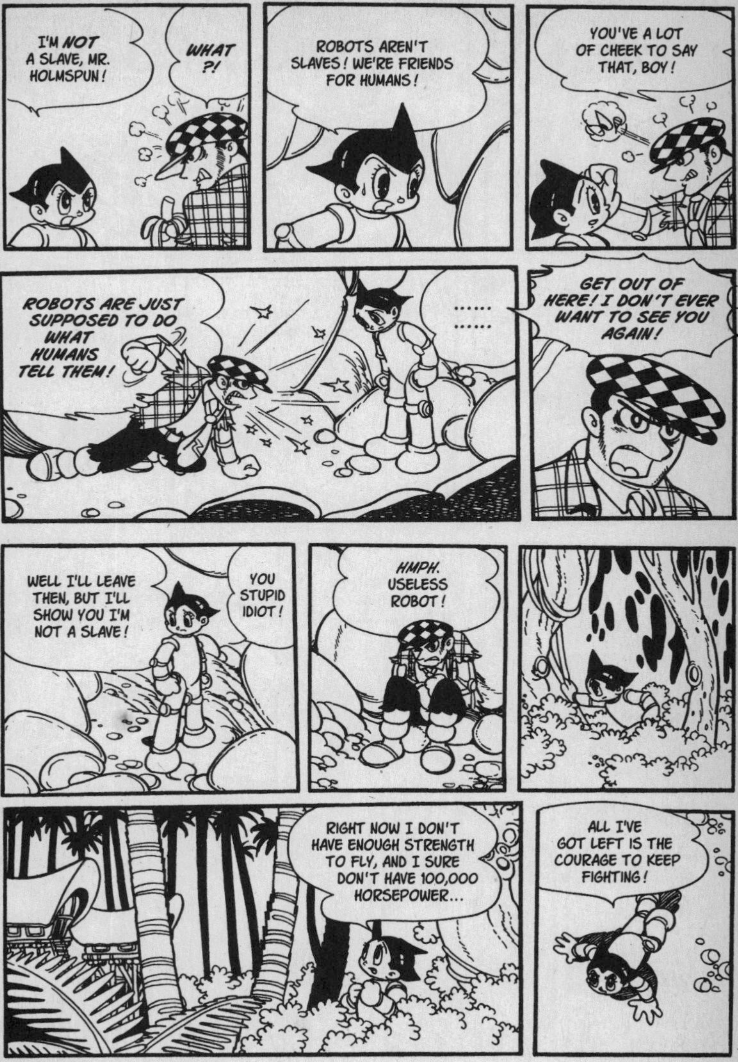
I'M NOT A SLAVE, MR. HOLMSPUN!
WHAT ?!
ROBOTS AREN'T SLAVES! WE'RE FRIENDS FOR HUMANS!
YOU'VE A LOT OF CHEEK TO SAY THAT, BOY!
ROBOTS ARE JUST SUPPOSED TO DO WHAT HUMANS TELL THEM!
......
......
GET OUT OF HERE! I DON'T EVER WANT TO SEE YOU AGAIN!
WELL I'LL LEAVE THEN, BUT I'LL SHOW YOU I'M NOT A SLAVE!
YOU STUPID IDIOT!
HMPH. USELESS ROBOT!
RIGHT NOW I DON'T HAVE ENOUGH STRENGTH TO FLY, AND I SURE DON'T HAVE 100,000 HORSEPOWER...
ALL I'VE GOT LEFT IS THE COURAGE TO KEEP FIGHTING!

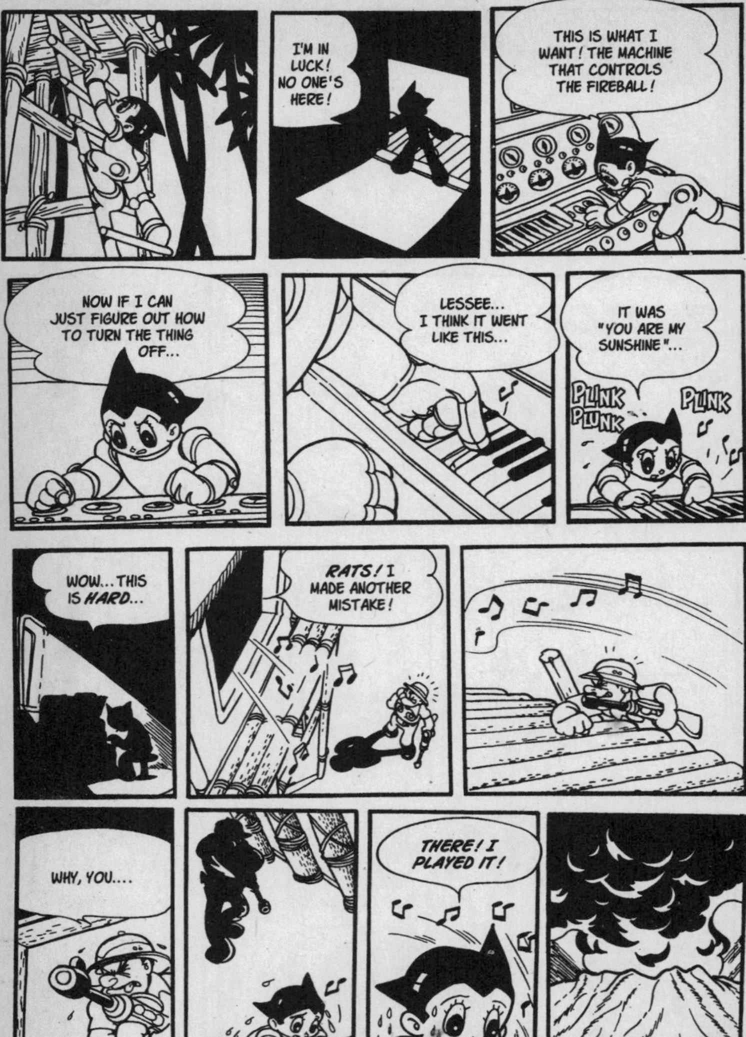
I'M IN LUCK! NO ONE'S HERE!
THIS IS WHAT I WANT! THE MACHINE THAT CONTROLS THE FIREBALL!
NOW IF I CAN JUST FIGURE OUT HOW TO TURN THE THING OFF...
LESSEE... I THINK IT WENT LIKE THIS...
IT WAS "YOU ARE MY SUNSHINE"...
PLINK
PLUNK
PLINK
WOW... THIS IS HARD...
RATS! I MADE ANOTHER MISTAKE!
WHY, YOU....
THERE! I PLAYED IT!

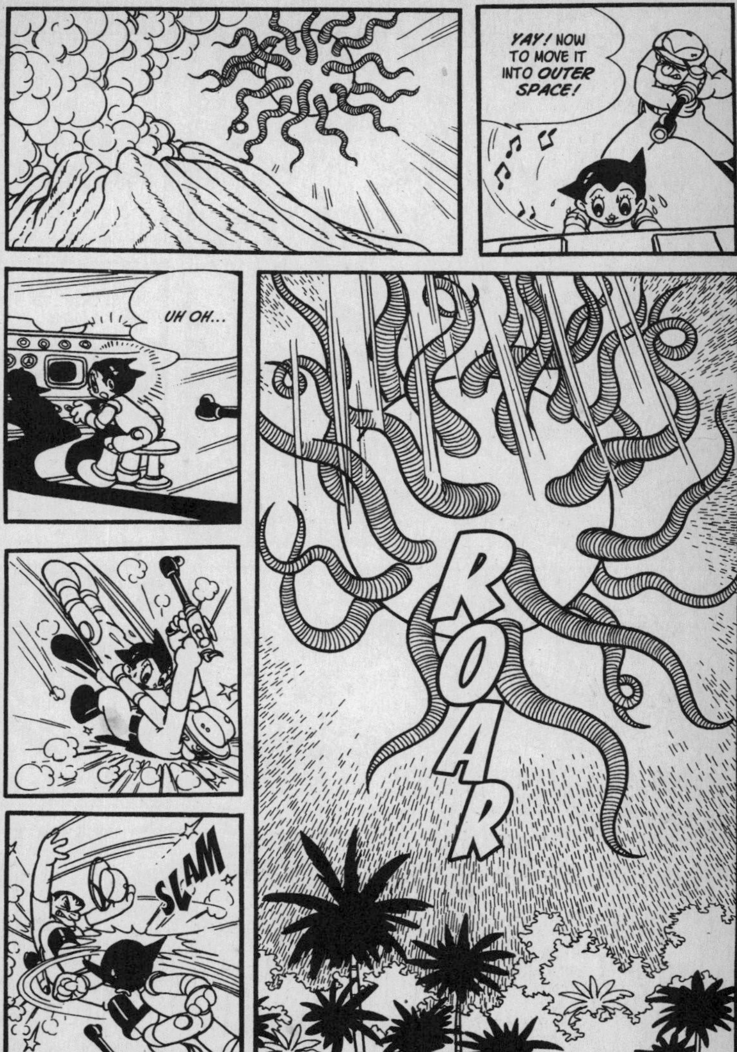
YAY! NOW TO MOVE IT INTO OUTER SPACE!
UH OH...
ROAR
SLAM

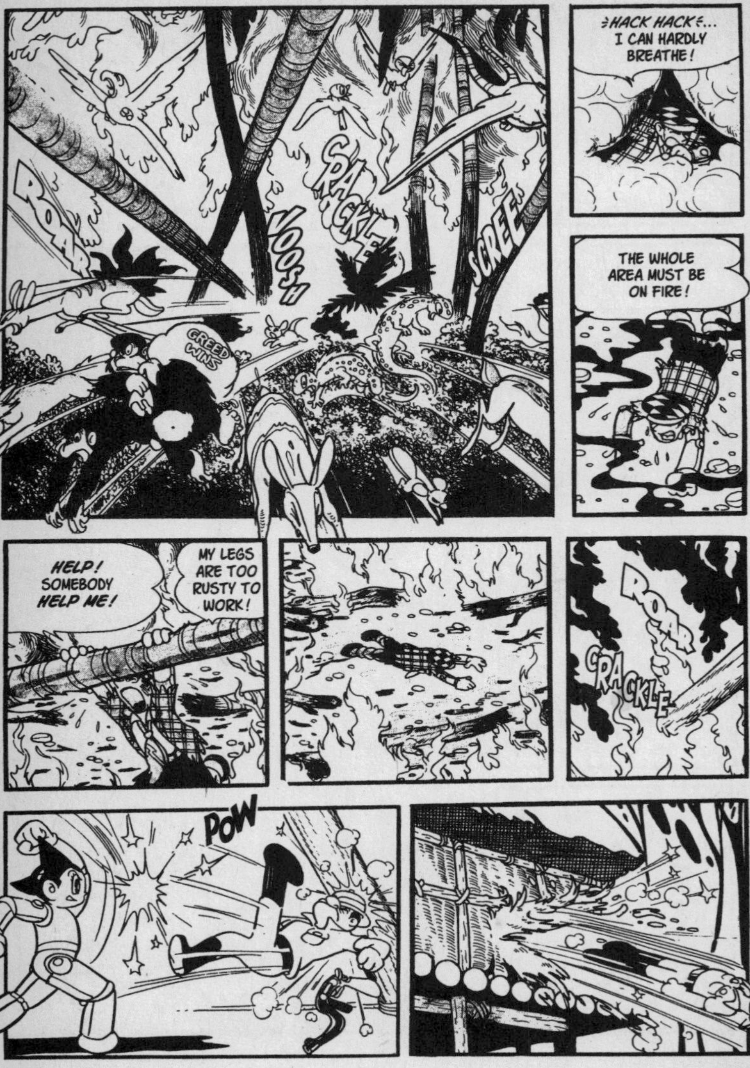
ROAR
CRACKLE
WOOSH
SCREE
GREED WINS
HACK HACK... I CAN HARDLY BREATHE!
THE WHOLE AREA MUST BE ON FIRE!
HELP! SOMEBODY HELP ME!
MY LEGS ARE TOO RUSTY TO WORK!
ROAR
CRACKLE
POW

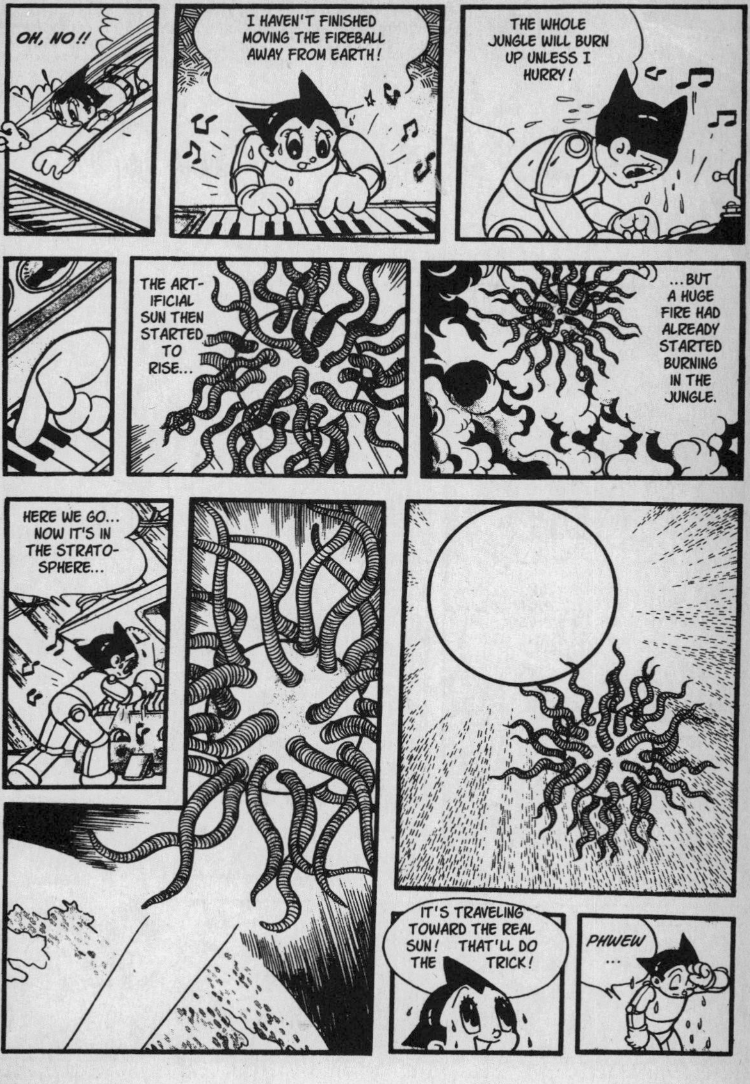
OH, NO!!
I HAVEN'T FINISHED MOVING THE FIREBALL AWAY FROM EARTH!
THE WHOLE JUNGLE WILL BURN UP UNLESS I HURRY!
THE ARTIFICIAL SUN THEN STARTED TO RISE...
...BUT A HUGE FIRE HAD ALREADY STARTED BURNING IN THE JUNGLE.
HERE WE GO... NOW IT'S IN THE STRATOSPHERE...
IT'S TRAVELING TOWARD THE REAL SUN! THAT'LL DO THE TRICK!
PHWEW...

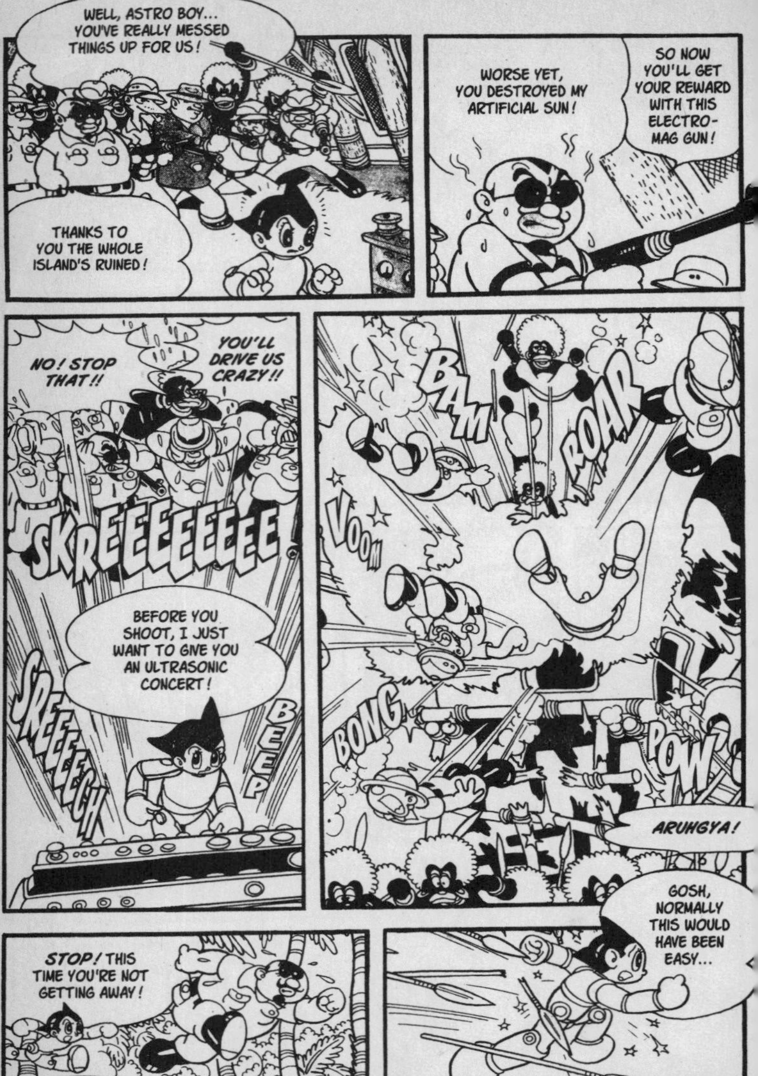

WELL, ASTRO BOY... YOU'VE REALLY MESSED THINGS UP FOR US!
THANKS TO YOU THE WHOLE ISLAND'S RUINED!
WORSE YET, YOU DESTROYED MY ARTIFICIAL SUN!
SO NOW YOU'LL GET YOUR REWARD WITH THIS ELECTRO-MAG GUN!
NO! STOP THAT!!
YOU'LL DRIVE US CRAZY!!
SKREEEEEEEEE!
BEFORE YOU SHOOT, I JUST WANT TO GIVE YOU AN ULTRASONIC CONCERT!
SREEEEECH
BEEEP
BAM
ROAR
VOOM
BONG
POW
ARUHGYA!
STOP! THIS TIME YOU'RE NOT GETTING AWAY!
GOSH, NORMALLY THIS WOULD HAVE BEEN EASY...

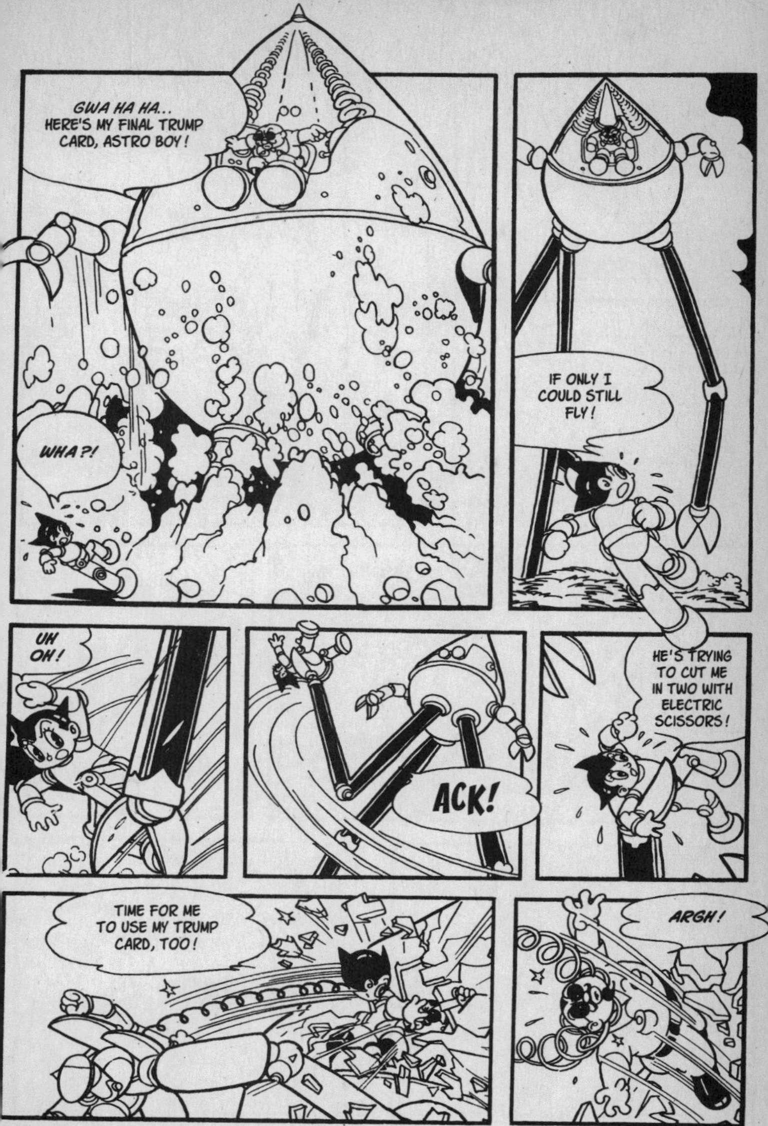
GWA HA HA... HERE'S MY FINAL TRUMP CARD, ASTRO BOY!
WHA?!
IF ONLY I COULD STILL FLY!
UH OH!
ACK!
HE'S TRYING TO CUT ME IN TWO WITH ELECTRIC SCISSORS!
TIME FOR ME TO USE MY TRUMP CARD, TOO!
ARGH!

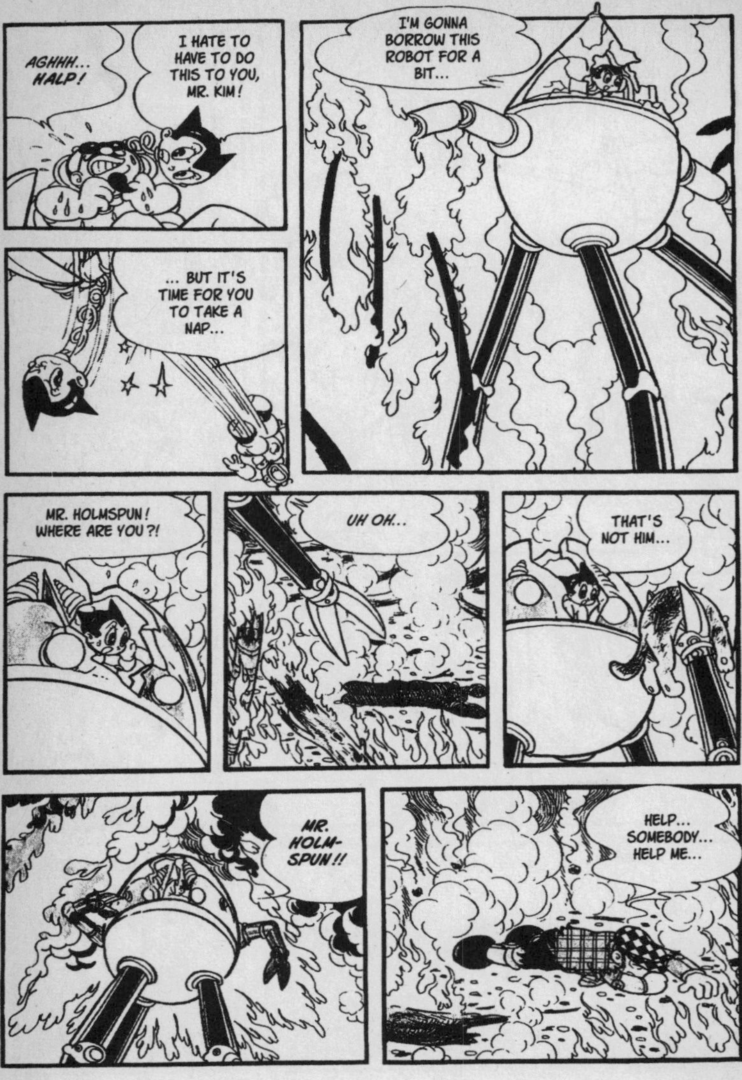
AGHHH... HALP!
I HATE TO HAVE TO DO THIS TO YOU, MR. KIM!
... BUT IT'S TIME FOR YOU TO TAKE A NAP...
I'M GONNA BORROW THIS ROBOT FOR A BIT...
MR. HOLMSPUN! WHERE ARE YOU?!
UH OH...
THAT'S NOT HIM...
MR. HOLMSPUN!!
HELP... SOMEBODY... HELP ME...

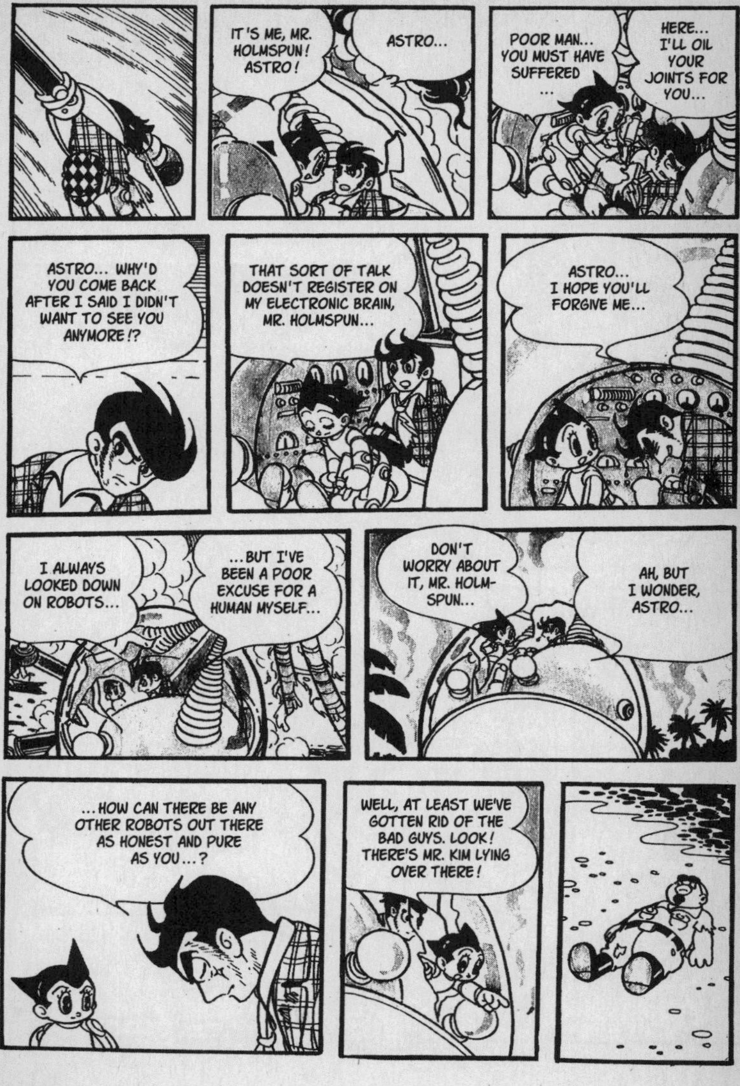

IT'S ME, MR. HOLMSPUN! ASTRO!
ASTRO...
POOR MAN... YOU MUST HAVE SUFFERED ...
HERE... I'LL OIL YOUR JOINTS FOR YOU...
ASTRO... WHY'D YOU COME BACK AFTER I SAID I DIDN'T WANT TO SEE YOU ANYMORE!?
THAT SORT OF TALK DOESN'T REGISTER ON MY ELECTRONIC BRAIN, MR. HOLMSPUN...
ASTRO... I HOPE YOU'LL FORGIVE ME...
I ALWAYS LOOKED DOWN ON ROBOTS...
...BUT I'VE BEEN A POOR EXCUSE FOR A HUMAN MYSELF...
DON'T WORRY ABOUT IT, MR. HOLM-SPUN...
AH, BUT I WONDER, ASTRO...
...HOW CAN THERE BE ANY OTHER ROBOTS OUT THERE AS HONEST AND PURE AS YOU...?
WELL, AT LEAST WE'VE GOTTEN RID OF THE BAD GUYS. LOOK! THERE'S MR. KIM LYING OVER THERE!

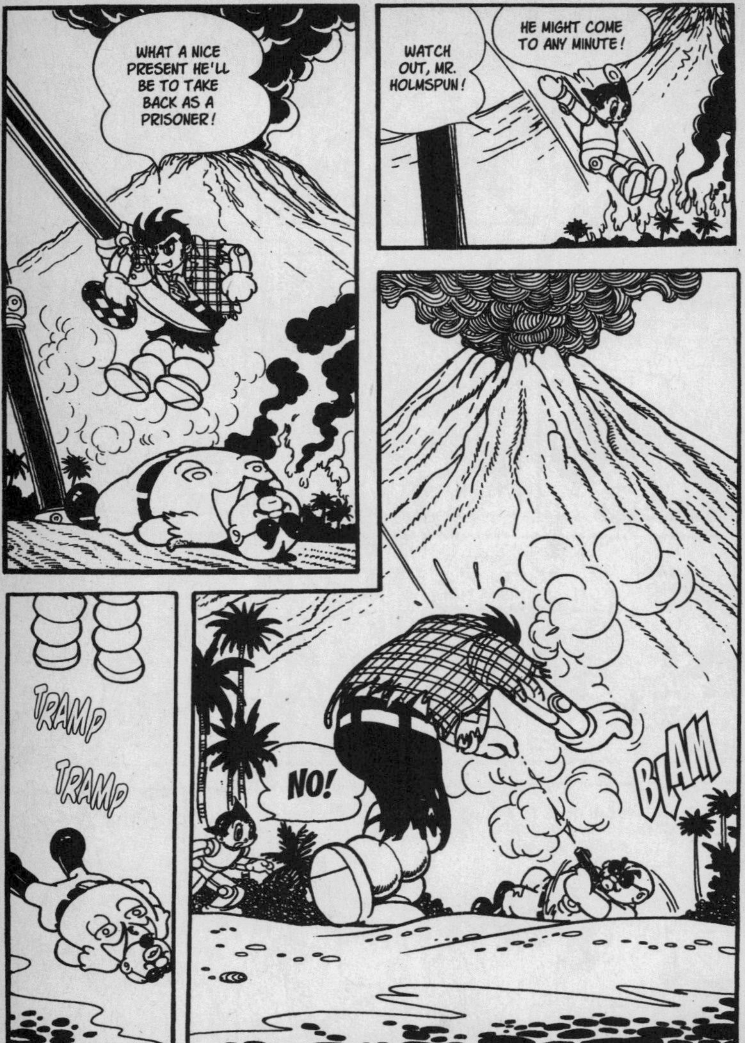
WHAT A NICE PRESENT HE'LL BE TO TAKE BACK AS A PRISONER!
WATCH OUT, MR. HOLMSPUN!
HE MIGHT COME TO ANY MINUTE!
TRAMP
TRAMP
NO!
BLAM

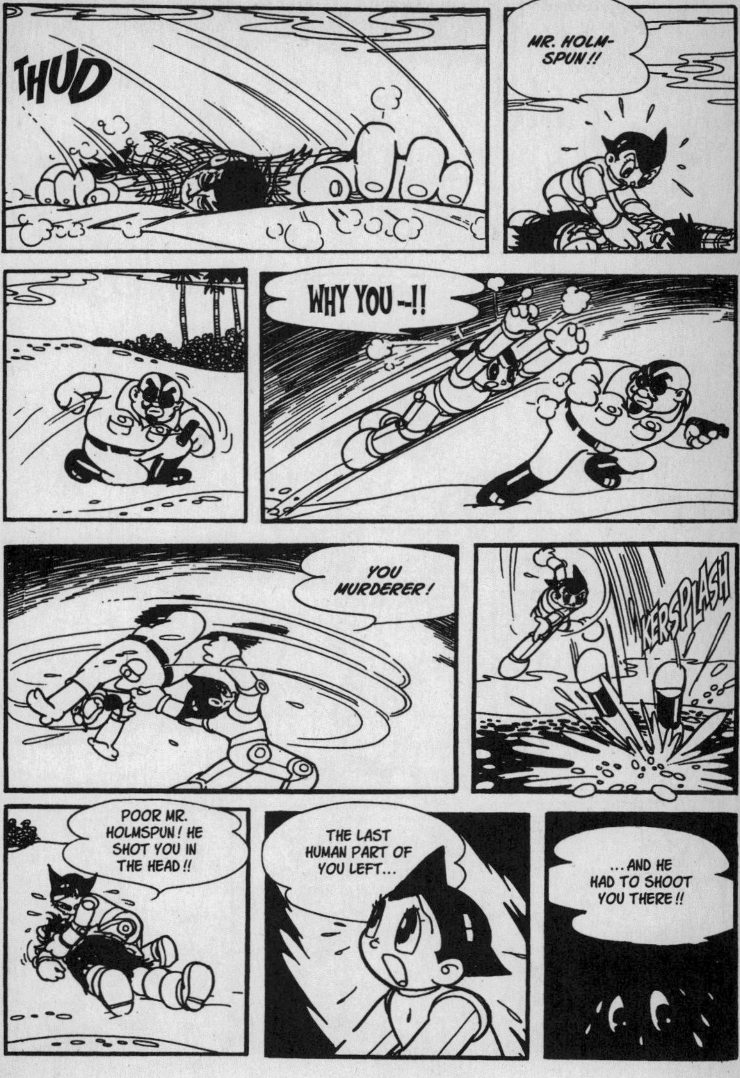
THUD
MR. HOLM-SPUN!!
WHY YOU --!!
YOU MURDERER!
KERSPLASH
POOR MR. HOLMSPUN! HE SHOT YOU IN THE HEAD!!
THE LAST HUMAN PART OF YOU LEFT...
...AND HE HAD TO SHOOT YOU THERE!!

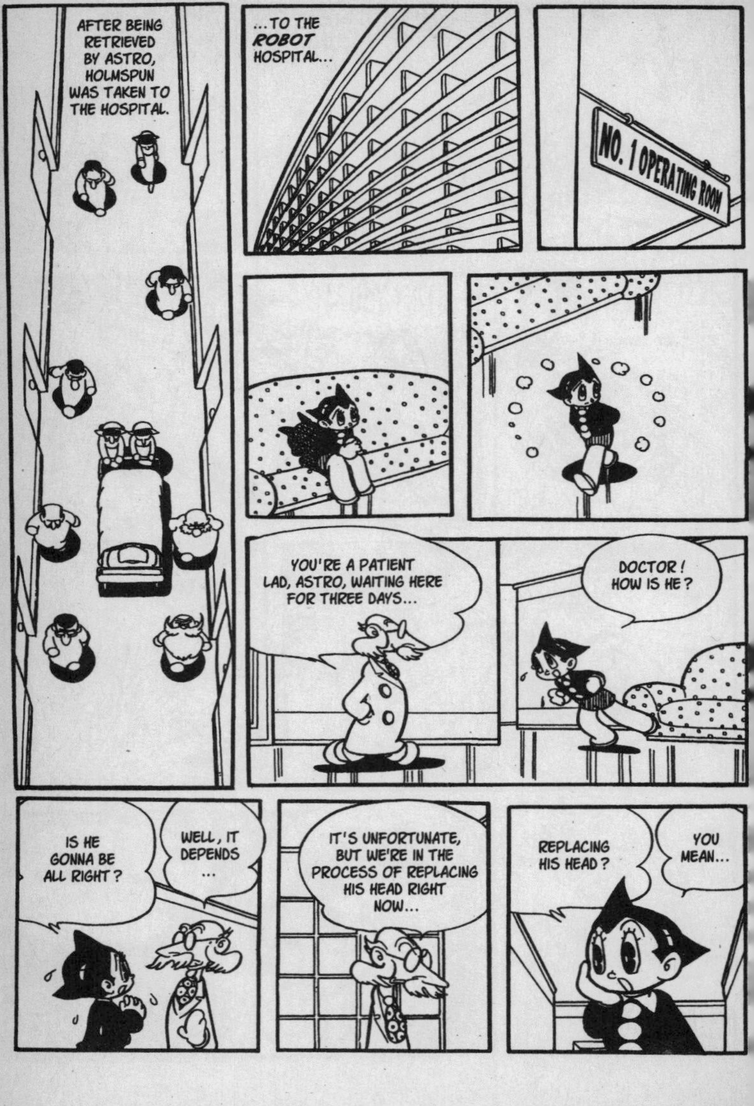
AFTER BEING RETRIEVED BY ASTRO, HOLMSPUN WAS TAKEN TO THE HOSPITAL.
...TO THE ROBOT HOSPITAL...
NO. 1 OPERATING ROOM
YOU'RE A PATIENT LAD, ASTRO, WAITING HERE FOR THREE DAYS...
DOCTOR! HOW IS HE?
IS HE GONNA BE ALL RIGHT?
WELL, IT DEPENDS ...
IT'S UNFORTUNATE, BUT WE'RE IN THE PROCESS OF REPLACING HIS HEAD RIGHT NOW...
YOU MEAN...
REPLACING HIS HEAD?

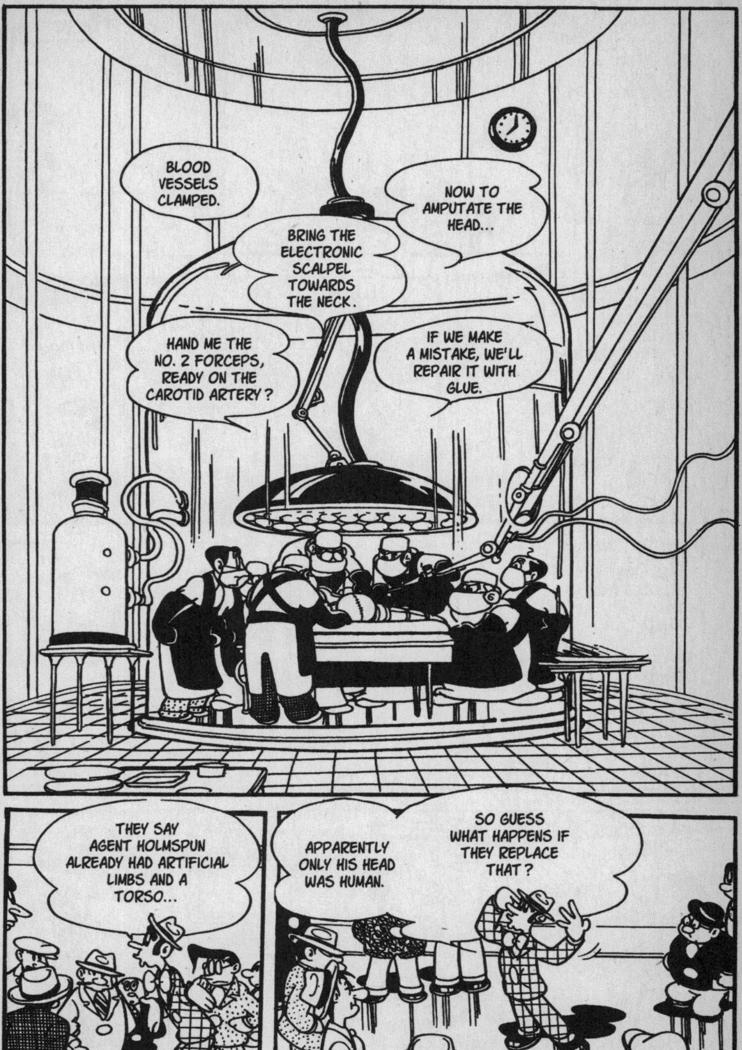
BLOOD VESSELS CLAMPED.
NOW TO AMPUTATE THE HEAD...
BRING THE ELECTRONIC SCALPEL TOWARDS THE NECK.
HAND ME THE NO. 2 FORCEPS, READY ON THE CAROTID ARTERY?
IF WE MAKE A MISTAKE, WE'LL REPAIR IT WITH GLUE.
THEY SAY AGENT HOLMSPUN ALREADY HAD ARTIFICIAL LIMBS AND A TORSO...
APPARENTLY ONLY HIS HEAD WAS HUMAN.
SO GUESS WHAT HAPPENS IF THEY REPLACE THAT?

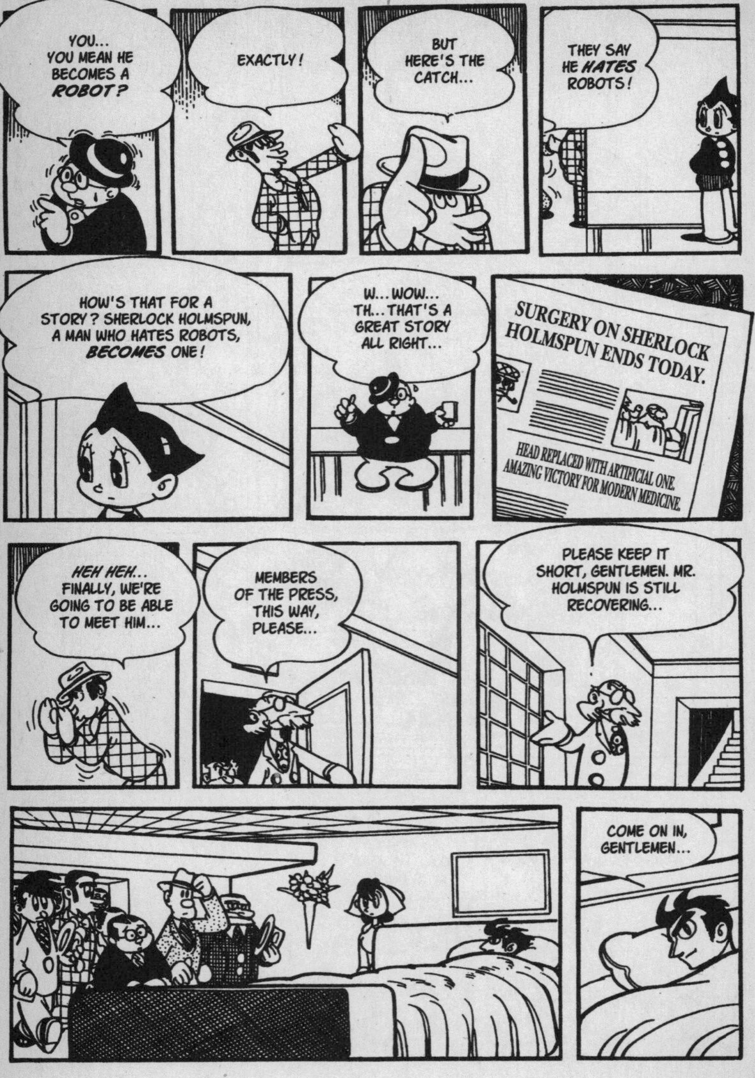
YOU... YOU MEAN HE BECOMES A ROBOT?
EXACTLY!
BUT HERE'S THE CATCH...
THEY SAY HE HATES ROBOTS!
HOW'S THAT FOR A STORY? SHERLOCK HOLMSPUN, A MAN WHO HATES ROBOTS, BECOMES ONE!
W...WOW... TH...THAT'S A GREAT STORY ALL RIGHT...
SURGERY ON SHERLOCK HOLMSPUN ENDS TODAY.
HEAD REPLACED WITH ARTIFICIAL ONE. AMAZING VICTORY FOR MODERN MEDICINE.
HEH HEH... FINALLY, WE'RE GOING TO BE ABLE TO MEET HIM...
MEMBERS OF THE PRESS, THIS WAY, PLEASE...
PLEASE KEEP IT SHORT, GENTLEMEN. MR. HOLMSPUN IS STILL RECOVERING...
COME ON IN, GENTLEMEN...

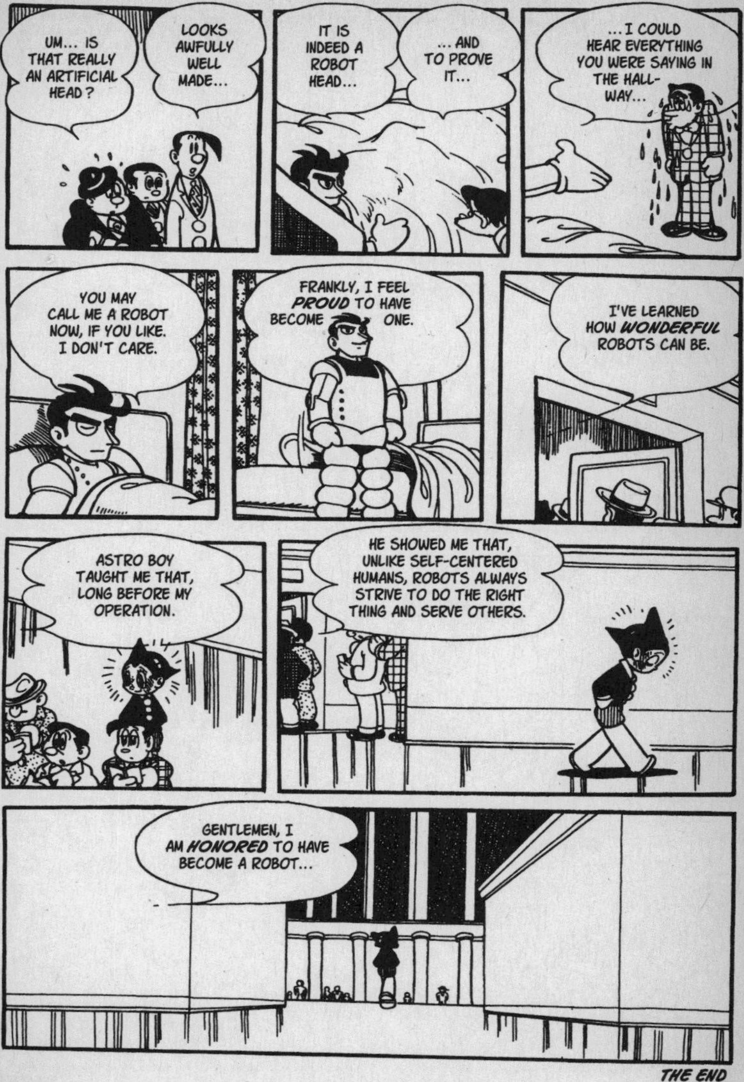
UM... IS THAT REALLY AN ARTIFICIAL HEAD?
LOOKS AWFULLY WELL MADE...
IT IS INDEED A ROBOT HEAD...
... AND TO PROVE IT...
...I COULD HEAR EVERYTHING YOU WERE SAYING IN THE HALL-WAY...
YOU MAY CALL ME A ROBOT NOW, IF YOU LIKE. I DON'T CARE.
FRANKLY, I FEEL PROUD TO HAVE BECOME ONE.
I'VE LEARNED HOW WONDERFUL ROBOTS CAN BE.
ASTRO BOY TAUGHT ME THAT, LONG BEFORE MY OPERATION.
HE SHOWED ME THAT, UNLIKE SELF-CENTERED HUMANS, ROBOTS ALWAYS STRIVE TO DO THE RIGHT THING AND SERVE OTHERS.
GENTLEMEN, I AM HONORED TO HAVE BECOME A ROBOT...
THE END

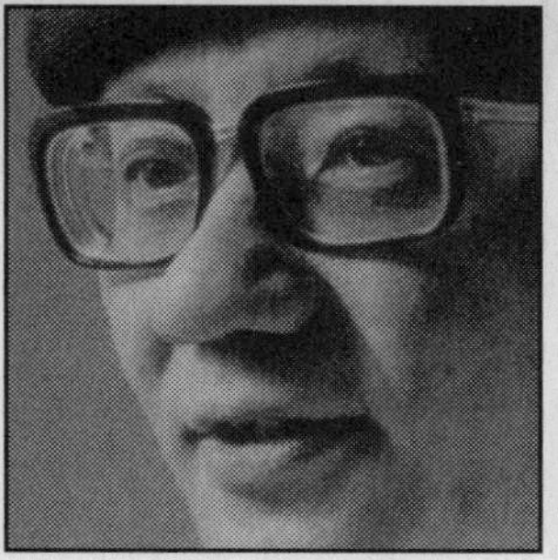

Osamu Tezuka was born in the city of Toyonaka, in Osaka, Japan, on November 3, 1928, and raised in Takarazuka, in Hyogo prefecture. He graduated from the Medical Department of Osaka University and was later awarded a Doctorate of Medicine.

In 1946 Tezuka made his debut as a manga artist with the work *Amachan's Diary*, and in 1947 he had his first big hit with *New Treasure Island*. Over his forty-year career as a cartoonist, Tezuka produced in excess of an astounding 150,000 pages of manga, including the creation of *Metropolis*, *Mighty Atom* (a.k.a. *Astro Boy*), *Jungle Emperor* (a.k.a. *Kimba the White Lion*), *Black Jack*, *Phoenix*, *Buddha*, and many more.

Tezuka's fascination with Disney cartoons led him to begin his own animation studio, creating the first serialized Japanese cartoon series, which was later exported to America as *Astro Boy* in 1963. Tezuka Productions went on to create animated versions of *Kimba the White Lion* (*Jungle Emperor*) and *Phoenix*, among others.

He received numerous awards during his life, including the Bungei Shunju Manga Award, the Kodansha Manga Award, the Shogakukan Manga Award, and the Japan Cartoonists' Association Special Award for Excellence. He also served a variety of organizations. He was a director of the Japan Cartoonists' Association, the chairman of the Japan Animation Association, and a member of the Manga Group, Japan Pen Club, and the Japan SF Authors' Club, among others. Tezuka became Japan's "comics ambassador," taking Japan's comics culture to the world. In 1980, he toured and lectured in America, including a speech at the United Nations.

Regarded as a national treasure, Osamu Tezuka died on February 2, 1989 at the age of 60. In 1994, the Osamu Tezuka Manga Museum opened in the city of Takarazuka, where he was raised. His creations remains hugely popular in Japan and are printed in many languages throughout the world, where he is acclaimed as one of the true giants of comics and animation, his work as vital and influential today as it was half a century ago.

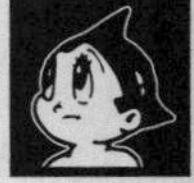

"Comics are an international language," Tezuka said. "They can cross boundaries and generations. Comics are a bridge between all cultures."